The University of the Future
Responding to Covid-19

Editors

Dan Remenyi
Kenneth A. Grant
Shawren Singh

The University of the Future: Responding to Covid-19
Eds. Dan Remenyi, Kenneth A. Grant and Shawren Singh

First edition, August 2020

ISBN: 978-1-912764-65-5

Published by: ACIL, Reading, RG4 9AY, United Kingdom, info@academic-conferences.org Available from www.academic-bookshop.com

Contents

Acknowledgements

The contributors of this book have responded to a request to produce suggestions as to how to cope with the current Covid-19 crisis and its aftermath with extraordinary speed, which of course was appropriate considering how quickly coronavirus descended upon the academic community. Academics, especially those in university management are not accustomed to facing such urgent challenges and perhaps the current crisis has demonstrated that when necessary universities and faculty can rise to the occasion as quickly as anyone else.

Once again the content of this book is the result of the thinking of the authors and their associates and colleagues and by this acknowledgement the editors wish to offer thanks to all those with whom they have discussed this subject and from whose input their ideas have developed.

The success of this book will be measured by the extent that it facilitates discussion and reflection by academics and others, and maybe even action by some, on how the university system works and how individuals and organisations might contribute to the future evolution of the university as an important institution in our society.

A Facebook page has been established to continue discussion on this subject at https://www.facebook.com/groups/2478159529151472

The Editors

After completing an MBA **Dan Remenyi** spent 15 years in business as an ICT consultant before undertaking a PhD. Since obtaining his doctorate he has held a variety of visiting professorships in the United Kingdom, the Republic of Ireland and South Africa. He originally researched and taught in the ICT management field, but for the past two decades he has increasingly focussed on research methodology and the sociology of research. He has had some 30 textbooks published. Some of his books have been translated into Chinese, Japanese and Romanian. He is the Academic Director of Academic Conferences and Publishing International Ltd (ACPIL) and also an Extraordinary Professor and the University of the Western Cape in South Africa. He holds a BSocSc MBA and PhD.

Kenneth A. Grant is a professor of entrepreneurship and strategy in the Ted Rogers School of Business Management in Toronto, Canada. He is a visiting professor in the UK, Europe and Asia. His research interests include strategy, entrepreneurship, knowledge management and innovation, and pedagogy. He is an active coach and supporter of student entrepreneur activity across the university and is currently working to facilitate the development of entrepreneurship programs in China. Prior to joining Ryerson, Dr. Grant had an extensive career as a management consultant and industry executive in Canada and the UK, leading global consulting practices in several major firms. He holds a BA degree from the Open University, an MBA from the Schulich School of Business and a DBA from Henley Business School.

Shawren Singh holds a B Com, B Tech, MSc and PhD and is an Associate Professor in the School of Computing at the University of South Africa, the largest university on the African continent. He has spent more than 20 years teaching and researching in the Information Systems space. In 2014 he obtained his PhD, based on research into eGovernment in South Africa, from the University of the Witwatersrand. His current research has focused on digital scholarship and e-Government. He is currently the chair of the Information Systems research committee in the School as well as serving on the Employment Equity Committee of the College of Science, Engineering and Technology of UNISA.

Contributing Authors

Author Name	Affiliation
Andrews Agya Yalley	Marketing and Strategy, University of the Cape Coast, Ghana
Arwa Z. Al-Riyam	Department of Haematology, Sultan Qaboos University Hospital, Muscat, Oman
Adi Arida	School of Health and Environmental Studies, Hamdan Bin Mohammed Smart University, Dubai, United Arab Emirates
Niyi Awofeso	School of Health and Environmental Studies, Hamdan Bin Mohammed Smart University, Dubai, United Arab Emirates
Lakshmi Balachandran	Faculty of Social & Behavioural Sciences, Utrecht University, Netherlands
Andrew D. Banasiewicz	Merrimack College, North Andover, MA, USA
Madelyn Blair	Pelerei, LLC, Washington DC, USA
David Bolton	School of Management, Swansea University, Wales, UK
Cathal MacSwiney Brugha	University College Dublin, Ireland
Marguarite (Reet) Cronk	Graduate School of Business, Harding University, Searcy, AR, USA
Gareth Huw Davies	School of Management, Swansea University, Wales, UK
Dima Moain Dayoub	The Higher Institute of Languages, Tishreen University, Syria
Gabriel Donleavy	UNE Business School, University of New England, NSW, Australia
Philip Dover	Babson College, Boston, MA, USA
Penelope Engel-Hills	Professional Education Research Institute, Cape Peninsula University of Technology, South Africa

Steven A. Gedeon	Ted Rogers School of Management, Ryerson University, Toronto, Canada
Kenneth A. Grant	Ted Rogers School of Management, Ryerson University, Toronto, Canada
Elizaveta Gromova	Peter the Great St. Petersburg Polytechnic University, Russian Federation
Andrew Hatch	Universidade Europeia de Lisboa, Portugal
Naomi Joyce	School of Medicine, Swansea University, Wales, UK
Isaac Kajja	Makerere University, Kampala, Uganda
Denise Lee	PwC, Washington DC, USA
Professor Mandla Stanley Makhanya	University of South Africa, Pretoria/Tshwane, South Africa
Francisco Maurício	Universidade Europeia de Lisboa, Portugal
Peter Mozelius	Department of Computer and System Science, Mid Sweden University, Östersund, Sweden
Maruff Oladejo	University of Lagos, Nigeria
Dan Remenyi	ACPIL UK and University of the Western Cape, South Africa
Martin Rich	City, University of London Business School, UK
Cees Th. Smit Sibinga	IQM Consulting, Zuidhorn and University of Groningen, Netherlands
Shawren Singh	Department of Information Systems, School of Computing, University of South Africa
Pedro Soares de Mello	Universidade Europeia de Lisboa, Portugal
Eduardo Tomé	Universidade Europeia de Lisboa, Portugal

Foreword

Universities worldwide are facing the most challenging period of their history, as this volume captures so vividly. Every year in the last 25 has seen books and conferences on topics like the 'future of the university' or the 'death of the traditional university.' But this is different, as the chapters that follow show. Whilst universities globally in 2020 look pretty much like they did in 2010, and in 2010 as they did in 2000, universities in 2030 will look nothing like universities in 2020.

The universities which will be flourishing will be those that embrace the change and re-imagine themselves in the new world. They will need to embrace five new realities.

Covid-19 isn't a disease that struck in the first half of 2020 then disappeared. There will be a second, a third and a fourth wave, there will be varieties of Covid-19 which will require new vaccines, and there will be other viruses. Universities will need to adapt to this new reality in the way that they teach and research, students learn and are cared for, and in the manner that they relate to their local communities, industry and beyond. Blended learning will have become ubiquitous. We will never go back to the old world where virtually everything happened face-to-face.

Artificial Intelligence (AI) embraces more than just machine learning. It is part of the 4.0 technologies which include virtual reality, augmented reality, the internet of things, blockchain and robotics which are already changing forward-thinking institutions. Universities to date have relied upon academic staff to teach, and support staff to administer and cater for student needs and their aspirations for the future. There will still be staff at universities in 2030, but AI technology will be all pervasive, in selecting students, offering individualised teaching and learning, marking, commenting and assessing student work and progress, looking after their mental and physical health, catering for their needs and career aspirations, enhancing research methodology and connecting staff to research communities globally. Linguistic barriers will be a problem of the past.

Homogeneity of universities will be gradually blown away. In 2020, most undergraduates globally studied in three or four year programmes which were residential, with long vacations and with most students studying after leaving school and before going on to work or to post graduate study. Most universities offered a wide range of subjects, undertook research, and for all their boasting of differentiation in their mission statements, they all offered fundamentally the same menu. By 2030, two year undergraduate and doctorate degrees, part-time and hybrid degrees will be far more common, as will adult education and students dipping in and out of universities. Universities in many countries will have started to differentiate, with a top tier of research-intensive institutions, a regional tier and local universities which are embedded in their communities. These will offer a range of technical and vocational qualifications in addition to traditional degrees. The standard model of the three- or four-year degree will have started to lose its hold.

Work will have changed beyond all recognition. Higher education has always been seen by governments as largely about providing the skills for employment, thereby creating a dynamic national economy. But the world of working is changing. As AI machines and automation take over many of the manual jobs, including in farming and manufacturing, the jobs of the future will be in sectors such as health, culture, social care and education where *human* skills are at a premium. But universities are still fundamentally teaching the knowledge and skills that machines and algorithms are already being able to replicate. A flight attendant on an airplane now needs more high-level and flexible skills than the pilot, who does little more than observe the technology to fly the plane. Already, increasing parts of the legal profession and accountancy are being taken over by machines which are far less likely to make mistakes, don't get tired and don't have bad days. Universities will be needing to teach a common core of future-proof skills which include human literacy, digital literacy, empathy and creativity.

Wellbeing and the environment finally are going to become increasingly important. Universities of the twentieth century accepted the dominant value system of the day, which was that quantities mattered far more than quality. Success was measured by material wealth, and universities were valued because of their size, turnover and proportion of top degrees. Little thought was given to the happiness of students and staff, or the sustainable quality of the local environment. University buildings the world over include some of the ugliest institutional structures anywhere, with green spaces sacrificed to concrete. Universities have been slow to embrace the well-being revolution and still more surprisingly, the green agenda. As president of the International Positive Education Network (IPEN) which links educational institutions to the best research on wellbeing, I am constantly surprised at the wilful ignoring of the evidence, that shows that happy and healthy staff and students achieve better results, and are more likely to engage in community activities. The full scale of the coming environmental disaster will hit hard into the 2020s and universities will be forced to embrace it in every single facet of their university design, teaching and research.

I commend these 20 chapters for their insight and imagination. This book needs to be studied by all in higher education globally. The future is hurtling fast towards us, and keeping eyes closed is no longer an option.

Sir Antony Seldon
Vice Chancellor
University of Buckingham, UK
July 2020

Foreword

The statement that 'prediction is very difficult, especially if it's about the future' has been attributed to many, but was probably first made by the nuclear physicist, Niels Bohr. It is particularly true when the change is brought about by so many different factors.

The great philosopher, futurologist and science fiction writer, Arthur C, Clarke developed an idea that he called, 'The 10 Factor Theory of Change'. He proposed that when the capacity of a technology increases by a ten factor, it changes radically all aspects of the society in which it is developing. As an example, he suggests that one might wish to consider transport – from simply walking to riding in horse drawn vehicles, to the invention of the steam engine and railways, to the internal combustion engine, cars and lorries and on to manned flight and the current capacity of aircraft.

The pace of change in the world is accelerating more and more rapidly Each ten factor change has taken place in a shorter and shorter period of time – 5,000 years from foot to horse drawn vehicle, a few thousand years to steam vehicles, one hundred to the combustion engine and then about fifty to the aircraft. Each of these shifts changed society immeasurably – travel, trade, politics, employment, social structure and of course education and access to it.

Every so often and generally unexpected new external factors also emerge to speed up change and there can be no doubt that the current Covid-19 pandemic is one such – though it is arguable whether its possibility could, should or did enter awareness much earlier. Although this book looks hard at aspects of the ways in which Covid-19 will affect Universities, it must not be forgotten that there have been many substantial pressures for change in the university sector for some time. It can certainly be argued that we have started to experience what T.S. Kuhn, the insightful and influential philosopher of science described as a paradigm shift.

Kuhn made several claims concerning the progress of knowledge and consequently society. Rather than solely progressing in a linear and continuous way knowledge undergoes periodic jumps and these paradigm shifts open up new approaches to understanding what people would never have considered before. Truth, at any given moment, cannot be established solely by objective criteria but is defined or agreed by a consensus of the relevant experts. Competing paradigms are frequently incommensurable and are thus not always reconcilable accounts of reality. This is now undoubtedly the case for education in general and for higher education in particular. Now is an opportunity for a radical revision of the whole educational process from pre-school through to the top end of research education.

There are those who see the use of technology in education as 'the' solution to solve all the coming challenges and it is said that artificial intelligence (AI) is the way forward. The is little doubt that improvements in AI are important and will have a role to play. However, education is not simply about the transmission of knowledge and its creation. There are many important psychological and social aspects that AI cannot now or possibly ever fulfil. On the other hand, there is the proposal by the psychologist Endel Tulving that, 'if something can be imagined, it will eventually happen and probably more quickly than might be forecast'.

The combination of the Covid-19 crisis, the potential of ICT including AI and the pressure to reform the University system leads us to ask a number of important questions. Included in these are: -

1. Should all tertiary educational institutions be called 'universities' or should this title be reserved for first class institutions with the highest standards required for entry and clear limitations on grades on graduation?
2. Should society be more careful about limiting the number of research focussed universities, and ensure that they keep their international reputations?
3. What percentage of young people should proceed to tertiary education, to study what subjects and to what level? What opportunities should be provided for those who will not engage with higher education? (J.K Galbraith has said that any society that can afford to have people unemployed should be able to afford to create a valuable satisfying life for them.)
4. Should more tertiary education be carried out in the workplace through internships and genuine apprenticeships?
5. How can programmes be made more flexible and adaptable to take account of the number of different roles that people may need to undertake in their lives? Also, how can tertiary colleges promote a desire for more effective lifelong learning.
6. Is outcome salary the best way to measure effectiveness?
7. What role can technology genuinely play in the delivery of effective learning and where should it take place?

Arthur C. Clarke, mentioned above, also formulated three adages that are known as Clarke's three laws, of which the third law is the best known and most widely cited. They were part of his ideas in his extensive writings about the future. These so-called laws stated:

1. When a distinguished but elderly scientist states that something is possible, he is almost certainly right. When he states that something is impossible, he is very probably wrong,
2. The only way of discovering the limits of the possible is to venture a little way past them into the impossible,
3. Any sufficiently advanced technology is indistinguishable from magic.

I am certainly not a distinguished scientist, but I am becoming elderly, or more experienced. I know that we must stop resisting change, accept its inevitability and venture beyond into the impossible and exploit the magic that is becoming available.

Aldwyn Cooper
Emeritus Vice-Chancellor
Regents University, London, UK
July 2020

Introduction

Business schools have been talking about continuity planning for more than a decade but the events which occurred in the first quarter of 2020 were truly unimaginable a year before. There was no way, in the normal course of events, in which the closure of the complete education system could have been forecast. Some extreme scenario planning might possibly have envisaged the Covid-19 pandemic crisis but even if this had been the case it was not possible to imagine how rapidly we were faced with these extraordinary circumstances. Nor was it possible to retrospectively put measures in place to mitigate the severity of the impact of the crisis on society. It seems that we forgot that in a globalised world anyone or anything, including a virus, can travel from almost anywhere on the planet to anywhere else in under 24 hours.

The unthinkable closure of the universities produces two enormously challenging outcomes. The first of these is the disruption of the educational programs which hundreds of millions of students were engaged in. This has all sorts of consequences not the least of which is the inability of many students to attend lectures and tutorials and complete assignments before the end of their academic year. This has led to some difficult problems with regards to the evaluation of student performance and thus the awarding of degrees. Proper completion of the academic year and the proper assessment of student achievements is a cornerstone of most professional activities in society.

The second consequence is much more prosaic but maybe even more disastrous to the universities. With their doors closed and in most cases with only Remote Emergency Teaching (RET) available (RET is what rashly conceived online teaching programmes are being referred to by some more sceptical academics) many of the students are asking for fee reductions. Like individuals and other organisations in society some universities are rich, but many others are poor. There is only a small number of rich universities. In general, the less well-off universities do not have great resources at their disposal and the disruption of an academic year accompanied by reductions in fees represents significant financial hardship which could lead to organisational failure. Putting it bluntly some universities might not be able to meet their financial commitments and therefore be forced to cease operation.

This Covid-19 crisis was sprung on universities at a time when they were already receiving considerable criticism. It is clear that our society no longer considers universities to be ivory towers which deserve special consideration and treatment. Universities are expected to be criticised and judged like any other institution in the complex reality of the 21st-century. In addition, many governments throughout the world are cutting back on their funding of higher education and this has been severely felt by a number of universities.

It is perhaps a truism that material change rarely occurs unless it is motivated by a crisis. As this is the case it does seem that Covid-19 might be a significant opportunity for universities to take some serious action to improve their real contribution to society. There is no doubt that universities have been one of the most successful groups of organisations in most countries in the world. Some universities have been in existence for hundreds of years, although it is true to say, that the form of the modern university owes its existence to educational reforms in the German-speaking states of Europe around the beginning of the 19th century. Nonetheless there are not many organisations which can claim to be as important to the general welfare of our societies as universities.

But this has been changing. Whereas 50 years ago most universities were public service, not-for-profit institutions where the focus was on education supported by some research, today universities are large complex multinational organisations where the emphasis is often as much on research as it is on the education of the students. Furthermore, many universities have adopted a corporate culture where financial success is seen as imperative. This is evidenced through the phenomenal changes in the way that universities function. The first of these is the cost of a university education which in many parts of the world has increased enormously. It is said that inflation in educational costs in the USA has outstripped even the remarkable increases in the cost of medical care. In the United Kingdom in a couple of decades the cost of acquiring a three-year university degree has changed from being free to about £50,000. Of course, both in the United Kingdom and the United States of America student loans have been available. It is now estimated that the total of UK student debt is about £17 billion and the equivalent in the United States of America is about $1.5 trillion. The second indicator of how the culture of universities has changed is demonstrated by the salaries paid to University Presidents in the United States of America and Vice Chancellors in the United Kingdom. According to Forbes,

> *The highest-paid public university president last year, James Ramsey, 69, of the University of Louisville, made a total of $4.3 million, according to The Chronicle of Higher Education's eighth annual survey of public university presidents' compensation. That's $2.5 million more than the next-highest-paid president, Jay Gogue of Auburn University in Alabama, and $3.7 million more than the $560,000 average compensation of the other 250 presidents in the survey, which showed average pay climbed 5% from the previous year*[1].

In the United Kingdom university Vice-Chancellors are not as well paid as their equivalent in the United States of America but nonetheless according to the Independent newspaper,

> *The average pay and benefits package for a vice-chancellor in the elite group is now £380,000 and the Imperial College London president, Alice Gast, tops the table with a total remuneration of £554,000*[2].

These salaries were unheard-of 20 years ago and are probably the most obvious indicator of how the university system has embraced the attitude of commercialism. Of course, universities have to pay their way like any other

---

[1] https://www.forbes.com/sites/susanadams/2018/07/15/the-highest-paid-public-university-presidents-no-1-is-engulfed-in-scandal/#64f26cfd66c1

[2] https://www.independent.co.uk/news/education/education-news/vice-chancellor-pay-university-russell-group-salary-students-fees-a9300286.html

institution in our society but converting universities from public sector organisations to commercial enterprises does not bode well for the development of the millions of professional men and women which are required to run a modern society. And even if this commercial attitude was more efficient or effective it flies in the face of other efforts to create a fairer and more open society to which easy access to education is an essential key. It is clearly time to examine the values which underpin this type of super-remuneration paid to some high office bearers and prestigious professors as well as reverse some of the trends that have been taking place within universities.

Indeed, there are many other concerns besides money which have surfaced in recent years which need to be addressed by the university sector and it is hoped that the current crisis may speed up the delivery of these much needed reforms. But for this to happen bold leadership is most definitely required and the university sector has often been slow in this respect.

This book addresses a wide range of these issues through different lenses perceived by the wide range of authors who have contributed to the text. In total there are 32 authors involved in the production of these chapters who work across 17 different countries including Australia, Canada, England, Ghana, Ireland, the Netherlands, Nigeria, Oman, Portugal, Russian Federation, South Africa, Sweden, Syria, Uganda, United Arab Emirates, United States of America, Wales. All these authors write with a degree of urgency and now is the time to do something about putting the university system back on track so that it delivers benefits to the community.

Each chapter in the book offers a different perspective on one or more of the many different dimensions involved in the operation of a university. These chapters have been inspected by the editors who have endeavoured to retain, as fully as possible, the voice of the authors. Consequently, very few changes have been made to the original text provided. Clearly, the views expressed in each chapter are those of the author/s and are not necessarily endorsed by the editors.

We have not attempted to standardise the English used by the different authors. Thus some of the papers have been produced using vocabulary and spelling for North American English and some papers have used other varieties of the language.

Each author or group of authors were asked to write a short statement which articulates the main thrust of their chapter. These are provided below, and it is hoped that they will be of assistance to readers in deciding which chapters are most interesting for them to study in some detail.

This book does not attempt in any way to forecast what will happen to universities in the future. It is the purpose of the book to point out the many complex issues which constitute the fabric of a modern university and to make some suggestions as to how universities might be conceptualised in the future in order to deliver the maximum benefit to all the various stakeholders.

The book has also been produced in the expectation that it may be of value to prospective students who are considering enrolling at a University and are not quite sure what a university education can deliver and how to choose the most appropriate university for their purposes.

Short statements about each chapter

ONE
Post Covid-19 Universities: Reformed or Reinvented
Dan Remenyi
Extraordinary Professor
Department of Information Systems
University of the Western Cape, South Africa

The Covid-19 crisis has been most disruptive to the university sector and it will certainly lead to material changes in the way in which universities will operate. Some universities may not survive and those that do will have to introduce new approaches to lecturing, tutorials, residences and general facilities on the campus. This crisis can also be an opportunity to re-conceptualise the nature of higher education and how universities could operate in an entirely different way so as to be far more beneficial to society. The structure of degrees could be overhauled as could the way student progress is evaluated. More collaboration with potential employers and the opening of access by the reduction or removal of fees should be addressed.

TWO
Ivory Tower to Ecosystem Driver: Transforming the University Business Model
Philip Dover
Emeritus Professor
Babson College, Boston, USA

The continued presence of Covid-19 highlights an existential threat facing many universities – their inability to generate sufficient revenue to cover burgeoning costs. The availability of digital technology platforms provides an environment where truly "disruptive" business model change offers a path toward economic survival. The notion of ecosystems encourages radical shifts in strategic and operational practice, stimulating multidisciplinarity, collaboration, open source activity and entrepreneurial thinking. Although technology-driven innovation hubs present powerful examples of ecosystems at work, most universities operate outside such settings and must become imaginative in driving institutional transformation. We describe two types of ecosystems – "bottom-up," catalyzed by students, faculty, alumni and entrepreneurs, and "top-down," working through established university structures. Shared ecosystem success factors include innovative university leadership, cross-disciplinary departmental cultures, and robust relationships with external partners. In particular, we argue for the adoption of an entrepreneurial mindset across the decision making process. In sum, universities must switch from market share competition to continual growth of the educational market.

THREE
The Impact of Covid-19 on University Teaching
Kenneth A. Grant and Steve A Gedeon
Ted Rogers School of Management
Ryerson University, Toronto, Canada

The Covid-19 pandemic has caused a dramatic forced experiment in remote teaching, with more than 90% of students across the world attending virtual classes. Universities and faculty have made an operational pivot in a matter of a few days to go remote, with students being very understanding of the unusual situation, but demanding a better experience when their next academic year starts. Professors have gained invaluable experience and participated in professional development on new teaching methods. Traditional universities must compete in the next academic year with online universities by delivering virtual real-time experiences appropriate to young fulltime undergraduate and graduate students, by going beyond lectures to provide active experiential learning. Looking forward, universities and faculty who are willing to be innovative and use their experiences and new learnings can create a new kind of university education that better fits the 21st Century.

FOUR
The Decimation: Not Yet the Implosion
Gabriel Donleavy
UNE Business School
University of New England, Australia

In the chapter I wrote for the book, University of The Future (Donleavy, 2019), I predicted that by 2030 the university sector would implode. That was because demand for university places had reduced far below supply. With 2020's Covid-19 keeping so many people locked down at home for the whole of semester one, overseas students were not able to study face to face abroad. Universities faced a financial crisis in proportion to their reliance on overseas student fee income. It is still too early to see a clear or comprehensive picture of the Covid-19 effects on universities. This chapter assembles some important early effects and early responses. The verdict is that the crisis will shrink the sector but not kill it.

FIVE

Turning Threats into Opportunities: A Hybrid Learning Model

Andrew D Banasiewicz
Merimack College, North Andover, MA, USA

The relentless march of automation is compelling broadening of the established conception of what it means to 'learn' as the rapidly evolving technological tools and capabilities now offer viable, and at times even superior, alternatives to the age-old reason-based learning mode; at the same time, the current global health crisis-caused physical contact restrictions are necessitating rapid learning modality adaptations. The hybrid learning model discussed in this chapter offers a reconceptualization of higher – i.e., university-based – learning, framed in the context of the interplay between the two broad learning modes and the two distinct learning modalities, while also expressly taking into account learning goals and outcomes. The reasoning that underpins the learning model outlined here argues that the combination of evolving technological and societal realities calls for institutions of higher learning to more fully embrace hybrid instructional approaches.

SIX

The Education Continuum: A Journey Interrupted

Madelyn Blair[1] and Denise Lee[2]
[1]Pelerei, LLC, Principal, Washington DC, USA
[2]PwC, Director, Washington DC, USA

Covid-19 has forced changes that have disrupted life at every level. We are all experiencing a journey interrupted. Both learning and working remotely has been shunned by a selection of universities and corporations over the years. With the Covid-19 tsunami crashing into the global economy, the future goals became immediate needs. All organizations that could move to 100% virtual collaboration rushed to do so. The impact of this sudden change on the workforce clearly demonstrated which universities had made the investments necessary to respond to this crisis and which were scrambling to catch up. This paper discusses the importance of revisioning the university's mission into a future story that builds resilience into the business model and the learning and teaching environment for students and the faculty. The paper also discusses how universities must provide alternative options for students to gain on-going competencies post Covid-19 to prepare them for the shifting career paths of the future.

SEVEN

Reflecting on Examinations: The Higher Education Examination Paradox

Shawren Singh
Department of Information Systems, School of Computing
University of South Africa

Covid-19 has forced the higher education system into overdrive. Universities have been caught wanting on several levels, not least of which is how do we examine our undergraduate candidates in the absence of traditional venue-based assessment? The purpose of this chapter is to reflect on the nature of examinations and how we as academics have approached them.

EIGHT

Smart Learning and Smart University Campuses in a Covid-19 World

Niyi Awofeso and Adi Arida
School of Health and Environmental Studies
Hamdan Bin Mohammed Smart University, Dubai, United Arab Emirates

Between March and May 2020, about 1.6 billion students — close to 80% of all primary, secondary and tertiary learners in 181 countries were unable to physically go to school due to the Covid-19 pandemic. Can traditional, campus-based universities adopt smart learning practices by choosing the right technologies and approaches for educating and engaging their students? Smart learning, as one of the key features of the University of the Future, promotes learning which is essentially personal, social, distributed, ubiquitous, flexible, dynamic and complex in nature. Hamdan Bin Mohammed Smart University, Dubai, exemplifies how universities of the future should integrate technology-based learning. In a Covid-19 world, the hitherto disruptive innovation of HBMSU's approach to Smart learning has become today's lifeguard, as online learning – a domain of smart learning - increasingly becomes mainstream in higher education. This chapter reviews the impact of Covid-19 on smart learning approaches in contemporary university education.

NINE
Envisioning Post-Covid-19 Higher Education
Reet Cronk
Information Systems Graduate Studies
College of Business Administration, Harding University, USA

This chapter looks at the past and the present, to help envision possible short and longer-term futures of higher education. It is suggested that the major influencer of the shorter- term vision will be financial pressure. Insight is gained from an examination of disruption-hardened business and their response to previous digitization driven disruption, as well as their current response to Covid-19 related disruption. Universities are already mirroring a similar transformation as they invest in digital infrastructure; employ emerging technologies and innovative business models. These investments and the resultant benefits will secure their place in the future. Technology will overtake finances as the major influencer of the shape of higher education towards 2030. A discussion of these technologies and their potential application is included. Challenges such as maintaining relationships, student/customer expectation, the digital divide, privacy and security, and product quality are identified and discussed.

TEN
Ensuring University Relevance in a Region's Post Covid-19 Knowledge Economy
Gareth Huw Davies[1], Naomi Joyce[2], David Bolton[1]
[1]School of Management, Swansea University, Wales, UK
[2]School of Medicine, Swansea University, Wales, UK

This chapter explores the case of Swansea University through Infrastructure and Activity initiatives, drawing upon experience of the initial Covid-19 crisis, with potential insight for other post-industrial regions. These initiatives emphasise the diverse interactions across innovation ecosystems to realise health sector innovation, aligned with knowledge-based regional economic development. Universities evolve over periods measured in decades and generations; however the recent crisis has required swifter response of university impact, beyond the longer-term Research Excellence and Knowledge Exchange Frameworks perspectives. This chapter demonstrates how the experience of early 2020 has shown university agility in the health crisis response which may be of further importance for the impending economic crisis.

ELEVEN

Covid-19 and Qualitative Social Media Data Collection

Lakshmi Balachandran
Faculty of Social and Behavioural Sciences
Utrecht University, the Netherlands

Qualitative social media data has immense potential to contribute to management research. This chapter familiarizes novice management student-researchers with the risks and benefits of qualitative social media data collection during Covid-19. With the help of examples from published studies, this chapter illustrates the concepts of availability (i.e. accessibility and timeliness) and relevance (i.e. significance and fitness) in the context of qualitative social media data collection. The implications of this chapter go beyond Covid-19 times by analyzing the risks and benefits associated with the use of feasible data sources, the efficiency of the research process and the trustworthiness of results can be ensured. This risk-benefit analysis of potential data sources is also vital for business schools, journal editors, funding agencies, and regulatory bodies who make policies and assess the value of research. Academics of the future should therefore explore the enormous potential of qualitative social media data rigorously, but wisely.

TWELVE

Post Corona Adapted Blended Learning in Higher Education

Peter Mozelius
Department of Computer and System Science
Mid Sweden University, Östersund, Sweden

The ongoing Covid-19 pandemic has increased the need for quality online teaching and learning in higher education. A wide variety of new tools and techniques are tested in an effort to provide quality online alternatives for all types of course activities. This is a challenge for almost all universities, but to what degree depends on their earlier design of blended learning. This chapter presents two different blended models, and how a successful redesign and enhancement of the models might be related to the five-factor model of personality (FFM). The main traits in FFM that seems to affect the learner and educator attitudes towards blended learning are: Openness to experience, Conscientiousness, Extraversion, Agreeableness and Neuroticism. The recommendation is to consider these variations in personality traits, to achieve a more inclusive redesign of blended learning in higher education. This could probably also lead to more interesting future discussions on the design changes that should be made permanent after the pandemic has resolved.

THIRTEEN
What is the Mix: Higher Education, Student Protests, a Virus and Ethics?
Penelope Engel-Hills
Professional Education Research Institute
Cape Peninsula University of Technology, South Africa

This chapter considers the university of the future in an environment of student protests and Covid-19 in South Africa, and the ethical challenges and questions arising from the current global crisis in an unequal society. To save the 2020 academic year meant transitioning to emergency remote teaching which exposed the gaps related to device and data access and again highlighted the need to transform the curriculum and decolonise the university. Sufficient time should be dedicated to ponder and glean the learning that could come out of this pandemic so as to ensure that we do not return to an equilibrium or settle on a new normal that closely resembles the old. Higher education must take this opportunity to shift from a structural, policy driven emphasis to a focus on human relations so as to meet the social needs and create an institution framed on ethical values.

FOURTEEN
Post Covid-19 University: *Quo Vadis*?
Mandla Stanley Makhanya
Principal and Vice Chancellor
University of South Africa, Pretoria/Tshwane, South Africa

21st Century higher education is stumbling into an uncertain future that is calling into question the notion, role and purpose of education and with it, the role of the university. Key drivers of the current dynamics of disruption include: accelerated technological innovation; concerns around sustainability, social justice and equity; a borderless yet increasingly divided and fragmented world influenced increasingly by changing demographics; a plethora of "actors" or stakeholders whose aims and objectives differ substantially from those which are currently assumed or provided for, and more recently, a global pandemic dubbed Covid-19, which has added new challenges and exacerbated many of the existing ones. The collective impact of these forces on society and institutions of higher learning is impelling leaders, management, staff and students of all ages to "unlearn" and re-learn (or learn anew) if they are to prevail and remain relevant in future. This chapter will provide some thoughts and insights on the future of the university in this fluid context.

FIFTEEN

Blended Learning as Response to Covid-19 in Syrian Universities

Dima M. Dayoub
English Language Teaching Department
Higher Institute of Languages, Tishreen University, Lattakia, Syria

The 2019 edition of this chapter presented the rationale for virtual and blended learning in the light of widening access through 1). creating inroads into higher education for the disadvantaged: those immobilized by heavy family or work commitments; and 2) enabling access to physically inaccessible higher education institutions whose infrastructures were destroyed by the war. Such educational modalities have been remedial alternatives for certain categories of students, unfettering them from geographical and time confinements. Today, with the unfortunate outbreak of coronavirus (Covid-19), blended learning is key to creating inroads for the masses, not just the disadvantaged. Most university students, lecturers and personnel have become temporarily immobilized and most higher education institutions inaccessible. In such times of unpredictability, we are in urgent need of certainty on the higher education front. Reflecting on the experience of the Syrian higher education system, this chapter proposes that planned blended learning is the emerging emergency response to potentially recurrent or unforeseeable higher education disruptions. However, for this modality to be robust enough, the concept of "emergency" needs to be synonymous with readiness, and continuity with quality.

SIXTEEN

Student Readiness to e-Learning Co-Production during Covid-19

Andrews Agya Yalley
Marketing and Supply Chain Management
University of Cape Coast, Ghana

The ongoing Covid-19 pandemic and its detrimental effect on traditional universities implies that universities of the future should substitute their usual face-to-face teaching and learning approach with e-learning technologies and platforms. This, thus, emphasizes the importance of understanding the factors for enhancing student readiness to engage in the co-production of teaching and learning through e-learning platforms. This requires that universities commit relevant resources and communicate effectively with students. It also requires that universities develop strategies that motivate students and enhance their self-efficacy to embrace these technologies. It is hoped that the successful implementation of these strategies will position and cushion universities of the future to survive Covid-19 and other turbulences that might affect universities in the future.

SEVENTEEN

Post Covid-19 Future of Universities in Low and Middle Income Countries

Cees Th. Smit Sibinga[1], Maruff A. Oladejo [2], Isaac Kajja[3], Arwa Z. Al-Riyami [4].
[1] IQM Consulting, Zuidhorn & University of Groningen, Netherlands
[2] University of Lagos, Akoka, Nigeria
[3] Makerere University, Kampala, Uganda
[4] Department of Haematology, Sultan Qaboos University Hospital, Muscat, Oman

Covid-19 has created a new world order requiring a shift in perspective and necessitating thinking in different ways, replacing the conventional strategic planning with a vision statement of intent, fundamentally different from a mission statement, as a description of the route to follow to realise the vision. Despite the disruption the Covid-19 pandemic has caused, there are opportunities for change and progress, e.g. changing from strategic to vision planning; developing new business models and financial options to stabilize the 'bottom line'; strengthening collaboration instead of competition. Additionally, there remains to be identified for the future beyond Covid-19 the rolling out of e-learning; less mobility, more students studying closer to home; embracing online enrolment methods; teleconferencing and video tele-congressing; diversifying supplies and capacities away from China. In fact, post-Covid-19 provides a 'golden' opportunity to change and attempt to narrow the existing knowledge gap in the seriously affected and deprived low and middle income world.

EIGHTEEN

Knowledge Management and the Post Covid-19 New Normal in Universities

Eduardo Tomé[1], Pedro Soares de Mello[1], Andrew Hatch[1], Francisco Maurício[1], Elizaveta Gromova[2]
[1]Universidade Europeia de Lisboa, Lisboa, Portugal
[2]Peter the Great St. Petersburg Polytechnic University, Russian Federation

In this chapter we analyse the "new normal" originated by the Covid-19 crisis from the point of view of knowledge management (KM) science; we furthermore refer to the specific case of universities and higher education. We find that the "new normal" is rooted in KM science. Crucially, a hybrid form of the "new normal" for universities will probably be more like the "old normal" than in some other sectors of economic activity, mostly because, in order for universities to maintain high standards and patterns of behaviour, they need some form of the "old new" where participants "rub shoulders" and walk (literally) together philosophising.

NINETEEN

Disruption and the University of the Future
Martin Rich
Faculty of Management
City, University of London Business School, UK

Disruption has emerged as a popular term to refer to radical change in an organisation, or in a sector, often prompted by major external factors. Inevitably this has led to some discussion of whether recent events might have a disruptive effect on universities. In fact disruptive innovation, as discussed in the Innovator's Dilemma written by Christensen in 1997 has a fairly precise meaning referring to cases where major technological innovations which have threatened the success of long-established businesses. The rhetoric of disruptive innovation has lessons for universities in the current climate where they need to adapt to a situation where long-held assumptions are no longer valid but this should be considered in conjunction with other concepts, notably double-loop learning as advocated by Argyris, which can rationalise the need to plan both for immediate actions and for an unknowable future.

TWENTY

The Idea of a University for the Future
Cathal MacSwiney Brugha
Emeritus Professor
University College Dublin, Ireland

There is a need for a radical change in the direction of governance in society. There are warning signs, challenges to face, problems to overcome, that could be researched, solved, and solutions taught to this and future generations. In the spirit of John Henry Newman, the future university would serve what is right for the good of all and, at this critical time, play a leading and beneficial role in preparing society to cope with its current and future difficulties. Newman believed university education could liberate people to think for themselves and, through this, develop their conscience, and inspire them to contribute to the betterment of people's lives. An internet-based globally connected university could facilitate giving people access to education, with equal effect everywhere in the world, regardless of any division, which they could use to empower themselves to help face the coming global challenges.

1

Post Covid-19 Universities: Reformed or Reinvented

Dan Remenyi
Department of Information Systems
University of the Western Cape, South Africa

The speed at which some universities have reacted to the Covid-19 crisis is hardly credible. Hariri (CBC 2020) told us that "the entire University went online" in a week. Mary Lidstrom Vice Provost for Research (Nature 2020) said that, "The notice went out on 6 March, a Friday afternoon. All classes at the University of Washington in Seattle - the city then the US epicentre of the outbreak of Covid-19 would shift online the following Monday. Instructors scrambled to set up remote learning options for more than 40,000 students". How that could have been possible is a mystery. More credibly, I am aware of a number of universities which paused for a few weeks and then resumed all their tuition online. It has been suggested that this fast response should be referred to as "remote emergency teaching" as clearly online teaching technology cannot be employed properly in such time periods. And perhaps, needless to say, these rushed conversions to develop online teaching have enormously increased pressure on the faculty.

Much of the transfer of university courses online was conducted through the video conferencing product Zoom. According to VB (2020) the number of Zoom's daily active users jumped from 10 million to 200 million and that 90,000 schools across 20 countries are using this one product to deliver online classes. This clearly smacks of panic. The Covid-19 crisis has indeed been the most astonishing gift to the remote educational technology sector with the value of companies in this business skyrocketing.

However, although delivering lectures and tutorials electronically may be part of the solution to the crisis it is by no means the answer to the dilemma in which the universities currently find themselves. This shakeup which is already apparent by the scramble described above to go online may well be a catalyst which could trigger a number of the more important changes which are required if the university is to become really relevant in the 21st century.

The changes required have been identified by the groundswell of discontent towards universities in various parts of the world. Universities seem to be regularly accused of a litany of unacceptable conduct. They have been accused of inter alia inadequately preparing their students for working careers. They have been accused of being elitist and not offering reasonable access to the less privileged members of society. They have been accused of being too expensive and especially not providing adequate tuition for the fees they are charging. They have been accused of remunerating their high office bearers and their prestigious professors excessively while at the same time restricting career opportunities for early career academics. There are few organisations which have been as thoroughly scrutinised as universities in the past few years.

Although these criticisms point to important failings in the university system they are also, in an important sense, unfair. The manner in which universities operate is in some respects a reflection of the culture within society. For many years society has adopted a neoliberal stance which insisted that efficiency is by far the most important consideration in the production of goods and services. Therefore, in following the efficiency mantra, universities have looked to introduce managerial techniques which optimise the employment of the resources at their disposal. The simplest example of this is the current tendency to employ contract staff instead of making full-time permanent appointments to faculty. This mean-spirited tactic simply costs the university less. At the same time universities have cut back on the intensity of tuition, thereby reducing costs. Universities have used the same neoliberal logic to determine the fee structures which are designed to maximise their income. In support of this logic universities have paid higher salaries to prestigious professors who attract more attention to the University in the media and thus, it is believed, will attract more students. It is the same logic that says that operating a large institution in this environment requires top management skills and therefore it is essential to pay Vice-Chancellors and other high office bearers international salaries. It is surprising that university councils or trustees or governors have allowed some of these salaries to be paid.

Some commentators have referred to the above changes in university culture as having acquired a corporate mind-set. Some academics have been opposed to this commercialisation or marketisation and have spoken out strongly against it. But it has been difficult to argue against a general tide of commercialisation in society. On top of this, while discontent has been developing with the issues mentioned above, there have been several high-profile law cases. Numerous complaints made by students have reached the law courts, which was totally unheard of a decade or two ago.

In 2019 the USA experienced a dramatic scandal when the criminal justice system brought prosecutions against 33 parents who had bribed elite universities to accept their children (Global News 2019). The problems experienced in other parts of the world are no less important with one particular case in the UK whereby a student successfully obtained a £61,000 payment for claiming that the university delivered a Mickey Mouse degree (The Guardian 2019). The value of some degrees had been questioned but it was startling to see the term Mickey Mouse degree come into use.

Meanwhile alongside these problems which could be considered to be external issues, there is perhaps an even greater internal danger facing the university sector related to their current cash flows. Clearly universities rely on students to pay fees. These differ for undergraduate and postgraduate degrees. There are also different fees for diplomas as well as for research students undertaking doctoral research. Universities also acquire substantial income from executive programmes which are sometimes run specifically for organisations on an in-house basis. These sources of fees are now in question as fear of the Covid-19 virus raises issues related to the safety of congregating in numbers. Universities are not easily able to respond to changes in their income. Unlike many commercial organisations which can reduce their costs in the face of declining demand, universities cannot easily follow such a strategy. The nature of the university establishment is that the vast majority of costs are fixed, i.e. irrespective of whether 1000 or 20,000 students enrol for an academic year, most of the costs remain.

There are rich universities with extraordinary large resources and these institutions will not be much affected, at least in the short term, by any reduction in fee income. But there are many more universities which do not fall into this category and which may well find themselves at risk of financial failure. The situation is, of course, made considerably worse by the fact that many institutions rely on the fee income from overseas students who customarily pay considerably higher fees. It is thought highly unlikely that a significant number of overseas students will be attracted in the future.

Because of these difficult financial circumstances, some Vice-Chancellors in the UK have appealed to the government for financial assistance during these troubled times. So far this appeal has been received with what might be described as lukewarm attention. The Telegraph (2020) reported that "the Universities Minister announced a £2.7 billion lifeline for universities but has stopped short of a generous bailout". Furthermore, it appears that there were to be some conditions attached to this lifeline. Of course, no one knows what the shortfall in the universities' budgets will be in the UK, but it is unlikely that £2.7 billion will be adequate to prevent some institutional failures.

To save the situation universities will probably have to make some fundamental changes to the way they function and these changes will be required urgently. But generally speaking, universities have been and will perhaps always be slow to embrace change. The acceptance of the current neoliberal attitude did not occur overnight, but was gradually absorbed by universities over some decades. The university mind-set is deeply rooted in tradition. They are prepared enough to launch a new degree or a new programme but to ask them to reconsider the model for education on which their activities have been based for hundreds of years presents major problems. This may largely be because the original principles on which universities were conceived included the fact that they should be self-regulating independent entities and not beholden to any outside authority.

This view of independence was not only applied to the relationship between the university and the community, but it was also perceived as being the basis of the relationship between individual faculty members and the university itself. This was best expressed through the concept of academic freedom whereby faculty members believed that they were entitled to independently determine what they should teach and how they should teach it. This philosophy may have served the university well in former times, but it is questionable whether it is appropriate in the 21st century. There are a range of strategies available to universities to cope with the circumstances in which they find themselves because of the Covid-19 crisis. However, it is instructive to consider two extreme courses of action which could be taken.

There are and there will be universities who believe that they have been on the correct path and that all that is required is to employ appropriate technologies to comply with the new social distancing rules. For these universities video conferencing software will be a central element in their new strategy. The practice of delivering lectures to several if not many hundreds of students in packed lecture theatres is clearly unacceptable. And of course, this type of delivery has been known for quite some time to be ineffective. It is simply not possible to absorb much knowledge in this way. This type of activity can easily be substituted by electronic delivery either in the form of video conferencing or by recording of the lecture and its being made available on the web. However, it is important that universities understand that there is still a digital divide and that it is wrong to assume that all students have access to appropriate Wi-Fi.

Tutorials by their very nature should be conducted in small groups and in many environments it would not be difficult to create circumstances which allowed appropriate social distancing. Tutorials could be timetabled to be in the evening or on the weekends or maybe during periods which are traditionally believed to be for vacation. Some universities are talking about students working in small groups or bubbles on a regular basis across an academic year. These new approaches to scheduling tutorials will have to be controlled and maybe some students will participate in tutorials in person while others will take turns to so do across the Internet. In the same way students could only be allowed access to the campus and thus the library on selected days of the week. Flexibility will be the key to success here.

Other activities such as laboratories, clinics and field trips, which cannot be delivered online, can also be re-timetabled, with some creative time management ideas, such as extending the number of hours worked during the day and perhaps working on weekends, in such a way that smaller groups are accommodated.

Such re-organisation requires a significant amount of reconceptualisation of the education experience as well as detailed planning and scheduling. It falls upon university leadership to be able to rethink the institutions modus operandi and to oversee the implementation of a new approach. Imagination will be one of the most important factors that will lead to success in this respect.

Alongside the purely academic dimension there is a whole raft of supplementary issues which affect important dimensions of student life. These range from on-campus catering to university residences, to sporting activities as well as socialising and entertainment. In fact, when all these activities are considered the typical university can properly be seen as a microcosm of society as a whole. All these issues now have to be addressed in the light of the new circumstances in which society finds itself.

It is quite unclear as to how restaurants will function in the near future and it has been suggested that, in society in general, many may have to close. An attempt to socially distance within university canteens or refectories will require some extraordinary measures to be in place which might make the experience challenging and could destroy the economics which makes campus catering possible. One idea could be to allow student access to these public facilities on a rotation basis so that students with names beginning with A to J could use the dining facilities on Mondays and so forth. On the other hand, maybe all campus catering will have to be refocused on takeaway food and refreshments which are consumed privately.

The way halls of residence will need to function has not yet been well addressed but it would appear that there will at least have to be much higher levels of hygiene than universities have generally been accustomed to achieving. Maybe special testing of students for the virus will be required. It has been suggested that perhaps students could hire their room by the week so that they could spend some time on the campus and some time away. Maybe the solution might be for the universities to divest themselves of this residence activity which is perhaps more suited to those with experience in the hotel or hospitality industry.

Much the same can be said for university sporting activities where crowd control could become an issue as well as the traditional facilities provided by students' unions for social gatherings. All these measures related to social distancing have negative economic implications which will threaten the financial viability of many universities.

The above describes how universities can try patch up the present system i.e. reform its operation and thus continue to make it work through the process of social distancing, rescheduling and greater control of student interaction on the campus. However, there will always be a significant number of young people who will find it difficult to sustain these types of restrictive practices and universities will have to be careful as to how they try to enforce the new regime. On the more optimistic side most of these suggestions assume that no vaccine will be available within the next few years. If a vaccine is produced and if effective treatment is established for Covid-19 many of these new restrictions will not be required.

There is however at the other end of the spectrum of possible university responses to the crisis an entirely different approach which could be taken to the reorganisation of universities and which could be seen as the universities reinventing themselves.

Crises are great drivers of change and Covid-19 represents an opportunity for major game changing strategies for the university sector. Thus, it is possible that we can now really rethink university education. Universities should not be regarded as a continuum in the education of the youth of the country. Perhaps on completion of secondary schooling young people should not look towards this type of institution but rather extend their knowledge in a different way. The original university model was created 900 years ago and then substantially reformed 700 years later. Thus, the current model of education delivery within the university operation is in most cases now 200 years old. It may be time for another major reform of how we think about higher education. The original model gives the universities an enormous amount of autonomy and it is not clear that this autonomy has always been used wisely.

Why not rearrange the structure of degrees so that students have far more freedom in deciding what to study, when to study, where to study (this is meant in a much broader sense than simply online learning) and how to study. Student performance could be evaluated on what they know about the topics they have chosen to study rather than what they have learnt, often by rote, from the lecturers.

The whole approach to examinations is regarded by many as being archaic. Assessment should not be based on what students can remember but rather on what they have achieved.

Universities need to distance themselves from the practices which allow them to appear to operate in a similar way to corporations in the business sector. Amongst other things it is essential that they need to stop referring to students as "clients". This mistake may be at the root of their mimicking other business values. They need to discontinue the practice of paying their Vice Chancellors a quarter of a million pounds or more. They need to carefully examine the amount of contract research which is undertaken and the conditions under which it is performed.

Universities need to stop taking advantage of junior contract and adjunct staff though sessional appointments. It is clearly understood that higher education leads to more interesting careers and therefore higher salaries and thus universities should be funded by levies on higher salaried individuals. This should be seen as a "pay-forward" rather than a payback procedure. It is after all patently obvious that the provision of education is essential in all modern societies and fees restrict access for many talented individuals.

The traditional approach of lecturing to large groups of individuals is an ineffective way of transferring knowledge and this could be immediately substituted by technology. In fact, a variety of different technologies can be applied to facilitate learning as well as increase the effectiveness of the teaching processes. In order to share knowledge across society, faculty could be required to teach at multiple institutions, thereby reducing the concentration of prestigious professors in elite institutions. Similarly, students from less established universities could be invited to participate in activities with students from elite institutions. This could be done by both physical visits as well as online activities.

Universities have taken for granted that the members of their community need to cohabit closely. Some universities had a rule that their students and faculty had to live adjacent to the campus. Of course, in the 21st century this has been extensively relaxed, but maybe more universities should be prepared to use technology to provide their members with knowledge and allow even greater freedom regarding attendance. It would also be possible to limit the competitive nature of the relationships between universities which would encourage much greater knowledge (and even faculty) sharing and remove one of the major blights on the face of the system of talking about elite and second and third tier universities. It was very refreshing to see several of the better-known universities make some of their lectures available on the web free of charge to the public which is a step in the right direction.

It is important to emphasise that university education needs to be continually updated so that it facilitates a smooth transition for graduates from a student's existence to professional life. It also must be born in mind that students are continually looking toward a university degree as a platform on which to build a career and as such the expense of acquiring the degree needs to obviously be value for money. Clearly it is seldom an easy task to balance the budget in an institution such as a university.

It is beyond the scope of this chapter to list all the possible initiatives which could be explored and thus suffice it to say that the central issue is one of imaginative reform. The question is can we reimagine a method of encouraging higher education in a way which does not produce the limitations which we have recognised in the current university system? There is a lot of work to be done in this regard and the current Covid-19 crisis could be used as a great stimulus to begin this difficult task.

However, it is necessary to be clear that there is so much invested in the current system that it will be difficult to undertake the root and branch reform which is suggested here. There will no doubt be resistance from faculty and maybe even students. Furthermore, any revolutionary type change is always dangerous as there are will inevitably be unforeseen consequences. But the universities truly need to take this opportunity to initiate substantial reforms and move towards reconceptualising, reformulating and delivering a better future for students and graduates and in the end themselves. There is little doubt that the universities now have more opportunity to reinvent themselves than they have had for many years. It really is time for bold leadership from university management and by those who have been trusted by society to advise them.

Reading list

CambridgeshireLive (2019) https://www.cambridge-news.co.uk/news/cambridge-news/anglia-ruskin-businesscourse-sued-pokwong-16367798

CBC (2020) https://www.cbc.ca/radio/thecurrent/the-current-for-april-1-2020-1.5517314/historian-yuval-noah-harari-says-we-can-choose-what-the-world-looks-like-when-the-pandemic-is-over-1.5518091

Global News (2019) https://globalnews.ca/news/5047211/felicity-huffman-lori-loughlin-college-admissions-scheme/

Nature (2020) https://www.nature.com/articles/d41586-020-01518-y?utm_source=Nature+Briefing&utm_campaign=0967852569-briefing-dy-20200605&utm_medium=email&utm_term=0_c9dfd39373-0967852569-44877893

The Guardian (2019) https://www.theguardian.com/uk-news/2019/jun/02/graduate-who-sued-university-says-payout-barely-covers-her-costs

The Telegraph (2020) https://www.telegraph.co.uk/news/2020/05/10/mickey-mouse-degrees-could-weeded-universities-face-financial/

VB (2020) https://venturebeat.com/2020/04/02/zooms-daily-active-users-jumped-from-10-million-to-over-200-million-in-3-months/

Dan Remenyi BSocSc MBA PhD is an Extraordinary Professor at UWC and has worked at 10 different universities over the past 30 years as a visiting professor where his main interest has been in the sociology of research. He has also acquired an interest in how universities function as educational and research organisations.

2

Ivory Tower to Ecosystem Driver: Transforming the University Business Model

Philip Dover
Emeritus Professor
Babson College, Boston, USA

The late Harvard Business School Professor Clayton Christensen consistently troubled leaders in higher education by predicting that 50% of colleges and universities in the United States would close or go bankrupt within a decade. And this was before the Covid-19 pandemic struck! The reasons for such difficulties are well-rehearsed. In the broadest sense, most colleges and universities are unable to bring in enough revenue to cover their costs. In the US, the average tuition discount rate was almost 50% for first-time, full-time freshmen in 2017-18 as competing schools scrambled to fill classrooms (Horn, 2018).[1] This practice leads to a "war for talent" in which universities aggressively poach students. This trend is exacerbated by the rapidly changing economic balance enabling universities in Asia, and particularly China, to become more attractive to students. On top of this, demographics are beginning to work against traditional colleges and universities. The pool of 18 year-olds is declining, with precipitous falls in many regions predicted over the next 5 to 10 years.

In the midst of these changes, another force is impacting universities even more. This is the rapid and disruptive introduction of digitization and artificial intelligence (AI). Indeed, Christensen has labelled online learning as the first truly disruptive innovation in education since the printing press! A recent McKinsey study (Bevins et al, 2020) revealed that almost 50% of US colleges and universities had no formal online education programs in 2018. Coronavirus has now made online capabilities imperative, with investment laggards finding it difficult to attract and retain students.

Such observations lead to the immutable conclusion that the long-established business model for colleges and universities is broken. The public increasingly questions the value of higher education, given the debts incurred by students and their poor prospects for employment. The Institute of Financial Studies calculated that a fifth of UK graduates would have been financially better off if they had not attended university (*Economist,* 2020). In order to ensure financial sustainability as well as marketplace relevance, more prescient higher education institutions are

---

[1] A tuition discount rate above 35% puts a college in the danger zone, particularly when it is heavily dependent on tuition for institutional funding. (Horn, 2018)

experimenting with changes to their operations. In addition to the commitment to online programming, intensified activities to increase enrollment and net tuition revenue, as well as efforts to reduce costs, are being implemented. For instance, some schools are changing their discounting policies and publishing much lower tuition prices; others are experimenting with fixed price guarantees, the length of time required to earn a degree (e.g., the University of Buckingham offers two-year undergraduate degrees), and the additions of new programs to both broaden and improve institutional attractiveness (such as pre-professional programs). Cost containment activities include reducing the percentage of full-time faculty, a decrease in tenured faculty, the fuller utilization of campuses year-round, increased consortia activity, and the application of open courseware.

Apart from the impact of digitization and AI, most of these concerns represent "incremental" issues that universities have been wrestling with for some time. It is the "disruptive" technology forces that will have the most profound effect on the future of universities. Covid-19 has raised the spectre of a once-in-a-lifetime opportunity for a radical political, economic and social reset of society. With heavy state intervention becoming the new political norm, the pursuit of a clean tech, high value economy becomes more feasible, as does the search for genuine social welfare policies (e.g., health care for all; universal basic income). Likewise, Covid-19 offers businesses the chance to reset and reshape the world in a more sustainable way. What will it take for business to achieve a symbiosis between people, planet and profit – the "triple bottom line" – in contrast to the familiar single bottom line of profit alone? Issues such as global warming, inequality and poverty should inform a new CEO leadership mandate. These same considerations must also resonate for college Presidents and Vice-Chancellors. The knowledge agenda for universities is rapidly shifting to giving the "grand societal challenges" a higher priority. Society is demanding that universities contribute more to solving the huge, applied problems civilization faces such as global climate change, migration, health care and the availability of food and water. But what business model adjustments are required to make such significant institutional changes? How can the university move from a narrowly focused functional operation to a truly societally engaged organization?

Digital technology reshapes, resizes, speeds up and complicates the environment in which universities operate. Technology dissolves existing boundaries between organizations and industries, allowing new collaborative links to be forged. In the search for both economic and social improvement, the university is encouraged to pursue multi-disciplinary activities that address the "grand challenge" issues. The research and teaching initiatives can be both horizontal – ranging across departments within or across academic institutions-- and vertical, where the university collaborates with the constituencies of business, government and civil society.[2] As we struggle to make sense of these developments, the notion of *ecosystems* becomes valuable. For global consultancy McKinsey, an ecosystem (Straub, 2019) is "a complex network of interconnected

---

[2] Often referred to as the Triple Helix Model of Innovation (university, business and government) or the Quadruple Helix Model (university, business, government and civil society). The inclusion of civil society encourages the social responsibility of partners within the network.

businesses that depend on and feed on each other to deliver value for their customers, to the end users, and their stakeholders." These multi-entity groups of players tend not to belong to a single unit but to involve shifting, semi-permanent relationships, linked by flows of data, services and money. Furthermore, players co-evolve as they redefine their capabilities and relations to others over time. Apple's scaling from its IOS digital platform to a multibillion-dollar app community provides an excellent dynamic example.

There are critical structural reasons why ecosystem design has become such a hot topic. These include the unprecedented deregulation of markets (e.g., the advent of for-profit degree programs), a blurring between products and services due to both deregulation and digitization (e.g., distance learning offered from home or the workplace) and technologies that revolutionize how players can serve their markets (e.g., instruction via AI). Given such shifts, it is unlikely that a stand-alone university can meet all needs of a growing customer base.

The implications of such trends for higher education providers are acute. Reviewing the mission of leading institutions, the following is typical – "an engaged university – interacting purposefully with people, organisations and communities to such concepts as engagement for change, sustainable innovation, disruptive creativity, interdisciplinarity, and entrepreneurial thinking." Strategic intent is clear and inspirational – "If ever there was a time for a great university to stand on the side-lines this isn't it."[3] In reality, the publication of smart strategy documents can be notoriously difficult to translate into an operational plan providing a customer-oriented decision process for portfolio selection. There are many inherent roadblocks in moving away from business models that have long focused on siloed teaching and research endeavours towards emerging systems that emphasize digitization, innovation and collaboration both within and beyond the boundaries of the university. This challenge is powerfully illustrated by the "rigor-relevance" research debate. A great divide exists between disciplinary focused, scientific research on the one hand, and practice-oriented research on the other, when addressing the question of meaningful academic knowledge for business and society. Scientific, rigorous research has long been the dominant focus resulting from faculty's relentless pursuit of academic careers, essentially driving the business model with limited regard for the broader needs of other stakeholders. However, there is growing acknowledgement that a sensible balance between scientific rigor and practical relevance must be sought. Cross-functional research aimed at social responsibility and public engagement issues will enable a rebalancing of quality research towards all stakeholders in society.[4]

How can the ecosystem concept serve to reset both the university's *raison d'être* and *modus operandi*? Can universities develop a new way of competing that challenges the conventional view of how to create and capture academic value? Can they *explicitly* position themselves as ecosystem players, within networks of

---

[3] Extracted from the Sussex University 2025 Strategic Framework.

[4] A global community of leading scholars, journal editors, and business school deans recently developed the Responsible Research in Business and Management (RRBM – https://rrbm.network) initiative. It advocates systemic change through the growth of academic quality research that stresses value and relevance to society.

customers, suppliers and producers of complimentary knowledge-based services? Let's examine the characteristics and key success factors of some early university-based ecosystems. We will use the term "entrepreneurship and innovation (E&I) ecosystems" in our discussion.[5] This embraces not only the established creation and commercialization of technology (e.g., the pursuit of a Covid-19 vaccine by Oxford University, GKN and others) but also the entrepreneurial and innovative application of digitally facilitated platforms to problem solve across the academic spectrum. Although most of our examples spring from the business-science interface, application of an *entrepreneurial mindset* allows disciplines from across the university to work together, and with external partners, to better serve their markets.

Innovation ecosystems can be split broadly into two camps. In the first, all governments are looking to technology innovation as a driver for national economic growth, and to universities as the incubators of this national capacity. Universities operating within established technology-driven innovation hubs offer robust models within these environments. MIT, Stanford University and the University of Cambridge are consistently cited as world leaders in this grouping. The second category comprise highly regarded university-based E&I ecosystems operating outside the established technology hubs. Such ecosystems must be nurtured in cultural, economic and socio-political environments that may not be naturally conducive to E&I. It is this group that will be of prime interest to most universities. However, a brief look at a leading technology hub ecosystem may be instructive.

The Cambridge Cluster: Today, Cambridge is Europe's largest technology cluster. Around 61,000 people are employed by more than 5,000 knowledge intensive firms in the area, which have combined annual revenue of over £15.5 billion. Much of the cluster's rapid growth can be attributed to the foundation of the Cambridge Science Park by Trinity College in 1970. In addition to the Science Park, the University and its Colleges have been integral to building the infrastructure that enables the cluster to continue to grow. University personnel and ideas are at the heart of many of the companies in the cluster.

Arnoud de Meyer, Director of the Judge Business School in Cambridge, identified a number of dimensions for technology cluster success.[6] These include access to good technological infrastructure (broadband, transportation, etc.), availability of affordable capital, presence of a sound legal system, a pool of locally available skills, and links with international markets. Of particular importance is evidence of an entrepreneurial/creative culture, existence of good role models and a positive attitude to failure and risk. Ecosystem growth also depends on the quality of networking "... where people meet, exchange ideas, develop new products, and encourage each other in taking risks."

Most universities operate in more challenging environments. How can these universities drive a process of institutional transformation toward E&I ecosystems? One path is a "bottom-up" and community led model, catalysed by students,

---

[5] The term E&I ecosystems was first used in an MIT report on the institutional transformation of universities toward a more entrepreneurial model (Graham, 2014).
[6] https://www.cambridgenetwork.co.uk/news/cluster-secrets-of-success-what-makes-a-successful

faculty, alumni and entrepreneurs in the surrounding economy. Often responding to economic and societal challenges, entrepreneurial development is triggered by a desire to stimulate regional economic growth, and thereby create graduate jobs, research opportunities and broader avenues for university support through the creation of a vibrant localized entrepreneurial ecosystem. Typically driven by the university grassroots, a dynamic and inclusive ecosystem is created through strong partnerships of trust between the regional entrepreneurial community and the university. The investment is focused on regional rather than institutional capacity with universities often downplaying the importance of IP ownership and start-up affiliation, regarding these as secondary to the overarching goal of developing the broader ecosystem. Two examples serve to illustrate this approach.

REMIT (Research on Economics, Management and Information Technologies) at Universidade Portucalense, Porto, Portugal: This is a young research unit founded in early 2017 with the goal of producing valuable applied knowledge for a set of shareholders – regional and national companies, science and technology organizations, public entities (banks, regional governments, etc.), social sector actors and the civil society. Output is strongly oriented to the creation of economic and social value in a rapidly changing environment, with a focus on businesses within the surrounding territories. Portugal, a fast-developing economy, places a heavy reliance on family owned businesses (90% of registered companies) which have struggled with the requirements of innovation, digitalization and professional management. These, and similar societal challenges, are addressed by multidisciplinary research teams across the University as well as through extensive collaboration with academic and non-academic partners (consultants, business clients, funding sources, etc.). The result is the development of valuable knowledge in a co-production model shared across all participants. Knowledge diffusion is tailored to the needs of academic, business and public policy audiences with success metrics weighted towards research relevance (e.g., start-ups, job creation, entrepreneurial platforms).

Babson Entrepreneurship Ecosystem Platform (BEEP) This initiative stimulates and supports entrepreneurship by developing scale-up ecosystems in cities, regions, and countries around the world—particularly in mid-income, advanced economies—where growth-oriented entrepreneurial businesses are present. Ultimately, the goal is stimulating economic growth, meaningful employment, and prosperity by creating measurable business development in a given locale. The program accomplishes this by helping regional leaders build the programs, policies, and culture that allow the entrepreneurial spirit to thrive. Partners may include government entities, foundations, private enterprises, universities, and public-private partnerships[7]. BEEP is the initiative of highly motivated and talented faculty with extensive experience of operating at the interface between academia and external constituents. The "university of the future" will depend on such wellsprings of inspiration from innovative faculty.

---

[7] An impressive example is BEEP's collaboration with the Colombian city of Manizales (Manizales-Más). More details on this and the Scale-Up program can be found at https://www.babson.edu/academics/executive-education/babson-insight/entrepreneurship/scale-up-to-drive-growth/

A second model for stimulating an E&I transformation is to take a "top-down" approach by working through established university structures. This model is often triggered by the desire to realise income and status from university research, with the E&I agenda driven by, and focused on, a strong and ambitious technology transfer office (TTO) or its equivalent. Although building on established university research strengths, this model can expose the danger that university E&I policies become synonymous with those of the TTO, leading to a culture where "only university-protected IP is seen as worthwhile." This may marginalize student, faculty, alumni and regional entrepreneurial communities.

An example of this model working well is Aalto University in Finland. It focuses its institutional vision on the areas of innovation, economic growth, employment and well-being. Research and teaching concentrates on the four core competencies of ICT, materials, arts and design, and business aimed at specifically addressing the broad societal challenges of energy, living environment and health. Notably this model is not the "all things to all people" approach taken by many universities but requires circumscribed research and learning infrastructures that allow intensive collaboration within the Aalto community, and with external users, fostering a growing innovation ecosystem that produces focused, differentiated, societally meaningful research output.

Despite the model differences in creating university-based entrepreneurial ecosystems, shared success factors are evident. Graham (2014) suggests the following:

- Strong university leadership, actively promoting a clear innovation agenda that is understood by staff, students and the appropriate external communities. Priority is given to establishing unique markets for the university's innovative outputs.
- An academic culture that acknowledges, supports and rewards innovation within a cross-disciplinary departmental context. Market facing personnel must act as champions for institutional change.
- At the university level, planners must distribute responsibility for E&I delivery across the multiple university agencies. This will include a range of support services and participation routes for both students and staff through all stages of entrepreneurial growth.
- Creation of an empowered, cohesive, inventive, bold and well-connected student-led entrepreneurial community. This requires, for example, sustained low level funding, seasoned entrepreneurial mentors, and direct connections to university senior management.
- Robust relationships built on trust and mutual benefits between the university and the regional/national E&I community, including a platform for these individuals to play a visible and influential role in university life.

A *small number* of university champions for change, whose conviction of the importance of E&I for the university and the region, as well as personal connections with industry and the regional entrepreneurial community, often prove crucial to the university's emergence as an entrepreneurial center. It is vital to identify and encourage such personnel as they represent a key to overcoming institutional inertia in the search for an improved business model. There are significant challenges in embedding E&I into the vision and mission of a university, not least the "rigor vs. relevance" research question. The incentives built into most universities, where research income and research rankings are the metrics that count, are rarely adapted to reflect the university's transition to an entrepreneurial institution. Widely accepted measures of university E&I (research-related invention disclosures, improved graduate employment, etc.) are relatively easy to capture. Additionally, metrics that reflect the university's institutionalization of and commitment to E&I, as well as its E&I culture, connectivity and influence on the regional and national community must be considered (e.g., satisfaction with university performance by key stakeholders).

We argue that colleges and universities that cultivate *multidimensional entrepreneurial ecosystems* can position themselves to thrive in a fast-changing marketplace. However, despite vocal commitment to an E&I agenda by university leadership and occasional high-profile entrepreneurial activities offered by various support functions, entrepreneurship remains virtually invisible in many university departments. How then to get students, faculty, staff and alumni to adopt an entrepreneurial mindset? A few thoughts follow:

Experiment continuously – try, fail quickly, learn and adjust. The iterative, action-oriented nature of the entrepreneurial mindset teaches that failure is neither permanent nor defining. This could lead to experimentation with the curriculum, introduction of new experiential learning opportunities, engagement with industry in ways that excite them, and exploration of new connection points with alumni through continuous learning opportunities.

Support entrepreneurial leaders – entrepreneurial thinking and leadership is essential at *all* levels in the organization. Transformational thinking should be normalized by supporting new ideas with actionable strategies and appropriate resources.

Collaboration – E&I is inherently collaborative. Internally, it produces efficiencies, builds multidisciplinary relationships and strengthens the learning environment for students and faculty. Externally, by identifying and pursuing strategic partnerships with individuals and institutions – whether academic, industry, non-profit, community or government – universities can create a multidimensional education ecosystem that supports a constellation of enhanced educational offerings at lower costs.

Build lifelong connections – collaboration and leadership within an ecosystem combine to create powerful lifelong connections that will sustain institutions, stakeholders and society. The educational experience is no longer linear. Rather, students seek a long-term, ongoing relationship with education, one with many connection points over the course of their lives.

Be market facing – the entrepreneurial mindset centers on opportunity recognition. Despite the serious headwinds that universities are facing, ultimately there remains a desire and imperative for learning. Constant change means that there is need for new knowledge all of the time. Continuous inquiry is needed to understand what students and employers are seeking and to explore ways to change the array of resources available to meet that demand. Ecosystem partners will prove an important source of this data.

As universities contemplate their future, those that explicitly position themselves as ecosystem players will play by a different set of strategy rules than traditional institutions. The old rules of competitive advantage required investment in what strategists called “deep moats.” This is what insulated the university from competitors. Sometimes it was based on access to scarce resources (outstanding faculty, facilities, etc.), sometimes based on customer loyalty and a strong brand (e.g., the Ivy League mystique), although for many institutions these positional benefits have been reduced to “me-too” claims in a crowded undifferentiated marketplace. The growth of E&I ecosystems challenges this thinking. The creation of opportunities and market value through network building allows ecosystem participants to continually grow the educational market rather than simply capture share in a static setting. Birkinshaw (2019) has used the metaphor of the “turnstile” to describe such players. Here the university can act as a hub linking networks of customers, suppliers and producers of complimentary services.

This shift from moats to turnstiles can be hard to grasp. For most universities, it is natural to protect existing assets and to keep competition at bay. However, a pure-play ecosystem orchestrator is happy to open up to competition and to share its intellectual property, as long as this keeps the ecosystem growing. As Birkinshaw notes, “the aim is to maximize the number of people coming through the turnstiles, rather than to increase the height of the fence or the width of the moat.” Why is this so important? It no longer becomes possible for a single institution to meet all elements of customer needs. “Its focus must turn to competition between digitally enabled ecosystems that span traditional industry boundaries and offer complex and customizable product-service bundles.” (Jacobides, 2019)

The ecosystem-based method may not be for everyone. As a way of working it is inherently more stressful and chaotic than the present, “go-it-alone” educational approach. It requires not only a radical re-definition of the competitive strategic space, but adjustment to organizational and cultural factors. Ecosystem players need the agility to respond quickly and effectively to new challenges and new challengers, require the analytical dexterity to understand rapidly changing customer and stakeholder needs, and to develop the ability to inspire an expanding array of business model partners. The skill base demanded of key institutional decision makers must shift towards an entrepreneurial mind set. Entrepreneurial leaders must be nimble, opportunity-driven, innovative and growth-oriented problem-solvers, as the nature of work swiftly and constantly evolves. To further complicate things, the split between the historically focused academic model and this emerging, eclectic ecosystem world is not absolute. The search for strong proprietary capability by discipline will continue despite a broader, cross-functional need for societal problem solving.

In conclusion, the rules of competitive strategy are becoming considerably more challenging within colleges and universities. A good first step to navigating this increasingly complex setting is to understand that the long-established individual, resource-based model that strives to capture as much of the existing market as possible does not work well in a world of platforms and ecosystems where participants are looking to continually grow both the input (number of students, broadly defined) and output (dissemination of knowledge, equally broadly defined) dimensions of the market. By looking afresh at the way emerging university ecosystem orchestrators operate, senior management in established institutions will be better positioned to compete through the cultivation of their own multidimensional entrepreneurial ecosystems.

References:

Bevins, F., Bryant J., Krishnan C and Law J. (2020). Coronavirus: How Should US Higher Education Plan for an Uncertain Future? *McKinsey.com.* Available at: https://www.mckinsey.com/industries/public-sector/our-insights/coronavirus-how-should-us-higher-education-plan-for-an-uncertain-future

Birkinshaw J. (2019). Ecosystem Businesses are Changing the Rules of Strategy. *Harvard Business Review* (Web Article). Available at: https://hbr.org/2019/08/ecosystem-businesses-are-changing-the-rules-of-strategy

Economist.com (2020). *Time to Think Small.* Available at: https://www.economist.com/britain/2020/04/30/the-government-ponders-bailing-out-universities

Graham R. (2014). *Creating University-Based Entrepreneurial Ecosystems: Evidence from Emerging World Leaders.* MIT: Skoltech Entrepreneurial Ecosystems Report. Available at: https://www.rhgraham.org/resources/Executive-Summary---MIT:Skoltech-2014.pdf

Horn, M. (2018). Will Half of All Colleges Really Close in the Next Decade? *Forbes.com.* Available at: https://www.forbes.com/sites/michaelhorn/2018/12/13/will-half-of-all-colleges-really-close-in-the-next-decade/#4fbe282152e5

Jacobides M. (2019). In the Ecosystem Economy, What's Your Strategy? *Harvard Business Review*, 97 (5). pp. 128-137

Straub R. (2019). The Power of Ecosystems. *Global Focus: The EFMD Business Magazine.* Available at: https://www.globalfocusmagazine.com/the-power-of-ecosystems/

Dr. Philip Dover is an Emeritus Professor at Babson College in Boston, MA, USA. His academic and business interests lie in the management of high technology products, entrepreneurial studies and strategic market planning. He has extensive executive education experience, leading programs on market strategy and corporate entrepreneurship for companies such as Sony, Siemens, Saint Gobain and Waters.

3

The Impact of Covid-19 on University Teaching

Kenneth A. Grant and Steve A Gedeon
Ted Rogers School of Management, Ryerson University, Toronto, Canada

Introduction

In recent months, universities across the world have seen an unprecedented pivot in how they operate. If we had suggested in our chapter on Teaching in the University of the 21st Century (Grant and Gideon, 2019), published only a few months ago that the vast majority of faculty in universities across the world would immediately and broadly embrace distance education, we would have been accused of hallucinations. Yet, as The Chronicle of Higher Education has observed, that is exactly what has happened (Zimmerman, 2020).

Previously, we argued that the most used form of university education – the lecture – was not fit for purpose in today's university. We also argued that good pedagogy called for a focus on learning outcomes and the use of active and experiential student-centric learning approaches, supported by new technology and improved physical spaces. Feedback from across the world on the rushed move to virtual delivery supports our argument for the limitations of the teacher-centric lecture approach and the need for improved use of technology.

As McMurtrie (2020) suggests: "Higher education has been granted good will these past couple of months by students and their families. But as with an unhappy marriage, everyone involved agrees that the patched-together system of awkward Zoom classes, glitchy technology, and uncertain expectations, among both students and professors, needs to end."

Here, we review key changes that have already been made, then address the immediate post-pandemic changes that should be made in order to improve the educational experience. Finally, we suggest some additional longer-term considerations to improve teaching in the 21st century university.

A radically changed environment

Kandri (2020), referencing the World Economic Forum, estimated that almost 90% of students globally were unable to attend university physically during the pandemic. He suggests that, "as painful and stressful a time as this is, it may fashion a long overdue and welcome rebirth of our education systems."

A disrupted student experience

Most students seem to have accepted the disruption of their 2020 winter/ spring/ summer semester experiences due to the Covid-19 pandemic. They recognized that their professors had to make a fast pivot and adopt new delivery and assessment methods overnight and, by and large, accepted the disruption. It is less clear that they will accept a similar quality of delivery in their next academic year. Indeed, students are demanding fee reduction to match the reduction in student experience. Almost 350,000 UK students have signed a Parliamentary petition to reduce fees (Quinn, 2020). Some students are considering taking a "gap" year (West, 2020).

The move to online delivery has had differing impacts on different groups of students. Students with disabilities, students from disadvantaged backgrounds, and international students are amongst those most impacted. They may lack the needed computers, Internet access, quiet study space, and support needed to participate in such sessions. Students needing part-time income to support their studies may not have jobs. These issues may have long-term social and economic impacts. While a bigger issue at the elementary/high school level (Dorn et al., 2020), this also has significant relevance at universities. The "Digital Divide" challenge is well known and the current situation exacerbates the problem (Maloney and Kim, 2020). Further, the move online has increased issues of isolation, well-being, mental health, lack of support networks and more.

Universities facing unprecedented strategic choices

Universities change very slowly. Important decisions have long-term implications and take years to implement. Since the pandemic struck, leadership teams have been struggling to respond, being expected to make major decisions on an urgent basis with limited information.

Universities in countries such as Australia, the UK and the USA, who depend heavily on international students for significant sources of funding face major revenue losses (The Economist Intelligence Unit, 2020). In addition, it is quite possible that domestic students may choose not to attend next year, particularly those expecting to be in residence. While signals are mixed, it does seem that many universities will continue in a virtual mode at least for their autumn semester.

Excepting a small number of online universities, most course delivery across the world has been face-to-face using traditional methods, with the lecture still the dominant delivery mode. When traditional universities adopt online education, they tend to do so in non-strategically-important specialized units, well separated from their mainstream activities. Michael Crow, president of Arizona State University points out even those universities who do provide online education do not use the "regular faculty" for these courses (Bothwell, 2020).

University business models for teaching and course delivery

There are three main strategic categories of university:

1. **On-line Universities**, whose delivery model is based on technology-enabled, distance approaches, usually asynchronously. Frequently, these serve more mature part-time students.
2. **Physical Universities**, whose main delivery model is face-to-face classes on a physical campus. Such universities may offer a range of strategically unimportant distance courses, but these do not form a major part of their course delivery and are often run for revenue creation purposes. Two main

types of physical universities exist - those whose students live in residence on/near campus (where the on-campus experience is a critical aspect of the student experience), and those where students live away from campus commuting to classes and other activities.

3. **Extended-Physical Universities**, those with a major presence as a physical university, who also offer complete programs in a distance format, in essence running an online university as a strategically important complement to their physical presence/delivery.

Suddenly, physical and extended-physical universities have been forced into direct competition with online universities without the infrastructure and support services that have been well established by online universities, and with faculty who have little experience of online/remote teaching and frequently have a negative view of this form of delivery. Further, at least at the undergraduate level, they are dealing with younger, less mature full-time students. Despite having survived the end-of-semester challenges, they need to respond to pressures from faculty and students to deliver a better quality product in order to compete with on-line universities. Ironically, many new undergraduates will have encountered more sophisticated teaching technology in high school than they will at their new universities.

Drawing on the University of Arizona's framework, (Bothwell, 2020) we see four basic delivery models:

1. Physical real-time classes
2. Virtual real-time classes
3. Asynchronous classes
4. Various hybrid/blended models, using elements of the first three

Since physical real-time classes are unlikely during the pandemic and effective asynchronous classes are likely to be beyond the capacity of most physical universities and their faculty, when compared to what is available from online universities, the option likely to be most considered is some combination of virtual real-time during scheduled class sessions and asynchronous hybrid components.

Suddenly, traditional Physical Universities have discovered the critical importance of distance education technology to enable them to compete with On-line Universities.

The strategic importance of technology

Most professors exposure to course delivery technology has been largely limited to the use of PowerPoint and some form of Learning Management System (LMS), likely chosen by their University.

Suddenly, this has changed. As Forbes magazine stated so simply, "And just like that, we're all using Zoom." In just four weeks during February and March, it became the most downloaded mobile app (Bellan, 2020). Zoom has seen its daily participant number leap from some 10 million in December 2019 to almost 300 million in April, 2020 (Wainewright, 2020). From primary schoolers to grandmothers, from boardroom to classroom, the adoption of Zoom is a social phenomenon. Along with similar video conferencing tools such as Skype, Microsoft Teams and Google Meet, it is clear that Zoom will form an integral part of the virtual real-time component of the upcoming fall 2020 and winter 2021 semester delivery strategies of most universities to fulfill their synchronous communication needs.

A professoriate in transformation

Watermeyer et al (2020) in a survey of more than 1,000 faculty in North America, the UK and Europe found that about 90% in the US and EU felt they had a good working knowledge of the needed technologies (less than 60% for the UK). However, only about half felt they had a suitable home environment for online teaching and many felt that the 24/7 digital world significantly increased workplace challenges.

Most universities have support units for learning and teaching and they typically provide excellent advice and resources. However, in the past, only a minority of faculty called on these services. Suddenly, this is no longer the case. Faculty who might never previously have considered going beyond their traditional delivery method are reaching out for help. In our own University, when workshops were offered to help in this transformation, the 200+ available places were filled within an hour of bookings opening. Indeed at most universities, the teaching resources and support for online pedagogy do not have the capacity to support the majority of faculty, rather than a small group of interested professors (Hodges et al., 2020). A professor's home office may now include computer, extra monitor, writing tablet for marking assignments, video camera/phone stand with lighting, green screen, over a dozen applications and editing software.

Just as university administrators have discovered the strategic importance of technology, so have most faculty, whose views and experience of technology are likely somewhat dated. Further, the well-established faculty resistance to adopt technology may be at an all-time low (Sharma, 2020). This is indeed an historic moment to seize in order to enhance the student experience in the 21st century university.

Enhancing synchronous course development and delivery using hybrid online learning

We are observing quite divergent approaches to reopening campuses. Some universities have already announced that their fall 2020 (and possibly their winter 2021) semesters will be taught remotely for most students. Others, particularly US universities who normally offer a residential experience, are projecting returns to campus, although at publication time, it is not clear whether they will succeed. Students and faculty at commuter campuses may be much less willing to travel to class. Regardless, it seems that the switch to remote learning that occurred during the pandemic's onset will continue for much of the next academic year but with higher expectations for a quality educational experience. As Hodges et al (2020) assert, "emergency remote teaching is not online learning"!

The Community of Inquiry (COI) Model of Online Learning (Rourke et al, 1999) is a robust framework conceptually grounded in theories of teaching and learning in higher education. It provides order, heuristic understanding and a methodology to define, describe and measure the elements of collaborative and worthwhile educational experiences (Garrison et al, 2010). Students' educational experience, satisfaction, learning and retention are primarily governed by their *Interaction with Content*, *Interaction with Instructors* and *Interaction among Students*.

Janicki and Liegle (2001) synthesized research results from many instructional design experts to compile best practices for enhancing the students' online *Interaction with Content*. These include using varying presentation styles, multiple exercises, learner control of pacing, frequent testing, clear feedback, consistent layout and clear navigation. Swan (2001) found that "the greater the consistency among course modules, the more satisfied students were, the more they thought they learned and the more interaction they thought they had with the instructors." Some specific recommendations around content, drawn from a variety of sources, include:

- Use of consistent pre-recorded lectures, using the flipped classroom approach which students can view at their own pace. Mix up the presentation style to provide variety when possible (e.g. videos, voice over PowerPoint, self-recorded Zoom sessions, audio podcasts, readings).
- Use publicly available videos and other supporting materials.
- Move beyond the typical course outline to a detailed description of each week's activities published, with the appropriate links, in the LMS (as a "one stop shop" to avoid confusion).
- If the course has complex assignment activities, consider recording separate videos to describe each stage of the work, supported by "how-to" documents within the LMS.
- If some issue was not well addressed in class, record a "quick and dirty" follow-up video to post within the LMS to address the issue. Timeliness is more important than quality.
- Increase the frequency of testing, feedback and interaction between the instructor and other students.

The importance of the student-teacher interaction on learning outcomes has been well established. In face-to-face classrooms, greater "immediacy" is established through behaviors such as giving praise, soliciting viewpoints, humour, self-disclosure, eye contact, facial expressions and gestures (Swan, 2001). Greater immediacy leads to enhanced learning outcomes and student satisfaction. It is often believed that these "social presence" and affective communication channels are more difficult to establish in an on-line context. However, researchers have identified three different aspects of the teaching presence that can increase student satisfaction and learning: direct instruction; facilitating discourse; and design and management (e.g. Coppola, Hiltz & Rotter, 2002). Specific recommendations around *Instructor Interaction* include:

- Videos showing the professor talking provide greater immediacy than audio-only.
- With pre-recorded videos, students prefer and pay more attention when seeing their instructors' faces close up rather than standing at a white board.

- Students prefer and learn more with shorter videos including authentic content rather than highly polished professional videos.
- Develop contingency plans, communicated to students in advance, of how disruptions to the virtual real-time delivery will be handled when they occur.
- Faculty must recognize that, whether they wish it or no, they have become part of a support infrastructure that expects them to do more than simply teach. They need to find ways to demonstrate empathy for the student situation by increasing formal and informal communication using virtual meetings, email and social media.
- Faculty need to share with their students the challenges they are facing in teaching and get the students' input in co-creating their Community of Inquiry.
- The professor is the first point of contact with the students' experiences well beyond the classroom itself. Recognise the challenges that they might be facing in terms of mental health, study environment, family situation and more. Be considerate and supportive, not leaping to conclusions about the reasons for their behaviour and be aware of the range of support services your university can provide when needed and direct students toward these resources.

Finally, *Interaction among Students* is seen as one of the most influential and well-researched aspects of online learning (Swan et al, 2000). This aspect of the educational experience can be superior in online courses because all students have an equal voice and no single student or instructor can dominate the discussion. Students perceive the online discussion as more equitable and democratic and the asynchronous nature allows students to take their time to be more mindful and reflective. Swan (2001) found that "the greater the percentage of the course grade that was based on discussion, the more satisfied the students were, the more they thought they learned from the course, and the more interaction they thought they had with the instructor and with their peers." Faculty should:

- Help students enhance their social presence by communicating purposefully in a trusting environment and developing interpersonal relationships. Find an appropriate medium, ideally within the LMS, to act as the discussion board for your class.
- Assign a percentage of the grade to posting on the LMS discussion board and frequently and meaningfully interact on the platform to help stimulate students to build a Community of Inquiry and develop relationships.
- Structure in-class sessions to include combinations of lecture, discussion, teamwork, breakout and feedback elements that enhance *Interaction among Students*.

Assessment

Assessment is one of the most contentious issues. The traditional assessment technique of the closed-book, time-constrained, scheduled examination does not lend itself to online adoption at scale and the various methods of proctored online exams are expensive, difficult to organize and not as secure as faculty might hope.

Obviously, a wide range of assessment options are available, and their choice is, at least in part, related to the expected learning outcomes.

Just as the lecture is an outmoded method of teaching, traditional examination approaches do not fit well with active and experiential learning and the development of students' abilities to achieve higher-level learning outcomes. A broad body of knowledge exists on how to embed assessment within the learning experience, both individual and group, rather than being independent of these experiences and such assessment techniques can work equally well in a virtual or physical environment. Where the purpose of exams is to test students' rote-learning, faculty may consider short, frequent, low-value quizzes rather than major examinations. Additionally, the use of non-credit quick polls can help assess students' participation and learning and can be used to create a more engaging learning environment.

As an example of the many online resources that have been established to assist faculty, Reimers at al (2020) developed, for the OECD, a useful set of annotated resources.

Longer term considerations

Prognostications for the longer term are speculative but we suggest there are both positive and negative scenarios.

On the negative side are concerns that universities, under significant financial pressure, will use the experience to reduce delivery quality and increase demands on faculty. For example, Watermeyer et al (2020) mention possible de-skilling of faculty and instruction and continuing challenges to student engagement. However, we hope that, rather than trying to impulsively blunder into the market space of the online university, physical and extended-physical universities might rather strategically invest in their resources and faculty to enhance the experiences and learning outcomes for their mainstream student population at both the undergraduate and graduate level.

Despite the explosion of trade press articles and academic journal papers addressing teaching responses to the disruptions of the pandemic, only a few look beyond the short-term to the potential long-term impacts. It is encouraging to see, in fields as diverse as anatomy (Pather et al., 2020), mathematics (Mulenga and Marbán, 2020) and education in Christian universities (Lim, 2020) some focus on how this experience can improve the future delivery approaches in their disciplines.

Despite Marshall McLuhan's argument that "the medium is the message" (McLuhan and Fiore, 1967), we would argue that the reverse is true for the consideration of longer term changes to the higher education teaching environment. Too often, we are focusing on the impact and demands of the medium rather than examining how the new technology enabled media can be used to better handle the delivery of our programs. (Ironically, this *was* one of Mcluhan's arguments way back in 1967!). New options are becoming available to go well beyond the restrictive LMSs that are used by so many universities. Flexible LMS platforms, evolving social media tools, the increasing capabilities and cost effectiveness of tools such as 3-D printing, artificial intelligence, telepresence and virtual reality are just a few examples of what are being used by creative professors.

Many faculty have received only limited training on how to teach and, in many universities, what goes on inside the classroom is subject to very little scrutiny as long as it addresses the course material in ways that follow the University's rules. This can be contrasted with how faculty approach research, which is often a team effort, subject to peer review and feedback on an ongoing basis.

Professors are now becoming part of a wider teaching community taking part in professional development activities at an unprecedented level and reading avidly how to adapt their teaching to meet the pandemic challenges. We hope that exposure to these challenges and the evolution in student expectations may cause faculty to reflect on how they might better handle their teaching responsibilities. This could be particularly impactful if universities recognize the strategic opportunity to help facilitate and support the constructive development of better teaching to cause changes that might benefit the organization and its budgets.

We had previously argued that good professors evolve from being the "sage on the stage" to become the "guide on the side". Perhaps now, we might aspire to becoming the "learning facilitator".

References

Bellan, R. 2020. What You Need To Know About Using Zoom. *Forbes.*

Bothwell, E. 2020. Michael Crow: crisis should herald cooperation and differentiation. *Times Higher Education*, June 10th, 2020.

Coppola, N. W., Hiltz, S. R., & Rotter, N. G. 2002. Becoming a virtual professor: Pedagogical roles and asynchronous learning networks. Journal of management information systems, 18(4), 169-189.

Dorn, E., Hancock, B., Sarakatsannis, J. & Viruleg, E. 2020. Covid-19 and student learning in the United States: The hurt could last a lifetime. McKinsey & Company.

Garrison, D. R., Anderson, T., & Archer, W. 2010. The first decade of the community of inquiry framework: A retrospective. The internet and higher education, 13(1-2), 5-9.

Grant, K. A. & Gedeon, S. A. 2019. Chapter 8: Teaching and Learning in the 21st Century University. *In:* Remenyi, D., Grant, K. A. & Singh, S. (eds.) *The University of the Future.* Academic Conferences and Publishing International Ltd.

Hodges, C. B., Moore, S., Lockee, B. B., Trust, T. & Bond, M. A. 2020. The Difference Between Emergency Remote Teaching and Online Learning. *EDUCAUSE Review* [Online]. Available: https://er.educause.edu/articles/2020/3/the-difference-between-emergency-remote-teaching-and-online-learning [Accessed March 27th, 2020].

Janicki, T., & Liegle, J. O. 2001. Development and evaluation of a framework for creating web-based learning modules: a pedagogical and systems perspective. Journal of Asynchronous Learning Networks, 5(1), 58-84.

Kandri, S.-E. 2020. *How Covid-19 is driving a long-overdue revolution in education* [Online]. World Economic Forum. Available: https://europeansting.com/2020/05/12/how-covid-19-is-driving-a-long-overdue-revolution-in-education/ [Accessed June 6th, 2020 2020].

Lim, H. 2020. Editorial: Post Covid-19 Christian Higher Education. *Journal of the Scholarship of Teaching and Learning for Christians in Higher Education,* 10.

Maloney, E. J. & Kim, J. May 21st, 2020 2020. The Challenge of Equity in Higher Education Under Covid-19. Available from:

https://www.insidehighered.com/blogs/learning-innovation/challenge-equity-higher-education-under-covid-19 [Accessed June 24th, 2020 2020].
McLuhan, M. & Fiore, Q. 1967. *The Medium is the Massage*, Penguin.
McMurtrie, B. 2020. Are Colleges Ready for a Different Kind of Teaching This Fall? *Chronicle of Higher Education*, May 5th, 2020.
Mulenga, E. M. & Marbán, J. M. 2020. Is Covid-19 the Gateway for Digital Learning in Mathematics Education? *Contemporary Educational Technology,* 12.
Pather, N., Blyth, P., Chapman, J. A., Dayal, M. R., Flack, N. A. M. S., Fogg, Q. A., Green, R. A., Hulme, A. K., Johnson, I. P., Meyer, A. J., Morley, J. W., Shortland, P. J., Štrkalj, G., Štrkalj, M., Valter, K., Webb, A. L., Woodley, S. J. & Lazarus, M. D. 2020. Forced Disruption of Anatomy Education in Australia and New Zealand: An Acute Response to the Covid-19 Pandemic. *Anatomical Sciences Education* May/june 2020.
Quinn, S. 2020. *Petition: Reimburse all students of this year's fees due to strikes and Covid-19* [Online]. UK Parliament. Available: https://petition.parliament.uk/petitions/302855 [Accessed].
Reimers, F., Schleicher, A., Saavedra, J. & Tuominen, S. 2020. Supporting the continuation of teaching and learning during the Covid-19 Pandemic: Annotated resources for online learning. OECD.
Rourke, L., Anderson, T., Garrison, D. R., & Archer, W. 1999. Assessing social presence in asynchronous text-based computer conferencing. The Journal of Distance Education/Revue de l'ducation Distance, 14(2), 50-71.
Sharma, C. V. K. 2020. Navigating the Crisis and Beyond Future of Higher Education – Impact Covid-19. Available: Navigating the Crisis and Beyond Future of Higher Education – Impact Covid-19.
Swan, K., Shea, P., Fredericksen, E., Pickett, A., Peltz, W. AND Maher, G. 2000. Building knowledge building communities: Consistency, contact and communication in the virtual classroom. Journal of Educational Computing Research, 23(4), 359-383.
Swan, K. 2001. Virtual interaction: Design factors affecting student satisfaction and perceived learning in asynchronous online courses. Distance Education, 22(2), 306-331.
The Economist Intelligence Unit 2020. Covid-19 and the crisis for higher education.
Wainewright, P. 2020. Zoom Q1 sees rocketing revenue as adoption soars, but what now? : diginomica.
Watermeyer, R., Crick, T., Knight, C. & Goodall, J. 2020. *Forced shift to online teaching in coronavirus pandemic unleashes educators' deepest job fears* [Online]. Nature Index. Available: https://www.natureindex.com/news-blog/forced-shift-to-online-teaching-in-coronavirus-pandemic-unleashes-educators-deepest-job-fears- [Accessed June 5th, 2020 2020].
West, C. 2020. *Coronavirus fears may lead to big gap year for college students* [Online]. PBS News Hour. [Accessed June 12th, 2020 2020].
Zimmerman, J. 2020. Coronavirus and the Great Online-Learning Experiment. March 19th, 2020.

Kenneth A, Grant is the Chair of the Department of Entrepreneurship & Strategy in the Ted Rogers School of Management at Ryerson University. He was the School's first Faculty Teaching Chair and was a partner in two major consulting firms before joining Ryerson.

Steven A. Gedeon is Chair of the Ryerson Entrepreneur Institute and Associate Professor of Entrepreneurship & Strategy at Ryerson University. He has designed and delivered entrepreneurship curricula and courses throughout North America and Europe

4

The Decimation: Not yet the Implosion

Gabriel Donleavy
UNE Business School,
University of New England, NSW, Australia

Introduction

In the chapter I wrote for the book, *The University of the Future* (Donleavy, 2019), I predicted that by 2030 the university sector would implode. That would be because demand for university places had reduced far below supply. With 2020's Covid-19 keeping so many people locked down at home for the whole of semester one, overseas students were not able to study face to face. Universities faced a financial crisis in proportion to their reliance on overseas student fee income. It is still too early to see a clear or comprehensive picture of Covid-19 effects on universities. This paper assembles some important early effects and early responses. The verdict is that the crisis will shrink the sector but not kill it.

Immediate impacts

Worldwide

The large market-oriented university systems in the US, UK, Australia and Canada are particularly vulnerable, as they have raised tuition fees and borrowed heavily to invest in things such as sporting facilities and accommodation to attract and house students. That has been underwritten by a belief in continued growth in the number of international students, currently more than 5m worldwide, who usually pay much higher fees than their domestic counterparts. (Jack and Smyth, 2020)

Students' lives have been seriously disrupted. When their campuses closed, many students were forced to leave their dormitories and hostels. Many students rely on their campus facilities as primary sources of meals, health care, and support services, including counselling. Also, many students work to earn money to cover expenses. Students who took a risk to leave home initially, who are not able to remain academically active or are falling behind better connected classmates, or who were employed at or near school and have had to take on new jobs in new locations—all will find it hard to uproot themselves once again and return to school when the pandemic restrictions are lifted. (Bassett and Arnhold, 2020)

The International Association of Universities (IAU) *Global Survey on the Impact of Covid-19 on Higher Education around the World* (2020) investigated the impact of Covid-19 on all aspects of higher education. It yielded 576 replies from 424 universities, 59% advising that their institution was completely closed, two-thirds that classroom teaching had been replaced by distance learning. The most common research impact of Covid-19 was cancellation of international travel and scientific conferences (81% of universities). 52% reported that scientific projects were at risk of not being completed and 21% reported that scientific research had completely stopped.

Impact in the USA

A study of first-degree students by Simpson Scarborough done in March 2020 in the United States found that 20% did not expect to return to the institution they left due to the pandemic closures. Many reported that they may enrol at an institution closer to home, but others will not return to their studies at all. (Bassett and Arnhold 2020)

Most companies and colleges and universities have banned all non-essential travel for employees. Teleconferencing opportunities will partially replace long distance travel as both faculty and administrators re-evaluate recruitment travel and attendance at academic conferences (Dennis 2020).

Cuts of more than 10% to both courses and jobs were announced by Minnesota State University and Northern Arizona University in the immediate aftermath of lockdown. Others are sure to follow.

The president of Harvard announced the self-imposition of a 25% salary cut, the president and provost of MIT each took a 20% cut. A survey of 415 fundraisers at 48 schools revealed that 43% do not expect to meet their fundraising goals. According to a recent report by the American Association of Collegiate Registrars and Admissions Officers, 60 percent of colleges and universities in the United States are considering or have already decided to remain fully on-line for the fall semester. A survey conducted by Tyton Partners revealed that only 57% of American parents surveyed would allow their children to continue at an institution if it offered only online education. When asked to respond to the quality of the remote instruction students were now receiving, on a scale of 1 to 10, they ranked the quality of online learning at 5.6. It also found that parents were less likely to pay the same tuition rates as were charged before Covid-19. (Dennis 2020, Leingang 2020)

Impact in Canada

In a survey of nearly 3,000 students intending to study in Canada, more than half (54%) are planning to defer their admission for a year. Another 15% are no longer planning to study in Canada. In a survey published in The Pie News on April 15th, 42% of students surveyed indicated they had no interest in studying online (Dennis 2020).

Most students in the Province of Nova Scotia do not want an online education, and many are calling for reductions in tuition fees to compensate for what they perceive might be a lower quality education and experience. Most professors do not want to teach in an online environment because they value engaging with students in discussions, debates, and laboratory demonstrations. Before Covid-19, it was thought that a year or more of planning and development was required for a single, high quality online course offering. Now that professors have scarcely three months to change over all their courses in time for the fall semester, quality is an issue. (Westwood 2020)

Mount Saint Vincent University announced a significant reduction in the number of contract academic staff, further increasing the workload of remaining academic staff. More will follow. (Westwood 2020)

Impact in Australia

The number of onshore international students in Australian higher education in mid 2020 sits at 330,000, a fall of 30 per cent on 2019. Universities are looking at losses of $4.6 billion or more in the second half of 2020, with 21,000 jobs on the line, including 7,000 in research. (Hunter 2000a). Redundancies and other cost-cutting measures have started at universities as vice-chancellors confront a major shortfall in revenue over the coming years. Universities Australia has projected losses of as much as $16 billion by 2023. (Hunter 2020b)

The losses will be concentrated at research-intensive universities such as the University of Sydney because income from international students often subsidizes research (Witze 2020). Deakin University said it will axe 300 jobs and not fill 100 vacancies. Southern Cross University has a "best-case" funding shortfall of around $40 million. The vice-chancellor has asked staff to forego the next two wage increases and to voluntarily reduce their workload. He said those measures would save the institution almost $6 million, equivalent to 50 to 60 jobs. 113 senior staff, including executives, already agreed to a pay freeze. (Herbert 2020). Charles Sturt University plans to axe 600 subjects as it tries to plug an expected $49.5 million hole in its 2020 budget. It will save money by cutting subjects that attract very few students. Apparently, 550 of the 4,751 subjects offered last year had no enrolments. (ABC 2020)

Impact in the British Isles

England

A report by London Economics forecasts the university sector could lose around £2.5bn in 2021 in tuition fees alone, along with the loss of 30,000 university jobs, if international and domestic students stay away with Covid-19 continuing unchecked. In addition, there would be the £790m lost in accommodation, catering and conference income, as identified by the Universities UK (UUK) group of vice-chancellors in its recent submission to the government calling for at least £2bn in bailout funding (Adams 2020). The Treasury, however, was said have blocked the appeal. Without it, UUK says some institutions (3 at least, 6 possibly) will go bankrupt (Fazackerley 2020). Ministers can (but need not) unilaterally allocate an additional 10,000 places, with 5,000 ring-fenced for nursing, midwifery or allied health courses (Stubley 2020). Also, universities in England can still charge full tuition fees if their courses are taught online because of the coronavirus outbreak, the government has confirmed (Stubley 2020). This decision appears unpopular with the students, as 63 per cent of postgraduates surveyed preferred a face-to-face course start in January to an online start in autumn (Roberts 2020).

Wales

Students from overseas bring more than £716m to the Welsh economy according to a report by Universities Wales in 2017. In Wales, universities could see a 13,250 fall in first year students causing income to plummet and 1,230 job losses, the report forecasts. Universities in Wales are proportionately more important to the economy of Wales than elsewhere in the UK generating £5bn of output and nearly 50,000 jobs (Wightwick, 2020).

Scotland

Universities Scotland said that it had lost about £80 million but that a plausible 50 per cent drop in the intake of international students would cost £435 million in 2020-21. A report last year by Audit Scotland said universities brought in £3.8 billion in 2017-18, meaning that they would lose about 11 per cent of their income under this scenario (Andrews, 2020).

A third of Scotland's universities could run out of cash by Christmas as a result of the coronavirus, ministers have been warned (Boothman 2020a). Universities Scotland has warned that the sector faces a £500m black hole, while the University and College Union has predicted that the pandemic will result in Scottish higher education losing out on 25,000 students at a cost of £250m (Boothman 2020b).

The Scottish government's approach to fees exempts Scottish and EU students but not English students. UK government sources believe it is untenable for taxpayers to continue to pay nearly £100m a year to give EU students free education in Scotland after Brexit (Boothman 2020b). Free tuition for Scottish undergraduates, however, has become a key component of the "social contract" ministers claim underpins the Scottish government's worldview (Times 2020).

Ireland (Ulster and Eire)

The seven traditional universities in Eire enrol some 17,000 international students a year, who pay €300m in fees, but they are facing a possible fee drop of up to €240m. This would occur if the Covid-19 restrictions are still in place at next term's enrolment time. Moreover, international students spend about another €100m a year in the economy (Donnelly 2020) .

Ulster's two universities have said they expect a loss of up to £100m as a result of the pandemic with a cumulative effect of a deficit of between £25-64m over the next three years" (McNeilly, 2020).

The UK in General

UK universities before Covid-19 were already in decline in the world rankings. A total of 62 out of 84 UK institutions saw their world ranking downgraded for the fourth consecutive year, according to the university guide compiled by Quacquarelli Symonds (Mathers 2020). More than half of the 132 UK universities ranked in the table saw a drop in their staff to student ratio, while 59 had fewer research citations. International students enrolling on courses had fallen at 51 universities (Mathers 2020). The slump has been attributed to unchecked expansion, over-stretched budgets, poor teaching, a reduction in research resources and the effects of Brexit. This is the country's worst-ever performance (Bromilow 2020).

Cavendish (2020) is sceptical of the case for UK taxpayers taking on the financial risk of bridging what will be a short-lived hit to revenue without a quid pro quo. It is not entirely universities' fault that they are in this position. They were encouraged by evangelists for undergraduate tuition fees across the political spectrum in the 1990s to act like businesses. Facing the loss of other government revenue alongside rising costs, they sought to become part of a market. Many decided this meant paying vice chancellors egregiously high salaries and hiring expensive senior managers. Between 2005 and 2018, the number of university marketing and public relations staff rose nine times faster than the number of academics. The irony is that tuition fees were supposed to make universities more responsive to undergraduates, with student choice driving up standards and producing a wider range of options. Yet far from seeing a profusion of differently structured courses at different prices, there was an almost uniform rush to maximum fee charging for traditional degrees. Instead of investing in teaching, many institutions racked up debt to build new facilities: sports halls, libraries and student flats. Borrowing by universities trebled to £12bn between 2010 and 2018 (Cavendish 2020). Unlike the situation with the banks in the 2008 crisis, few politicians in 2020 are declaring that UK universities are too big to fail.

Impact in the EU

Most European higher education systems primarily depend on public funding (Estermann et al 2020). Systems where university income depends significantly on domestic tuition fees (e.g. Spain and Romania) will be impacted by reduced family income, depending on the scale of corrective measures implemented by national governments (e.g. subsidised loans, unemployment benefits, student aid) (Estermann et al 2020). The frequency of university mergers increased across Europe in the aftermath of the 2008 crisis. Between 2013 and 2015 notably, a spike in merger processes was observed in France, Greece and Lithuania. Previous EUA work has shown that mergers of higher education institutions cannot be considered to reduce costs or serve as a quick fix to economic difficulties. Their main purpose is to create new synergies and opportunities to achieve common goals in research and teaching (Estermann et al 2020, Witze 2020).

Broader perspectives

Online for-profit colleges in the USA have increased enrolments during the coronavirus pandemic. Their flexible programs attract students displaced by the Covid-19 crisis. The colleges' parent companies often have substantial cash reserves that they can pump into tuition discounts and marketing at a time when public universities and non-profit colleges are seeing their budgets disintegrate. These schools often attract low-income, non-traditional college students who tend to have low completion rates. For-profit schools made a play for students during the 2008 recession, as people searching for work in a shrinking job market sought new credentials at low cost., so that enrolments at for-profit colleges climbed 24%. (Butrymowicz and Kolodner, 2020).

Private universities are closing their physical campuses and moving to online learning along with their public counterparts. With one in every three students in the world enrolled in private institutions, they have arguably a certain responsibility to answer the immediate challenges posed by the closure of campuses. There are wide differences in the penetration of private enrolments into tertiary education across developing countries. Brazil has one of the highest footprints at 75%; other countries like the Dominican Republic have a more balanced distribution with 57%, and in China it is a surprisingly high and rising 25% (IAU 2020).

New business models have been emerging. The Hasso Plattner Institute of Design at Stanford launched its 'Open Loop University'. Instead of a four-year degree course starting at 18 for a few, it promised six years over a lifetime, where constant acquisition of new skills enables the frequent career pivots people would need. University would be more like a Netflix subscription and less like buying a house (Marmolejo 2020).

Driven by growth in middle classes in Asia and Africa, the "demand" for higher education is set to increase from 160m students in 2015 to more than 414m by 2030, according to Unesco. To meet that, the world would have to build four universities, each serving 80,000 students, every week, every year. (Johnson 2020)

On April 19, 2020, in the Nikkei Asian Review, it was asserted that China and South Korea are surging ahead in the international brain race for world-class universities. China has already surpassed Japan in world rankings and is closing the gap with the United States. China has poured more than $20 billion in funding into more than 100 Chinese institutions. However, according to a report in The Chronicle of Higher Education, 91 percent of Indian students want to continue studying abroad even in Covid-19 lockdown (Dennis 2020). India is likely to gain more international students as key study destinations continue to struggle with the Covid-19 pandemic. Indian universities said they have increased their online outreach to target Asia and Africa to attract more students. India is home to nearly 48,000 international students as of now, and the country aims to take that number to 200,000 over a period of time. (Mint; 2020)

Conclusion

As unbundling of units from courses and subjects from programs becomes more general, so the acquisition of taught degrees could come to resemble more and the acquisition of badges (literal ones) in the boy scouts and girl guides. Badges would be awarded for units, bigger ones for hopefully coherent clusters of units constituting whole courses (after a target number of credits have been earned) and the fully integrated course with few electives would be a minority but one which still has a substantial market among the professions. Such unbundling and badging would make it easier to credentialize each and every one of the soft skills and character traits many employers have long complained to be lacking in current graduates. Communication, presentation, negotiation analytical thinking, creative thinking, interpersonal skills in general, and becoming a more affable person, are examples of what future students will learn and employers appreciate.

The 2030 implosion of universities was foreseen as the ultimate result of increasingly bitter competition for shrinking cohorts and shrinking reservoirs of funds. Graduate unemployment will rise as more students become qualified for jobs that do not exist. Jobs for which a degree needed in the teens and twenties of this century, but which did not have degrees as entry tickets in the nineteen eighties, will find that market forces have made their degrees useless. The university industry all round the world is utterly unprepared for the implosion and present-day university board members and executives will be long retired by the time it eventuates. It will be unprecedented in the history of higher education and will be go down in history's Hall of Infamy to sit alongside the Wall Street Crash, the Black Death or Passchendaele. The institutional carnage will be comparable to those disasters, even though the deaths through mental illness, suicide and poverty that follow the implosion will not be so great. The universities have never had a mass catastrophe before. It will be the ultimate result of unabated massification that lacks the common sense to cut its supply coat to fit its demand cloth. Has Covid-19 moved the date of the implosion forward? This chapter is written as countries come out of first wave lockdown and the initial impact of Covid-19 on universities is clear. If recovery is rapid so that we are back to 2019 normal by the end of 2021, then implosion is deferred. We will have a little decimation and universities will mostly shrink in enrolments, campuses and income. They will not die though. Whether the implosion occurs with the force I envisaged in the 2019 book chapter (Donleavy 2019) depends inter alia on the lessons universities learn from 2020. Universities may yet surprise us by being institutionally capable of learning as well as teaching.

References

ABC (2020) (Australian Broadcasting Corporation) Regional News; Sydney: ABC Television 16 June.

Adams, Richard; "Coronavirus UK: Universities face £2.5bn tuition fee loss next year"; *The Guardian*; London 23 Apr 2020: p17.

Andrews, Kieran (2020); "Universities facing a £500m shortfall as virus costs mount": *The Times*; 10 Apr: p2.

Bassett, Roberta Malee, and Arnhold, Nina; (2020); "Covid-19's immense impact on equity in tertiary education"; *World Bank Blog* April 30, Accessed on June 20 at https://blogs.worldbank.org/education/covid-19s-immense-impact-on-equity-in-tertiary-education

Boothman, John, (2020a); "Virus could leave Scots universities on brink by Christmas Covid-19 causes a university cash crisis": *Sunday Times*; 3 May 2020:a p1.

Boothman, John, (2020b); "End to 'fee discrimination' is price for Scots universities' bailout"; *Sunday Times*; 7 June 2020: p7.

Bromilow, Ryan (2020): "UK universities record worst performance to date in international league tables"; Ex*press (Online); London* 10 June .

Butrymowicz, Sarah; and Kolodner, Meredith; (2020); "For-Profit Colleges, Long Troubled, See Surge Amid Pandemic"; *New York Times (Online)*, New York: New York Times Company. Jun 17.

Cavendish, C. (2020). "Universities are pleading for a bailout to paper over their failures: Some pursued a high-risk strategy of debt and expansion; now they must work together or go to the wall". *Financial Times*; London 04 Apr 2020: 12.

Dennis, Marguerite, (2020); "The Impact of Covid-19 on Higher Education"; Posted on May 12/26, Accessed June 19 at https://mjdennisconsulting.com/the-impact-of-covid-19-on-higher-education

Donleavy, G D, (2019); "Common Sense and the Future Proofed University" chapter 1, pp1-14 in *The University of the Future* (Dan Remenyi, Kenneth Grant and Shawren

Singh, eds.), December 2019, Reading, UK: Academic Conferences and Publishing International. ISBN 978-1-912764-51-8

Donnelly, Katherine (2020); Universities brace for a devastating blow to finances as revenue dries up; *Irish Independent*; Dublin 16 Apr 2020: 12.

Estermann, Thomas; Pruvot, Enora Bennetot,; Kupriyanova, Veronika; and Stoyanova, Hristiyana; (2020): "Briefing : the impact of the covid19 crisis on university funding in Europe: Lessons learnt from the 2008 global financial crisis"; *European University Association online*: Brussels.

Fazackerley, Anna (2020); "Loss of international student fees could decimate UK research";*The Guardian (Online)* , London: Apr 24.

Herbert, Bronwyn; (2020); "Southern Cross University vice-chancellor says job losses 'inevitable'": *ABC Regional News*; Sydney 17 June.

Hunter, Fergus (2020a); "Never waste a crisis: will Covid-19 be a catalyst for change at Australia's universities?"; *The Sydney Morning Herald*, May 3.

Hunter, Fergus (2020b); "Regulator says universities will shrink but survive"; *Sun Herald*; Sydney, 14 June.

IAU International Association of Universities (2020), *Global Survey on the Impact of Covid-19,* Paris:IAU.

Jack, Andrew; and Smyth, Jamie (2020); "Universities face harsh pandemic lesson"; *Financial Times*; London 22 Apr, p19.

Johnson, Jo. (2020). Higher education can turn this threat into an opportunity [europe region]. Financial Times Apr 13 p17.

Leingang, Rachel (2020); "More than 100 faculty members lose jobs at NAU"; *Arizona Republic*; Phoenix, Arizona, 18 June.

M2 Presswire (2020); "Government to protect UK research jobs with major support package"; M2 Presswire ; Coventry, 29 June.

Marmolejo, Francisco, (2020): "Reimagining Education: Grasping what change really means"; 9 June, *Forbes*

Mathers, Matt (2020); "Majority of British universities fall in global rankings table:" *The Independent (Online)*; London; Jun 10.

McNeilly, Claire (2020); "Universities brace for £100m loss as they fight to keep foreign students"; *Belfast Telegraph*, 25 May: p8.

Mint (2020): "Covid-19: India may see get more foreign students as US, Europe struggle";. Mint New Delhi, 31 May.

Roberts, Lizzie (2020); "Universities face £463m funding drop after third of East Asian students plan to cancel or delay offers": *The Telegraph* (UK); London 8 June.

Stubley, Peter; (2020); "Universities can charge full fees for online classes"; *The Independent*; London 5 May 2020: p18.

Times (2020); "Degrees of difficulty: Scotland's universities are the pride of the country but increasingly depend on foreign income." *The Times* (Apr 22, p29).

Westwood, David A (2020); "University courses can't go digital in just 3 months"; *Chronicle - Herald*; Halifax, Nova Scotia, Canada, 15 June.

Wightwick, Abbie (2020); "'Urgent action' needed to protect Welsh universities"; *South Wales Evening Post*; Swansea 24 April. p10.

Witze, Alexandra (2020): "Universities will never be the same after the coronavirus crisis"; *Nature*, 1 Nature 582, 162-164. DOI: 10.1038/d41586-020-01518-y

Gabriel Donleavy has four decades of university teaching and managerial experience in Australia, England and the Far East. He is currently at Australia's University of New England in Armidale as Professor of Accounting and President of the Teachers' Union branch there.

5

Turning Threats into Opportunities: A Hybrid Learning Model

Andrew D Banasiewicz
Merrimack College, North Andover, MA, USA

Introduction

Institutions of higher learning have been a part of the fabric of society for centuries, with some of the oldest universities tracing their roots to the Middle Ages, perhaps best illustrated by the University of Bologna, Italy, which has been continuously operating since 1088 AD. As a consequence, many of those institutions 'lived' through anything from devasting conflicts, such as the Hundred Years' War or the two World Wars, to pandemics, such as the Black Death or the Spanish Flu, to crippling economic meltdowns, such as the General Crisis of the 17th and 18th century or the Great Depression of the early 20th century. And while the world crumbled and changed time and time again, those institutions kept on, largely unchanged. Why? Perhaps because as centers of knowledge creation and dissemination they were seen as unique and irreplaceable, which enabled them to transcend socio-politico-economic upheaval. That favored status, however, slowly began to be called into question with the rise of the Internet. The new communication medium not only made information more accessible – it also spurred the flow of technology-based learning alternatives that have been slowly but persistently eroding universities' grip on all-things-knowledge. The resultant democratization of learning took many forms, none more visible than the emergence of massive online open courses, or MOOCs, developed and offered by a host of non-traditional learning centers, all of which forced established educational institutions to think more creatively about teaching. By and large, however, colleges and universities were able to adapt to the new multi-modal teaching realities by augmenting their traditionally synchronous, place-bound instructional methods with asynchronous, online offerings, including MOOCs.

It is tempting to see the current Covid-19 pandemic as a yet another adverse development that will, ultimately, be absorbed by higher education without changing its general trajectory. However, the crisis' reach and duration, the full scope of which are still not fully known and appreciated, suggest that the current global pandemic might turn out to be a lot more than just another bump in the road. The reason for that is the massive and, likely, long-lasting disruptions in traditional institutional functioning have the potential to re-shape the key aspects of learner behavior. Online education, once merely a sidekick to the traditional educational model, is now emerging as a viable, lower risk, mainstream alternative to place-bound, face-to-face instructional models. That development has the potential of permanently altering the conception of 'higher learning' for a large enough segment of (prospective and current) learners to materially alter the operating economics of many, maybe even most, institutions of higher learning. The threat in such a change is that online programs are subject to more commodity-like cost pressures, simply because that instruction delivery modality robs universities of the (physical) 'institution' part of their value proposition, stripping away their ability to charge 'institutional premium' for their offerings.

In my earlier article titled *Higher Learning in the Age of Data* (Banasiewicz 2020) I outlined a typology of learning distinguishing between reason-based and technology-based learning modes. The ideas encapsulated in that framework were inspired by desirability of expressly framing multiple, and possibly even competing ways of knowing, and by doing so to enable learners to reach balanced, but ultimately all-points-considered conclusions. However, the current Corona pandemic causing en masse migration to remote learning is posing an interesting question: What is the impact learning *modality*, specifically, physical classroom-based vs. remote, on distinct learning *modes* (experiential, theoretical, computational and simulational), discussed earlier in the aforementioned *Higher Learning in the Age of Data* essay?

The not-so-new distance learning

While it can be taken for granted that the traditional, physical classroom-based teaching and learning modality needs no description, the Internet-enabled online learning that is now nearly synonymous with remote education cannot be appreciated without understanding its roots, and those are surprisingly deep. In 1728, Caleb Phillips, a Boston, Massachusetts teacher began advertising private shorthand correspondence-based lessons, which can be considered the forebearer of modern remote education. However, it was the expansion of postal services in the 1800s that truly fueled the growth of correspondence courses in the US, while also contributing to the emergence of distance learning in countries such as Sweden (1833), UK (1840), Germany (1856), and South Africa (1873). Those courses were initially trade (e.g., stenography) oriented, but the 1858 creation of the External Program by the University of London marked the beginning of formal, university level distance education (although the term 'distance education' was coined by the University of Wisconsin in the US in 1892, which in 1906 also began to record and distribute lectures in phonograph form). The emergence of radio and television presented new course delivery modalities which were quickly noted by academic institutions, with Pennsylvania State College (now University) becoming the first to broadcast courses using radio in 1922, and not long after, in 1934, the University of Iowa becoming the first institution of higher learning to use television as the mode of academic course delivery. Television proved itself particularly popular with universities, compelling the US Federal Communications Commission to create Instructional Television Fixed Service, which dedicated 20 television channels to university use and instruction. However, all those early distance learning modalities – mail, radio, and television – suffered from the same core shortcoming: they were one-way forms of communication, where students were not able to ask questions or interact with other students. That changed with the emergence of the Internet, which enabled distance education to evolve from alternative mode of lecture delivery to a dynamic teaching and learning environment encompassing a mixture of asynchronous (e.g., lecture summaries and readings, pre-recorded videos, discussion blogs, etc.) and synchronous (e.g., webinars) content.

Today, remote learning is synonymous with online modality – in fact, 'online' is the most commonly used characterization of distributed learning, and terms like 'distance' or 'remote' are now rarely used due to their detachment connotation. Given the self-evident convenience and the ever-expanding interactivity of online learning, especially since the release of the first electronic learning management system (LMS), WebCT 1.0 LMS, in 1997, online enrollments have been steadily increasing. In the US, in 2003 about 16% of undergraduate students were enrolled in at least one online course, a number which grew to about 60% a decade later, and undoubtedly is noticeably higher today (2020).

Not just delivery

On the surface, online learning is just another knowledge delivery modality, but deeper consideration suggests far richer possibilities, perhaps even mirroring the rapid evolution of the Internet itself. Initially, the Internet was seen as just another communication channel, but now it is a lot more than that – it is an essential part of modern commercial, governmental, and social functioning. What makes the Internet different from traditional mass communication media such TV, radio or print is its unparalleled interactivity and richness, the combination of which empowers users to reach deep understanding of anything ranging from mundane daily events to the most transcendental truths. That is because traditional communication, which includes in-classroom teaching, tends to be perspective laden, whereas the Internet offers raw materials (broadly defined data) and tools (access, synthesis and disambiguation means) that empower audiences to construct their own understanding. And that is both a threat and an opportunity for institutions of higher learning.

It is a threat because, as noted earlier, it robs institutions of higher learning of that something uniquely special, the 'institution' part of their educational offerings. The traditional path to becoming, let's say, an attorney, a teacher, an art historian was a rite of passage through an institution of higher learning culminating in a formal degree – an institutional 'seal of approval.' Online learning, however, shifts the attention away from institutional credentialing and toward the attainment of specific competencies – higher learning not as W.B. Yeats' 'lighting of a fire', but as practical skilling. Already, some of the leading technology companies are emphasizing competencies in areas such as programming over the attainment of formal degrees, as they see more predictable economic benefits emanating from defined technical skills. And while the majority of organizations still value formal university education and rely on those credentials as a key selection criteria, voices demanding academic training that is better aligned with the needs of the employment marketplace are growing louder, and non-traditional (i.e., not affiliated with established institutions of higher learning) educational offerings keep proliferating...

The above notwithstanding, the upside of online learning is profound, but it is also somewhat complex. To start, as argued by philosopher I. Illich, much of university education is built around programmed instruction, which, as a process is designed on the assumption that there is a secret to everything in life and that those secrets need to be learned in orderly succession, under the guidance of instructors. And while it might be an overstatement to suggest that it leaves no room for creative, out-of-the-box thinking, the traditional framework of higher education conditions learners to equate learning achievement with the ability to assimilate fed-to-them facts. Permeated by a web of assumptions that govern what constitutes 'knowledge' and 'educational value', the centuries-old model of higher learning effectively traps students into having to assimilate content chosen for them in a manner that pays little-to-no attention to them as individuals, or even to the utility of that which they are required to learn. All told, in the world in which the already overwhelming amount of information is expanding at an exponential rate, the traditional higher education model favors assimilation of hand-picked elements of knowledge over open-ended, individual-level construction of a new and deeper understanding of the world – and that is the essence of the current crisis-precipitated opportunity. *Infusing* more balance between structured instruction focused on enduring truths, or universal and timeless elements of knowledge such as rules of mathematics, and online-based immersion and pursuit of individually-framed construction of new knowledge holds the promise to push institutions of higher learning toward a more discovery and creativity-minded hybrid teaching and learning model. Given how entrenched the traditional higher education model is, such dramatic change is unlikely to take place without a powerful jolt – Covid-19 could be that jolt.

Higher learning revisited

In *Higher Learning in the Age of Data*, and graphically summarized in Figure 1 below, I proposed a typology of learning built around two meta-categories: 1. reason-based learning, which embodies cognitive and behavioral acquisition of knowledge by human learners, and 2. technology-based learning, which reflects machine systems' translation of data patterns in data into performance of tasks. The stated intent of that conceptualization was to expand the definition of what it means to 'know' by pointing out distinct ways of knowing, and by doing so to contribute to learners' ability to more fully develop evidence-based decision-making capabilities.

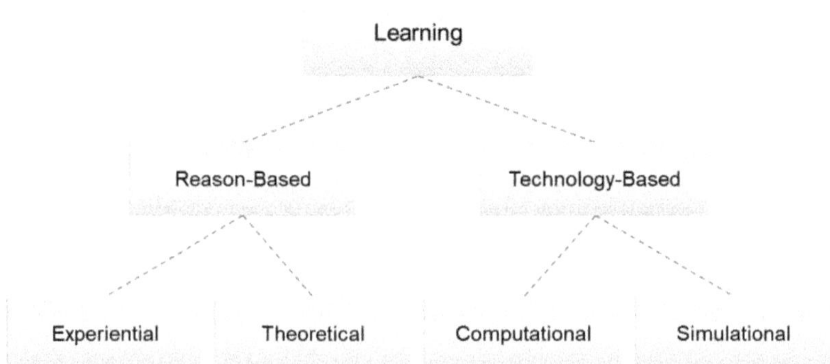

Figure 1: The Typology of Learning

The four manifestations of learning summarized above – experiential, theoretical, computational and simulational – were depicted as separate and distinct, primarily because the emergence of each can be seen as an expression of the evolving state of science and technology. That distinctiveness as well as the progressively greater scientific sophistication were captured in the original wording, '...from early man gazing at the stars and trying to make sense of natural phenomena (experiential learning), to early philosophers and scientists discerning the underlying laws of nature (theoretical learning), to modern data- and technology-enabled investigators identifying new and testing presumed relationships (computational learning), to the now-emerging means of simulating reality as a mean of learning that transcends experience and physical reality (simulational learning)...'. Also noted, however, was that '...it is important to think of those four distinct learning modalities as complements, not replacements, in the same way that airplanes, automobiles, bicycles and simply walking all offer complementary means of traversing distance...'. An important consideration that was not addressed in those characterizations, but one that was thrust into the spotlight by the forced en masse migration to remote learning was learning modality, which captures the 'how', or the systemic aspects of teaching and learning.

The Opportunity

Figure 2 offers an expanded reconceptualization of ideas summarized in Figure 1.

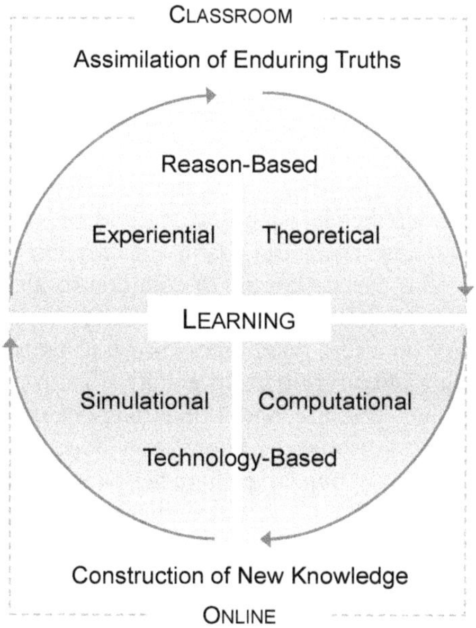

Figure 2: Learning modes vs. learning modalities: The multi-element hybrid learning model

It expressly differentiates between *learning modes*, framed as four distinct but interdependent mechanisms of knowledge creation, and *learning modalities,* which take the form of two distinct knowledge transfer formats. The former is comprised of experiential and theoretical learning, together comprising the reason-based meta-category, and computational and simulational learning, together comprising the technology-based meta-category (all discussed at length in the *Higher Learning in the Age of Data*, (Banasiewicz 2019)), while the latter expressly differentiates between the two alternative teaching and learning formats: 1. physical classroom-based modality, and 2. online modality, as a modern day successor of what was originally known as distance or remote learning. The interplay between learning modes and learning modalities is at the center of the current health crisis precipitated evolutionary opportunity for higher education.

As graphically summarized in Figure 2, the classroom-based learning model lends itself to acquisition of what can be broadly framed as *enduring truths*, a broad category of generally agreed on, foundational, objective body of knowledge, as exemplified by rules of mathematics, fundamental concepts of physics or biology, or principles of social justice. As implied in their characterization, enduring truths are largely unchanging, across time and contexts, which means they transcend individual experience and thus need to be understood the same way by all learners, a goal which is well-served by the centuries-old physical classroom-based teaching model. Perhaps somewhat less obvious is that while those 'tried and true' elements of general knowledge play an important role as tools of everyday rational reasoning, enduring truths are also the foundation on which pursuit of new knowledge is built. As famously noted by one of the greatest scientific minds, Isaac Newton, 'if I have seen further, it is by standing on the shoulders of giants.'

Online learning, on the other hand, lends itself to construction of new knowledge. It is due to extensive reliance on rich, interactive and multimedia content (e.g., videos, recordings, readings, self-assessed exercises, data analyses, intelligent artificial agents, etc.), coupled with students' consumption of content being guided, rather than shaped by instructors, all of which ultimately heightens creative thinking potentiality. In other words, the underlying instructional model is implicitly discovery-minded, because it allows individual learners more freedom in how they approach and make sense of available information. Interestingly, the contrast between classroom-based learning of common-to-all enduring truths and online-based construction of individual-level knowledge notionally parallels the logic of dual-aspect monism, more commonly known as body-mind duality. Classroom-based learning of enduring truths is body-like in the sense that it has a clearly defined essence and structure, and it functions in a predictable manner, whereas technology-enabled discovery of new knowledge can be seen as mind-like because its inner workings defy objective characterization, and it can yield quite unexpected outcomes. This is the realm in which great ideas are born, ones that go beyond or altogether break with established beliefs, as exemplified by scientific leaps of Copernicus, Newton, Einstein or the creative genius of da Vinci or Mozart. There is little doubt that the ability to go beyond what is currently known or believed – the enduring truths – cannot be taught (in a traditional classroom or elsewhere), because teaching is focused on the transfer of 'what is' and new ideas stem from imagining 'what *could be*.' In the words of Albert Einstein, 'imagination is more important than knowledge', and while the Internet is certainly not a proxy for imagination, the virtually unbound informational environment it brings to bear (in the form of countless sources of raw data, as exemplified by the CERN Data Centre) allows individual-level cognition, really consciousness, to dive into the richness of those informational raw materials in a way that is largely unconstrained, a sort of a sandbox for imagining minds. All told, online learning has the potential to stimulate more great breakthroughs more often.

In closing, it is worth noting that universities are, of course, already focused on original, discovery-minder research – in the US alone, the Carnegie Classification of Institutions of Higher Education currently designates 131 universities as 'Research I' institutions (characterized by 'very high research activity'); on the global scale, the most recent QS World University Ranking counted 1,011 research universities. However, the institution's overt research orientation should not be confused with general teaching philosophy, as the commonly seen distinctiveness between 'research' and 'teaching' realms of university functioning are quite pronounced. In other words, even heavily research leaning institutions tend to be rooted in traditional (i.e., classroom-based) teaching modalities. Why not seize the opportunity offered by the unexpected en masse immersion in online learning to make the research lab-like unstructured knowledge discovery a bigger part of the general university education? More on that to come…

Andrew Banasiewicz is currently the Director of Data Science & Analytics programs at Merrimack College and the Founder of Erudite Analytics, a consultancy; formerly, he spent more than two decades as a senior level quantitative analyst.

6

The Education Continuum: A Journey Interrupted

Madelyn Blair[1] and Denise Lee[2]
[1]Pelerei, LLC, Principal, Washington DC, United States
[2]PwC, Director, Washington DC, United States

A journey interrupted

"The future will not, in crucial ways, be anything like the past, even the very recent past of a month or two ago." (The Guardian)

Covid-19 has forced changes that have disrupted life at every level. We are all experiencing a journey interrupted. Social distancing may have saved 530 million lives to date as stated in a recent UC Berkeley Study compared to the 1917-1919 Great Pandemic, and Covid-19 is not over yet. The difference between that time and 2020 is technology and the tools that have enabled us to share information, stay connected and even work and learn remotely in our homes. Both learning and working remotely has been shunned by a selection of universities and corporations over the years. With the Covid-19 tsunami crashing into the global economy the future goals became immediate needs. All organizations that could move to 100% virtual collaboration rushed to do so. Suddenly workers and students all over the world were working from home in different ways. Bill Gates stated on a recent CNN Town Hall that "what I expected to happen over the next 10 to 15 years happened in two months when suddenly large percentages of the workforce were working from home". The impact of this sudden change on the workforce clearly demonstrated which organizations and universities had made the investments necessary to respond to this crisis and which were scrambling to catch up. Can universities use this moment to rethink the story that has dominated the design of higher education? Can universities use this time to select a new future, a new identity, a new business model, a new set of values?

A compelling future story

"Those who do not have power over the story that dominates their lives, the power to retell it, rethink it, deconstruct it, joke about it, and change it as times change, truly are powerless, because they cannot think new thoughts." (Salman Rushdie)

Higher education has been thrust into a liminal moment that will certainly see the demise of some institutions. The rapid onset of the pandemic has highlighted what happens when the environment of the organization changes radically. Universities face the need to assess their viability. They have been slow to respond to declining demographics for years with business models that have become too costly for most students and families. The slow trends were ignored by universities. Will Covid-19 prompt them to imagine a new future story?

Developing a future story begins with revisiting the mission of the university and refining it by creating a scenario, an image that everyone can aspire to. A future story enables the organization to define what it wants to be. The future story captures that vision in a compelling, transmittable and energizing way. People learn and make sense of the world through stories. Future stories have been used by strategists, politicians, religious leaders and others for centuries. There are many techniques (Hutchens 2015) and methodologies (Hammond and Royal 1998) that can assist a university in developing their future story.

An organization or a university that cannot articulate their future story, especially in the current pressing environment, will seriously jeopardize their viability.

The mission of a well-respected major university is to contribute to society through the pursuit of education, learning and research at the highest international levels of excellence. This is a broad and important mission. The 'future' on the university's website is emphasizing more facilities. A university at the 'highest international levels", needs a future story that tells the potential student and faculty what it means and what highest international levels means. Stories have that amazing ability to explain things that cannot or even should not be explained explicitly or measured precisely and do so to effectively inspire and guide those who must take the journey to make it happen.

Resilience is imperative

> *"Between stimulus and response there is a space, and in that space lies our power to choose our response."* (Victor Frankl)

Universities must not continue as if the status quo will carry on. Consider the core of the university to be its faculty where knowledge is preserved and co-created. Consider that students are the future repositories of that knowledge. Covid-19 has driven a wedge between faculty and the students. Universities must innovate to maintain that dynamic flow of knowledge. Universities must be ready to adjust to the changes and disruptions imposed. This calls for resilience that draws upon different strategies, leadership approaches and behavioral norms just to name a few.

Resilience is called upon when there is a sudden change that creates discomfort. At these moments, we are called upon to make a choice. As Victor Frankl says, "Between stimulus and response there is a space, and in that space lies our power to choose our response." Covid-19 has interrupted our journey. We are in that space where we must choose. That space where we must lead. That space where resilience resides.

Resilience is being able to make a choice even in the discomfort of radical change. Today, universities must call upon whatever resilience reserves they have, but they must also work to assure that the reservoir of resilience is constantly built up and encouraged.

It is critical to understand that resilience depends on two elements – energy and knowledge. Energy comes out of a vision – the future story of the university and its purpose. Knowledge is enriched by an open atmosphere that encourages questions and free exchange across all levels, where mistakes can be made, and unusual ideas are accepted for the value they may bring.

The university

Universities must be resilient to provide the flexibility and motivation to make the necessary adjustments to remain viable through today's Covid-19 crisis and for the future. With the right strategies put into place, possibilities will open up for decisions to adjust to Covid-19, and, likewise, provide an infrastructure for robust decision making for future onslaughts.

Knowing who you are and what you want to be are essential to resilience. Story is the strongest way to express that identity. Covid-19 has challenged every story, and our very identity is being tested. Now is the time to review and refine our identity, our intentions, and the future story of the university. "Knowing who you are broadens the scope of what you can do" (Blair 2019).

The mission must be clear and actionable. There is no simple solution. Universities must do the work to clarify the deep purpose of the university so that students as well as faculty will be energized by the vision. The future story must be embraced by faculty, students, alumni, and donors.

An example of how to craft a future story includes funding. With the disruption of this year by Covid-19, universities must assess how funds are used. Revenues have been curtailed from cancelled classes. Universities must rethink how their portfolios are used. An implication is that universities, like any organization in the future, will need to have greater margins that will allow them to be more resilient when radical change occurs. The risk should be tempered with the reality that major disruption may not be mitigated entirely, but that normal disruption can be. Rethinking the business model of the university from the ground up including how endowments are used and the balance of online vs face-to-face teaching could be part of that redesign beyond Covid-19.

Resilience is about making a decision when things are not at their best, when fear can subvert good intentions, when inaction can be fatal. Responding to Covid-19 is about making good decisions even when under stress.

Students

Early experience in offering virtual learning options found that completion rates were dramatically less than in face-to-face options (Blair 2020). Covid-19 mandated a rapid move to virtual learning. If the university of the future must embrace more virtual learning, then the focus must be on how to create energy and motivation for students learning virtually so that they will remain excited about their course work enough to finish the course. Keeping student energy high is the focus.

Resilient universities found ways to retain the community of connections that so easily flourish in classroom discussions, dorms, and the quad. These communities of collaboration energize students in their learning journey despite a virtual environment. Leveraging a cohort model that encourages relationship building and team projects enables students to engage with others and more closely emulate the on-campus experience where, "spontaneous conversations build understanding."

Resilient universities encourage enquiry, i.e., on-going curiosity, into subjects even when the enquiry is virtual. The settings may be virtual, but curiosity in the subject is what energizes students to learn more on their own when faculty and fellow students are not around to encourage learning.

Neuroscientists have found that high performing athletes and professionals are most successful when they practice under mild stress. The resilient university provides opportunities for students to experience learning challenges that are mildly stressful and develop resilient students. When individuals encounter mild stress, they are not overwhelmed with the challenge and are willing to 'give it a try'. Every 'try' builds resilience through the confidence gained from the experience. Making mistakes that are examined for lessons (critique must also include things done well – especially important in virtual environments) is built into the experiences of students. This builds an atmosphere of mutual support – essential for resilient behaviour.

Faculty

To be a faculty member in a Covid-19 world requires rethinking how to teach and how to engage with students. Faculty will need to design courses that enable students to build relationships and connect with the subject matter that finds different and multiple ways to engage with the students.

For example, one such virtual program is the PhD in Management program at the College of Management and Technology at a leading, virtual university. This university is 100% virtual. Designed prior to Covid-19 explicitly to keep the student in the driver's seat of learning and promote self-directed learning within a context, this program integrates scaffolded research skills into the curriculum where students are expected to delve into the content literature of their designated specializations. Through a theme-based approach, students identify current topics and trends to create research-based projects. The role of the faculty is to demonstrate content expertise, facilitate the process and coach the students as they develop into self-directed scholar practitioners. This changes the role of the teacher to one of coach and mentor along with being the subject matter expert (SME) to even undergraduate students. Faculty must move further from didactic presentation of their knowledge to means that enhance the student's ability to discover knowledge for themselves. This is a major shift in faculty perception of themselves. This shift offers more options when the need to change (return to quarantine) is enforced.

Moreover, faculty are the models for students. They need to be willing, as many are today, to show vulnerability, connect emotionally and build relationships both face-to-face and virtually. Creating an environment where mistakes can be made is part of supporting the free sharing of ideas. This may be the hardest challenge moving to the post Covid-19 university. Publishing has been a cornerstone of promotion even when teaching should be. Connection between and among people and groups leads to an enhancement of the whole. "We develop ourselves best in relationship with others" (Blair 2019). Connections facilitate knowledge creation and sharing – the very heart of a university's story. Building easy ways to connect and to communicate with trust represents a different attitude for universities. When publishing is critical to success, a competitive attitude pervades actions and behaviours. This curtails creativity and innovation – both called for in times of crisis.

Remaining challenges

The hard sciences offer great challenges. The quick response to Covid-19 and higher education is that the teaching can be done online. Experience has shown that even when core courses in the sciences are carefully designed and supported by reliable infrastructure, failure rates of students were higher than when delivered in the traditional on-campus format.

Scientific and engineering subjects that require laboratory work have no alternative than to be done in the lab. When on campus, research can include undergrads as well as graduate students. This creates the setting where knowledge can be created at the same time as experiencing how (and thus learning how) knowledge is discovered or created. Losing this aspect of higher education would limit science advancement directly in terms of knowledge and indirectly by the loss of inspiration of young minds. There are research laboratories outside of university, but few are involved in fundamental research. Moreover, they are not designed to accommodate undergraduates. Ironically, fundamental research as well as applied research will continue to be essential as Covid-19 is just the current virus event and unlikely the last. Universities that primarily identify as engineering and science organizations face ever greater challenges when exploring their future story. When virtual reality is used to teach surgeons, it suggests that universities must challenge themselves to see other mechanisms for solving this aspect of virtual learning. When the entire world is confronting this crisis, solutions to this challenge may come from unlikely sources and look unfamiliar.

A university degree must lead to more than a job

> *Industry sees the future of work as skills where degrees are not the main issue. (this is misinformed) "More inclusive means of hiring the best and most talented people to meet the needs of our rapidly changing economy."*
> (Jamie Dimon)

> *Intentionally shortening and fragmenting educational and personal development in the name of bolstering economic productivity now is shortsighted and does a catastrophic disservice to individuals, our national prosperity, and the long-term well-being of a civil, democratic society.*
> (George D. Kuh)

Several months ago, it was recognized that workers can anticipate that they will change careers more times than their parents changed job titles. The days of committing to one employer, just out of high school or college, and then working their way up the ladder is becoming more and more an unlikely career path. With the onset of Covid-19 the path forward is even more unclear. In the United States over 40 million people have applied for unemployment. The new university graduates are facing a job market never seen before, even in the Great Depression. When we examine different industries, and the jobs they support we find that they are changing so fast it is forecasted that 40% of jobs today will not exist, or will have been significantly modified, in just 10 years. Covid-19 has now introduced the concept that white-collar workers can perform their jobs from home with little impact on productivity. On the other hand, blue-collar workers are facing massive unemployment as they represent restaurant workers, ride-share drivers etc. The predicted massive amount of change in the job market with many jobs being eliminated in just 10 years has accelerated as organizations layoff and consolidate. How people plan, not only their formal education, but their careers is creating a tremendous amount of stress and uncertainty.

How do we plan for constant change in a pandemic with no end in sight? With this much change and not only an existing trend in the reduction in the recognized careers of today, how do we navigate the path forward? In the past people looked to their career and formal education to guide their path forward and establish stability in their lives. A student would select a university degree that would credential them to pursue a career in that discipline, sometimes following family traditions. Today, young people are graduating with degrees that may be immediately needed in the workforce such as engineering and cyber security but there are a vast number of other degrees that are hitting a wall with the shrinking job market.

Just a few months ago, we were seeing the different forces that are impacting the workforce of the future being frequently discussed in the corporate boardroom. Now many corporations are focused on their immediate survival when corporations such as a large car rental company are going bankrupt. The question is - how is this new short-term workforce trend information being communicated to today's students to help them make decisions? How are universities responding to the crisis? Many universities are struggling with just how to hold classes in the fall of 2020. Enrollments may be down significantly. Prior to Covid-19 the cost of education was on the rise and student debt at crisis levels therefore selecting the wrong path forward could have critical ramifications. Now the path forward is even more fuzzy. In fact, the mindset shift required of today's students is increasingly one of flexibility and mobility. We have to be prepared for the fact that jobs and careers will continue to evolve. This is especially important for universities as they design programs that matrix different disciplines and meet the needs of the current workforce and the fallout of Covid-19 where jobs will be scarce for at least the next few years.

Resilient universities need to respond by mirroring the need for flexibility and mobility. The fact that the individual worker must plan a solid path forward from the choice of formal education through the organizations they choose to join leads to the need to embrace lifelong learning. With the increasing changes in the marketplace, the skills that people have today will need to be upgraded continuously over their lifetime and universities have a role to play. It is important for students today to understand they are starting on a lifetime journey that will not end in four or eight years and for universities to offer programs that support that journey such as Certificate Programs. Students and Universities must be prepared to understand that careers will continue to evolve and the need to supplement learning will never end.

Closing thoughts

> *"Moving boldly doesn't mean moving thoughtlessly... Bold action and the ability to learn are highly interrelated."* (Blackburn et al.)

As discussed, Covid-19 has forced changes that have disrupted life at every level. We are all experiencing a journey interrupted. With the Covid-19 tsunami crashing into the global economy the future goals became immediate needs. The impact of this sudden change on the workforce clearly demonstrated which organizations and universities are resilient. Can universities use this moment to rethink the story that has dominated the design of higher education? Yes, if they embrace the principles of a resilient university. Can universities use this time to develop a new future story, a new identity, a new business model, a new set of values? Yes, if they craft a future story that builds a resilient organization that is flexible, innovative and intricately linked to the needs of the students and their careers.

References

Bird, Jane. "How Robots and Holograms Are Bringing Online Learning to Life," March 5, 2019. https://www.ft.com/content/4b8a810c-1a88-11e9-b191-175523b59d1d.

Blackburn, Simon, Laura LaBerge, Clayton O'Toole, and Jeremy Schneider. "Digital Strategy during the Coronavirus Crisis | McKinsey." Accessed July 7, 2020. https://www.mckinsey.com/business-functions/mckinsey-digital/our-insights/digital-strategy-in-a-time-of-crisis

Blair, Madelyn, 2020. Interview with University Administrators and Academic Directos, June 12 2020.

Blair, Madelyn, 2019. Unlocked: Discover how to embrace the unexpected, Pelerei Publishing, Jefferson, MD.

Dynarski, Susan. "College Is Worth It, but Campus Isn't." *The New York Times*, June 29, 2020, sec. Business. https://www.nytimes.com/2020/06/29/business/college-campus-coronavirus-danger.html.

Fortune Editors. "25 Ideas That Will Shape the 2020s: Economy, Markets, Tech, Health, A.I., Work, Society and More | Fortune." Accessed July 7, 2020. https://fortune.com/longform/ideas-shape-2020s-tech-economy-markets-ai-health-work-society/?utm_campaign=fortunemagazine&utm_medium=social&utm_source=facebook.com&xid=soc_socialflow_facebook_FORTUNE&fbclid=IwAR37L24JoHrr7fwB0RjOMv3FLilXdPpqoAMxn3dtltWKh7jiCaL5GdqfLpI

Govindarajan, Vijay, and Anup Srivastava. "What the Shift to Virtual Learning Could Mean for the Future of Higher Ed." *Harvard Business Review*, March 31, 2020. https://hbr.org/2020/03/what-the-shift-to-virtual-learning-could-mean-for-the-future-of-higher-ed.

Govindarajan, Vijay, and Anup Srivastava. "A Post-Pandemic Strategy for U.S. Higher Ed." *Harvard Business Review*, June 2, 2020. https://hbr.org/2020/06/a-post-pandemic-strategy-for-u-s-higher-ed.

Hammond, Sue Annis and Cathy Royal, 1998. Ed. Lessons from the Field: Applying Appreciative Inquiry, Practical Press, Plano, TX.

Hsiang, Solomon, Daniel Allen, Sébastien Annan-Phan, Kendon Bell, Ian Bolliger, Trinetta Chong, Hannah Druckenmiller, et al. "The Effect of Large-Scale Anti-Contagion

Policies on the Covid-19 Pandemic." *Nature*, June 8, 2020, 1–9. https://doi.org/10.1038/s41586-020-2404-8.

Hutchens, David, 2015. Circle of the 9 Muses: A storytelling Field Guide for Innovators and Meaning Makers, John Wiley and Sons, Inc., Hoboken, NJ.

Kuh, George D. "Why Skills Training Can't Replace Higher Education." *Harvard Business Review*, October 9, 2019. https://hbr.org/2019/10/why-skills-training-cant-replace-higher-education.

Ogbunu, C. Brandon. "The Pandemic and the Protests Are Mirror Images | WIRED." Accessed July 7, 2020. https://www.wired.com/story/opinion-the-pandemic-and-the-protests-are-mirror-images/.

The Guardian. "'The Impossible Has Already Happened': What Coronavirus Can Teach Us about Hope," April 7, 2020. http://www.theguardian.com/world/2020/apr/07/what-coronavirus-can-teach-us-about-hope-rebecca-solnit

---

Denise Lee is a Director at PwC with clients in the public and private sectors. Her projects focus on the development of knowledge strategies that enable effective and efficient sharing of knowledge. Ms. Lee has taught at Johns Hopkins University, University of Maryland and Kent State University in the US.

Madelyn Blair is a business owner and faculty member specializing in unlocking resilience for individuals and work teams. Dr. Blair is faculty at Columbia University, blogger on Psychology Today, author of five books including her new book Unlocked. She holds a PhD from the University of Tilburg.

7

Reflecting on Higher Education Examinations

Shawren Singh
Department of Information Systems, School of Computing
University of South Africa

> *"even successful, able and committed students – those who become university teachers – have been hurt by their experiences of assessment, time and time again, through school and through higher education"*
> (Boud, 1995)

Introduction

The University has long been recognised as the pinnacle of our education system. University education begins with admission into an undergraduate program, which for many is the foundation for postgraduate studies. In some rare circumstances, recognition of prior learning would allow some individuals access to undergraduate programs or certain postgraduate degrees. Generally, however, postgraduate courses are sophisticated research-driven degrees that are built on the foundation of an appropriate undergraduate degree. The research candidate is expected to identify a researchable problem, then use appropriate technologies and methods to develop a better understanding or solution to the problem. Before the Internet, and in the tradition of undergraduate shared "group" work, postgraduate research candidates would work in small communities of practices or groups and would share their research findings within those groups. The Internet has changed the secretive culture of universities meaning that increasingly undergraduate and postgraduate candidates are seeking refuge in the bosom of the Internet.

It is important to note that apart from governments, universities have been at the forefront of adopting or developing technology. The work of Babbage[1] and Fessenden[2] transformed our society, but also had an impact on the nature of contemporary scholarship. Universities have over the years invested billions of Euros in hardware, software, networking infrastructure, online databases, and mobile platforms. Despite this investment university technology may have appeared fragmented or disorganized, but due to the Covid-19 pandemic university systems are being revitalised and a new form of scholarship is taking root - 'digital scholarship'. Remenyi & Greener (2016) refer to digital scholarship as the use of the internet, the Web as well as other electronic technologies to facilitate the

---

[1] Professor of Mathematics and "father" of computing.
[2] In the 1899's Professor Fessenden successfully use a telephone link to transmit human speech via radio waves.

development of research. They confine their definition to the postgraduate journey, but the Covid-19 pandemic has encouraged us to see digital scholarship with a wider lens and to include the undergraduate journey as well.

Context: The author, ODel and digital scholarship

Within the higher education space, there are two broad approaches to education: the first is the residential university with face-to-face teaching and the second is distance education. The author is an academic and academic manager at the largest and only Open Distance e-Learning (ODel) university in South Africa. In 2018, the University enrolled 373,747 candidates, of which 247,462 were female and 126,285 were male and delivered 52,318 graduates (University of South Africa, 2018). The ODel model aspires to develop a community of practice between the key-stakeholders, i.e. the academics, candidates, and the institution (Manyike, 2017) by actively using technology (Ngubane-Mokiwa, 2017). The unintended consequence of the ODel model is that the entire community has become digital scholars. During this pandemic, social distancing to prevent the spread of Covid-19 was not an issue because the university follows an ODel model and the university management agreed that all examinations will proceed as scheduled, the caveat being that they would be online and that examination papers would be modified to suit the online environment.

Reflection on the ritual of examinations/assessments

Examinations/assessments[3] are the bedrock of our contemporary education system (Hickey et al, 2006). Remarkably at the undergraduate level, very little has changed with the manner of examinations over the years. Imperial Chinese examinations are the first known written examinations (Wilbrink, 1997). Much like in the Chinese tradition, sophisticated memorisations of material to be regurgitated at high stakes examinations are still the order of the day. It was not uncommon for aspiring Chinese scholars to "collect essays by successful candidates in previous examinations" and try to replicate these essays in their examinations. Within the Chinese system, several insidious practices developed (Hu, 1984), such as:

- Anticipating questions and developing canned solutions,
- Cribbing,
- Impersonation,
- Substitution of exam papers,
- Bribery.

As a countermeasure to these practices, the authorities introduced measures such as:

- Frisking the examinees from head to toe, (today's equivalent is signal jamming technology)
- Constant patrolling of the examination hall, (we still invigilate examinations in person and with technology)

---

[3] The term examination and assessment are used interchangeably in the chapter. No special attempt has been made to define these concepts.

- Anonymity of the examiners, (we still use second examiners, moderators, and re-mark examiners)
- Reproducing essays to avoid recognition through handwriting, (we have developed sophisticated multiple-choice questions as one deterrent)
- Re-examination of successful essays, (we still use the moderator and external examiner) and
- Execution, (today's equivalent is trial by social media[4] (Singh & Mendy, 2019).

The University of Paris and the University of Bologna were the first to introduce examinations in the western world. The candidates knew the examination questions in advance and were required to demonstrate their ability to memorise the material (Madaus & O'Dwyer, 1999). Joan Cele is credited with creating the European examination model, with the objective of promoting candidates based on merit (Wilbrink, 1997). It was not uncommon, much like in the Chinese tradition, for 'examination compendia' containing model solutions to past questions to be made available to candidates. Within the European model, failing a student was a rare event, and the system experienced the same challenges as the Chinese system, namely, fraud, stress, coaching, cheating, and lying (Wilbrink, 1997). Both with the Chinese and European models of examinations, one obtained a small sample of the examinee's understanding of the material under a high-stakes environment (Madaus & O'Dwyer, 1999). Within the European system, the practice of payment by results emerged as teachers were offered an additional reward for each student that passed. This reward practice still exists today in the form of government subsidies for candidates that successfully graduate.

Much like in the past, contemporary academics still struggle to develop authentic examinations (Madaus & O'Dwyer, 1999). In an effort to develop authentic examinations at the author's ODel university a variety of new tools are used (Hickey et al, 2006):

- Portfolio Assessment – a purposeful written/electronic collection of the candidates' learning journey.
- OverAll Test – a sophisticated test that measures the extent to which a student can analyse and problem solve in a defined context.
- Self-Assessment – candidates make judgments about their success and challenges through the learning journey.
- Peer-Assessment – a process where individual candidates or groups of candidates rate their peers.
- Co-assessment – both candidates and academic staff are involved in the assessment process.

These are sophisticated, labour intensive examination tools. It may be argued that at the undergraduate level some of the examinations are an intellectually barren exercise. We have not progressed much from the early Chinese and European systems. What has been successfully achieved is the development of sophisticated

[4] The internet is unforgiving; naming and shaming a university stays on the internet for perpetuity leaving a digital scar against the good name of the university.

examinations using tools such as Bloom's Taxonomy. Examinations at the undergraduate level, driven by the massification of the education system, appear to serve a ritualistic function – a rite of passage to the next level.

Several compelling arguments have been put forward as to why examinations are important. From the perspectives of the candidate, the academic, the university, and external stakeholders', examinations are considered important. From the candidate's perspective to successfully pass an examination indicates a level of mastery of the required academic material. Focusing on the academic, the examination is used as a tool to measure the effectiveness of the academic's teaching ability. The university uses the examinations as a vehicle to promote candidates to the next level of the learning journey as well as claim funding from government agencies. Finally, external stakeholders trust that the examination process has produced capable graduates that can be recruited. The role of examinations within the higher education space is complex.

Within the academic space, cheating in examinations is frowned upon at best, or regarded as a disciplinary matter leading to expulsion at worst. The question is why is cheating in examinations frowned upon? There is the argument that the cheater is being given an unfair advantage and the examination process is being undermined. This view is probably driven by the long-standing moral imperatives of "Thou shalt not steal" and "Thou shalt not bear false witness against thy neighbour"[5]. Is it not plausible that these traditional moral imperatives are less appropriate for our contemporary society? In Information Systems and Computer Science, we teach programming and the notion of reuse. There are several repositories on the Internet that provide free programming code that can be "copied, cut, and pasted" into a software artefact with little to no recognition of the original programmers. The Open Access movement is arguing for the lifting of restrictions on academic research. The Free and Open Source software movement is also championing the lifting of restrictions on software. Websites like SCI-HUB[6] provide free access to research papers. These are some examples of the blurring in attitude to the idea of originality (Simons, 2011). Within our learning spaces, we are developing learning communities and we are encouraging the sharing of knowledge, sometimes without acknowledging the original authors of these ideas. Is this a bad phenomenon? Possibly the question we should be asking is: Why not cheat?

Reflecting on online examinations

Online examinations have introduced a different level of trust issues for the candidate. With traditional examinations, universities would develop strict policies that for example:

- Banned mobile devices in examination halls,
- Provided pre-seating for candidates,
- Ensured reasonable distancing to minimise communication.

---

[5] The Church has had a long-standing relationship with the university and has influenced university culture.

[6] SCI-HUB (https://sci-hub.tw/)

In some bizarre situations, the cheating deterrents can be described as inhumane, see Figure 1 for examples of demeaning examination practices.

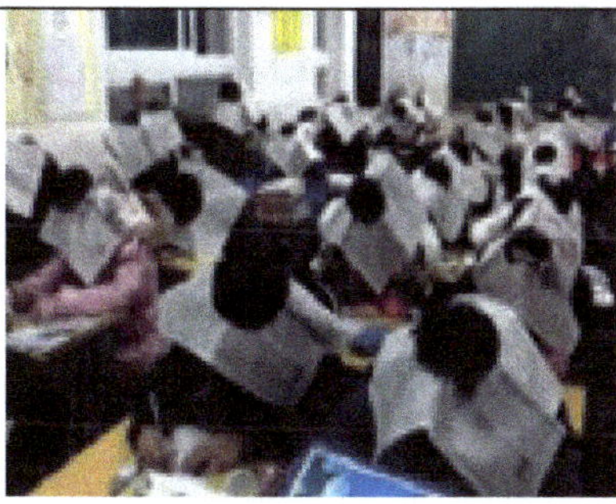

Source (W1, 2017)
Candidates wear newspaper hats to prevent examination cheating

Source (W2, 2020)
Candidates wear boxes on their heads to prevent examination cheating

Source (W1, 2017)
Army recruits were asked to strip off their clothes, as a deterrent to prevent examination cheating, and appear at the examination venue in their underwear.

Figure 1: Inhumane examination conditions

Inquisition, which interestingly is the origin of the word question (Nelson & Dawson, 2014) conjures up uncomfortable images of torture during the Spanish Inquisition, which was more inhumane than answering examination questions in a field, see Figure 1. Nevertheless, in our contemporary online high-stakes examinations, all key stakeholders have been tortured. University infrastructure in the form of ICT struggled, academics had to develop "alternate" assessments at short notice and/or reschedule assessments, candidates had to deal with the failing infrastructure (the universities' and their own) and unfamiliar ways of taking examinations.

Before embarking on the online examination journey, academics in the authors' School were asked what would be required for successful alternative assessments. From Table 1 it can be seen that overall the academics displayed a distrust of their candidates. This is not unexpected based on the evidence shown in Figure 2.

Table 1. A snapshot summary of alternative assessment opinions

Theme	**Response**	**Other Concerns of academics**
Plagiarism	Turnitin for all students and staff	Students will need to complete an MCQ exam, but this is still a risk
Technology and proctoring	Access to Teams, where sessions can be recorded and students will also have to hand in a 10 min. video via the Dropbox as part of the assessment	ICT system stability is an issue, as is access by all students to a computer with an internet connection
Sophisticated application of Blooms Taxonomy	If possible, require justification for MCQ answers for additional marks	
Cheating	Timed assessment	There is no way to maintain integrity – It is not possible to know if a Computer Science student gets help from an experienced programmer.
Proctoring	Skype Oral, student card verification.	Some modules are technical and venue-based is the only way to maintain the integrity

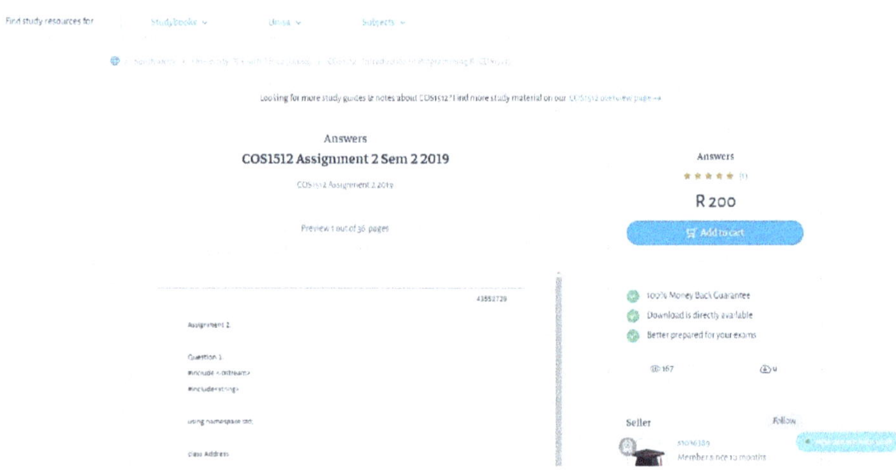

A website that sells solutions (https://www.stuvia.co.za/)

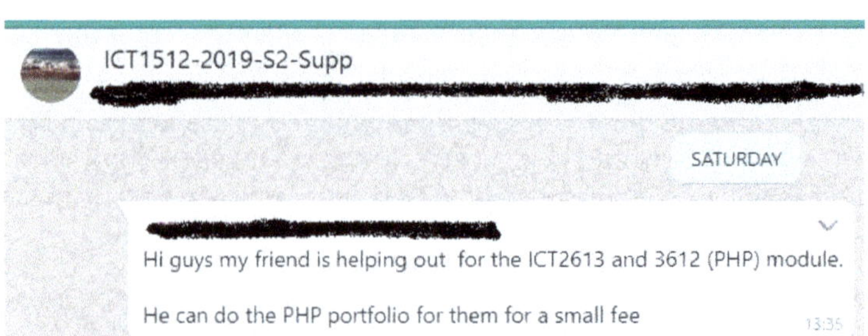

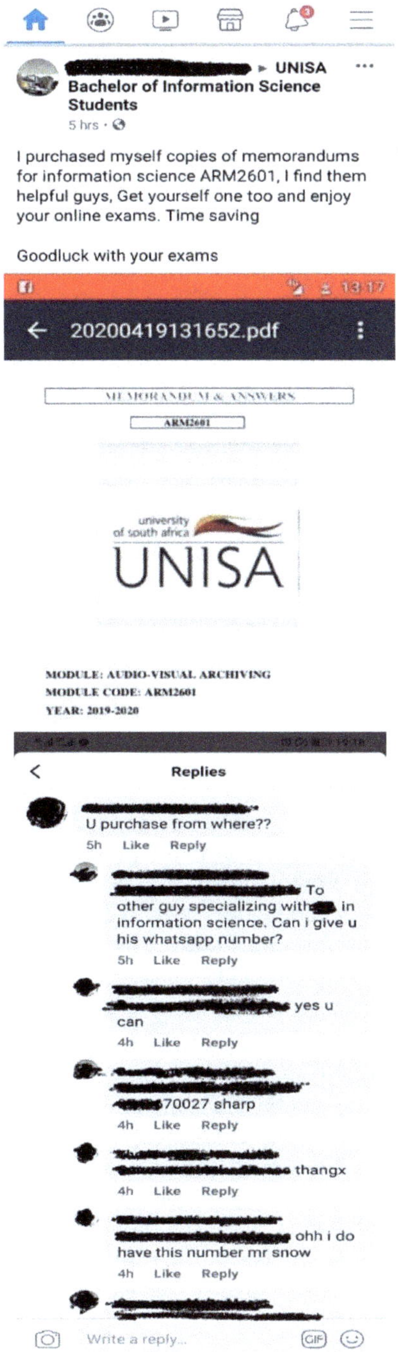

A Whatsapp teaching group

Figure 2: Technology-driven cheating

So, the evidence suggests that digital scholars have already begun to outsource some of their learning activities, demonstrating that the intellect has become lethargic during examinations.

Using Twitter tweets an analysis of key stakeholders' sentiments to online examinations at the university indicated that there are mixed sentiments. Figure 3 shows the results of the sentiment analysis. It is notable that the word exam appears in all 4 quadrants. This is no surprise as candidates react differently to examinations (in our case online examinations).

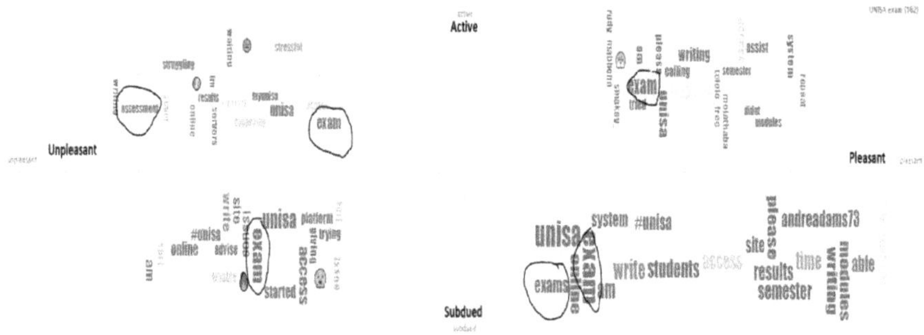

Figure 3: Sentiment Visualisation

Discussion

It is evident that cheating is not a new concern during the learning journey and the Internet has only given the prospective cheater a greater opportunity to indulge in this insidious practice. Our reaction to the Covid-19 pandemic has exposed some uncomfortable truths about our universities, which are:

(1) *Universities can be considered as a trust system*. The community trusts the university's research and the graduates that it produces. However, within the university system, there is a mutual distrust between students and academics. Why is it that we do not trust our candidates? Why is it that we as academics spend so much time on the lower performing student who may cheat? Should we not invest this time on the above-average student? Cheating will happen, but this is a self-correcting system, the cheaters will be exposed sooner or later.

(2) *South African universities, in a panic to avoid the loss of the academic year, resorted to supplying undergraduate candidates with free laptops and free data.* This practice of scaffolding candidates is not uncommon. The Chinese education system significantly supports their candidates, for example in the form of free meals, while the western education system exposes its candidates much earlier to the harsh realities of life. Of course, candidates should be supported, but instead of giving to candidates hand downs, the focus should be on giving them a hand up. South African universities have invested significantly in technological support for candidates, but do not appear the have skilled candidates to take advantage of this support.

(3) *The bureaucracy within the university system does not support innovation in examinations*. Staff have outdated technology, university procurement is challenging, and the university legal services could be paralysed by the legal implications of using technology-enhanced examinations.

(4) *Academics are knowledge workers and therefore it is entirely plausible for academics to work from home.* However, this introduces the challenge of how or whether to invigilate examinations. Some academics have resorted to using tools such as MS Teams, Zoom, and Google Hangouts to invigilate large examinations. These invigilation practices are driven by external key stakeholders who have a vested interest in the quality of the examination (engineering councils, certification boards, or professional societies). Other academics prefer using tools like Skype for one-on-one examinations, but this is not realistic for large cohorts. The premise is that technology will assist in reducing the tendency to cheat. In reality, however, it just introduces other challenges such as those related to the digital divide; human resource constraints, and technology challenges for candidates, academics, and the university. The result is that academics are using new technologies to mirror old practices.

(5) *Communication channels within the university during high-stakes examinations have become blurred leading to catapult versus slingshot communication.* With catapult communication candidates communicate directly with university top management, and vice versa, about online examination queries, bypassing department and academic managers. The disenfranchised academics are informed by candidates about some of the university's decisions or via the press. With slingshot communication the student catapults an individual examination concern directly to university top management, by-passing the responsible academic and academic managers. The university top management in turn slingshots the student query to the structures below, typically: student query to principal/Vice-Chancellor, principal/Vice-Chancellor to the dean, dean to the school director, school director to the chair of the department, chair of the department to responsible academic. This ineffective type of communication creates a stressful hyper-reactive environment which is open to abuse.

(6) *With traditional examinations, the candidates received the examination paper and at the end of the examination, all papers were collected from the candidate.* The university had a policy permitting candidates to query aspects of the examination. In the case of online examinations, candidates are taking screenshots of all questions. They analyse the questions and then pointedly query the examination questions and the marks that are awarded. Before this, we as academics had a safety net to make "adjustments". It is also plausible that candidates are taking screenshots of the examination questions and sharing the questions with candidates in other countries or with candidates in different time zones.

(7) *Universities have a long history of operating as independent entities and have become so independent that they have begun to compete with each other for limited resources and candidates.* There is a significant amount of duplication at universities, particularly when it comes to setting examinations. Perhaps there should be a union of universities that share the responsibility to develop high-quality assessments?

These seven uncomfortable truths should compel us to rethink our ritual of examinations. Possibly the question that we should be asking ourselves is "How can we efficiently get undergraduate candidates to demonstrate proficiency during the undergraduate learning journey?"

Conclusion

Covid-19 has made it clear that technology must play a greater central role in the learning journey as opposed to a supportive role, but it is also clear that technology cannot be used as a band-aid solution for replicating intellectually lethargic examination practices. We need to develop context-appropriate examination strategies for our contemporary society. Our current reality of the examination journey, as shown in Figure 4, will be:

- characterised by social distancing,
- inappropriate examination venues, and
- hyper hygiene requirements

In a society plagued by time poverty (Walker 2013) surely there are better ways of assessing young adults' grasp of knowledge that does not create a stressful high-stakes environment.

Source (W3, 2020)
Jobseekers in South Korea undertake examinations in a football stadium to reduce the spread of Covid-19.

Source (W4, 2020)
Cleaner disinfects examination venue

Source (W5, 2020)
Candidates take outdoor examinations and maintain social distancing

Figure 4: The New Reality

References

Boud, D. (1995). "Assessment and Learning: Contradictory or Complementary." In Assessment for Learning in Higher Education, edited by P. Knight, 35–48. London: Kogan Page

Hickey, D. T., Zuiker, S. J., Taasoobshirazi, G., Schafer, N. J., & Michael, M. A. (2006). *Studies in educational evaluation ELSEVIER. 32*(1), 180–201.

Hu, C. T. (1984). The Historical Background: Examinations and Control in Pre-Modern China. *Comparative Education, 20*(1), 7–26. Retrieved from http://www.jstor.com/stable/3098649

Madaus, G. F., & O'Dwyer, L. M. (1999). A Short History of Performance Assessment: Lessons Learned. *Phi Delta Kappan, 80*(9), 688–695.

Manyike, T. V. (2017). Postgraduate supervision at an open distance e-learning institution in South Africa. *South African Journal of Education, 37*(2), 1–11. https://doi.org/10.15700/saje.v37n2a1354

Nelson, R., & Dawson, P. (2014). A contribution to the history of assessment: How a conversation simulator redeems Socratic method. *Assessment and Evaluation in Higher Education, 39*(2), 195–204. https://doi.org/10.1080/02602938.2013.798394

Ngubane-Mokiwa, S. A. (2017). Implications of the University of South Africa's shift to open distance e-learning on teacher education. *Australian Journal of Teacher Education, 42*(9), 111–124. https://doi.org/10.14221/ajte.2017v42n9.7

Remenyi, D., & Greener, S. (2016). *Social media and digital scholarship for academic research: a user's guide.* Reading, UK: Academic Conferences and Publishing International.

Simons, J. (2011). Why we should abolish the university exam. Retrieved July 8, 2020, from The Conversation website: https://theconversation.com/why-we-should-abolish-the-university-exam-1329

Singh, S., & Mendy, J. (2019). Academic Dishonesty: A Preliminary Researchers View. In A. Stacey (Ed.), *Published by Academic Conferences and Publishing International Limited* (pp. 294–304). Johannesburg: Published by Academic Conferences and Publishing International Limited.

University of South Africa. (2018). 2018 Integrated report. *Year Report*, 1–207. https://doi.org/https://www.unisa.ac.za/static/corporate_web/Content/News & Media/Publications/Annual reports/docs/unisa-annual-rpt2018.pdf

Walker, J. (2013). Time poverty, gender and well-being: lessons from the Kyrgyz Swiss Swedish Health Programme. *Development in Practice, 23*(1), 57–68. https://doi.org/10.1080/09614524.2013.751357

Wilbrink, B. (1997). Assessment in Historical Perspective. *Studies in Educational Evaluation, 23*(1), 31–48.

Pictorial Evidence

W1. (2017). Newspaper hats' used to stop cheating in China: Steps taken against cheating in India. Retrieved July 9, 2020, from India Today website: https://www.indiatoday.in/education-today/featurephilia/story/cheating-in-examinations-953205-2017-01-04

W2. (2020). Students wear boxes on their heads during exam to prevent cheating. Retrieved July 9, 2020, from CNN World website: https://edition.cnn.com/videos/world/2019/10/22/indian-students-wear-boxes-heads-prevent-cheating-school-apology-vpx.hln

W3. (2020). South Korean Jobseekers Take Written Exam In Football Stadium To Avoid Coronavirus. Retrieved July 9, 2020, from https://www.ladbible.com/news/news-south-koreans-take-exam-in-football-stadium-to-avoid-coronavirus-20200405

W4. (2020). Degree without exam: Bombay High Court says UGC be made party to PIL. Retrieved July 9, 2020, from The New Indian Express website: https://www.newindianexpress.com/nation/2020/jul/07/degree-without-exam-bombay-high-court-says-ugc-be-made-party-to-pil-2166662.html
W5. (2020). Asia Today: Sri Lanka reimposes curfew; India eases lockdown. Retrieved July 9, 2020, from ABC News website: https://abcnews.go.com/Health/wireStory/asia-today-sri-lanka-reimposes-curfew-12-cases-70343358

Dr Shawren Singh B.Com, B.Tech, MSc, PhD. He is an associate professor and Chair of Information Systems in the School of Computing at the University of South Africa. His research focuses on digital scholarship and e-Government.

8

Smart Learning and Smart University Campuses in a Covid-19 World

Niyi Awofeso and Adi Arida
School of Health and Environmental Studies
Hamdan Bin Mohammed Smart University, Dubai, United Arab Emirates.

Background

The emergence and metamorphosis of Novel Coronavirus (Covid19) into a pandemic in 2020 has created crises and opportunities for the higher education sector globally. With 1.8 billion students (about 90% of total enrolment), from primary to university level unable to physically attend school between March and May 2020 globally, the need for innovative approaches to sustain educational activities despite Covid-19 related movement and assembly restrictions is self-evident. One of the most commonly applied smart strategies to sustain learning in the Covid-19 era is a (temporary) shift from physical to online learning mode. For example, the largest single migration from classroom to online education took place in Wuhan with 900,000, or 85% of K-12 students attending classes via Tencent (730,000 enrolees) and several other online platforms. At China's prestigious Tsinghua University, migration from physical to online learning occurred from February 2020. A total of 4,254 courses, taught by 2,681 faculty members to more than 25,000 students, are now being successfully delivered online. The migration was relatively smooth partly because of the university's commitment to online learning to complement on-campus learning since 2013. In contrast, most Australian universities continue to struggle in the transition to online learning, with adverse implications for student enrolments, teaching staff job security and university revenue (Johnson 2020).

Domains of smart campus and smart learning

The concept of a smart university campus is an extension of the concept of smart cities; The Smart Campus actively learns from and adapts to the needs of its people and place, unlocking the potentials of technology and enabling world-changing learning and research (Future Cities Catapult, 2018). At United Arab Emirates' Hamdan Bin Mohammed Smart University (HBMSU), a partnership with Phillips enabled the development of state-of the-art connected LED lighting controlled by its Interact Office system[1]. HBMSU recently migrated all its technology resources to the public cloud via Amazon Web Services. (HBMSU, 2020b). In Australia, Deakin University implemented an artificial intelligence system named Genie. It is

[1] https://www.signify.com/global/our-company/news/press-release-archive/2018/20180319-state-of-the-art-lighting-controlled-by-interact-office-at-hbsmu

a digital assistant, in the form of a Siri-style voice-activated smartphone app, with information on assignments, timetables, and referencing (IBM, 2017).

Smart learning is a broad term for education in today's digital age. It reflects how advanced technologies are enabling learners to digest knowledge and skills more effectively, efficiently and conveniently. Smart learning comprises transformations in four components of tertiary education: the learner becomes a proactive leader rather than a static follower of the educational process; academic faculty focus on being mentors and coaches rather than just being teachers; the curriculum is overhauled to better reflect how knowledge is evolving both in form and delivery, and the learning environment is expanded to consider new realities (Al Awar, 2017). Smart learning aligns with the perspective of Chatti et al (2010) that the university of the future should promote learning as essentially personal, social, distributed, ubiquitous, flexible, dynamic and complex in nature.

Core attributes of smart learning environments include; (a) context-awareness, implying that the system is able to provide learning support based on the learner's online and real-world status; (b) adaptive and prompt support to learners, using analytics-based assessment of the needs of individual learners from different perspectives (e.g., learning performance, learning behaviors, profiles, personal factors); (c) adaptable user-interface, the ways of presenting information) and the subject contents to meet the personal factors (e.g., learning styles and preferences) and learning status (e.g., learning performance) of individual learners. Learners in smart universities can interact with the learning environment via mobile devices (e.g., smartphones or tablet computers), or wearable devices (e.g., Google Glasses or a digital wristwatch). At HBMSU, the state of the art virtual learning environment – Smart Campus[2] – is available in major app stores for use by stakeholders with required log in credentials, and acknowledged by the United Nations Educational, Scientific and Cultural Organization as a best practice virtual learning environment .

Learner domain

The smart learning concept comprises learners who are proactive in accessing and utilising ubiquitous, predominantly digital learning objects, and in experiencing personalized and seamless learning. Smart learning is focused on learners and content more than on devices. The personal and smart technologies make learners engaging in their learning and increase their independence and proactiveness in more open, connected and augmented ways by personally richer contexts. According to Duran-Sanchez et al. (2017, p2); "*the objective of smart learning is to improve the learning quality and student outcomes throughout the student's educational process; it focuses on contextual, personalized and transparent learning capable of encouraging the emergence of students' intelligence and facilitating their ability to solve problems in real environments; students are provided with personalized education where they can learn flexibly, in any place and at any time, and work collaboratively.*" Bring-your-own-device technologies in smart learning contexts eliminate the barriers to learning of time and space, but

---

[2] https://www.albawaba.com/business/pr/hbmsu's-'smart-campus'-wins-first-place-middle-east-regional-awards-category-2015-wharto

may be limited by cost (e.g. of internet data), learners' digital literacy skills, and ability to innovate.

Academic faculty domain

At HBMSU, it is mandatory for all teaching staff to undertake a university funded, customised certificate course in online curriculum and instruction. Feedback from HBMSU lecturers who undertook this training program attest to its usefulness in preparing academic faculty for teaching roles to facilitate smart learning. Technological tools embedded in e-learning platforms such as Moodle assist faculty to monitor progress with smart learning activities. Teaching presence refers to the methods that an instructor utilizes to promote a quality online environment and facilitate an effective community of inquiry. It is composed of design and organization, facilitating discourse, and direct instruction. Anderson et al. (2001) described the design and organization aspect of teaching presence as the planning and design of the structure, process, interaction and evaluation aspects of the online course.

Curriculum domain

Smart learning curricula require redefinition to promote deeper, challenging, motivating learning tasks, moving away from content memorisation towards authentic, situated, real-world application. Learning objectives need to be carefully crafted to reflect core knowledge, skills, and roles in real life contexts. At HBMSU, the library department as well as the technology support department utilize the virtual learning environment (including Ellucian's Banner system for curriculum integration and learner information) to develop metadata and make them easily accessible to users. HBMSU is currently an accredited Banner training centre for the Middle East region[3]. Preferred smart learning assessment modes include e-assessments, adaptive testing, and feedback methods that are personalized, automated, real-time, evidenced-based, and data-driven.

Learning environment domain

A smart learning environment, then is one that is effective, efficient and engaging. Key features of smart learning environments include location-awareness, context-awareness, social awareness, interoperability, seamless connection, adaptability, ubiquitousness, multimodal interaction, and high engagement. Emerging adaptive learning environments include adaptive, intelligent tutoring systems, and ambient intelligent environments. At HBMSU, the smart campus is an internationally acknowledged technology-rich one-stop shop for learners as well as teaching and administrative staff. The smart campus is complemented by a Cloud Campus, a social smart learning initiative which provides high quality life-long learning services using social media channels.

Covid-19, smart learning and smart universities

As with any major challenge that requires intellectual and scientific rigour to address, in line with their "Third Mission" universities are working individually and collaboratively with philanthropists and industry in smart ways to address the

[3] https://www.hbmsu.ac.ae/news/hbmsu-kicks-off-training-sessions-at-banner-training-center

Covid-19 pandemic through research for therapeutics and vaccine as well as social research on mental health (Universities UK, 2020). The impacts of Covid-19 on universities are multifaceted. Whether it is in the area of applications and admissions, tuition, teaching, or assessments, Covid-19 is a game changer in the higher education landscape globally.

With regards to teaching and learning, a core component of smart universities which requires widespread adoption in order to deal with Covid-19's impact on on-campus learning is a steep transition to an online learning mode for most coursework teaching activities (Cruickshank 2020). Such a transition will require reforms in each of the four domains of smart learning. With regard to academic faculty, HBMSU recently launched two free online training courses titled "How to become an online tutor in 24 hours", and "Design an online course in 24 hours". The courses were translated into English, Arabic, French, Spanish and German. To date, 82,000 course completion certificates have been issued to 92,000 participants from 63 countries (HBMSU, 2020).

Learner preparation for the migration to online learning entails getting them to understand that online programmes constitute an innovative and equally effective platform to on-campus learning through which access to higher education can continue despite Covid-19-related disruptions. Online education should be designed to promote autonomy, initiative and creativity for students while encouraging reflection, critical thinking and collaboration. With job losses and global economic meltdown detracting from the motivation of students to learn, they require individualised attention and smart advising in order to optimise their learning mind-set. University libraries need to be remodelled to provide prompt and high-quality online support to students. Students' learning etiquette requires careful attention to assure fidelity with course and program objectives and promote ethical scholarship, devoid of plagiarism and other forms of academic dishonesty.

In the learning environment domain, the ecosystem may comprise four integrated facets: (a) The university community itself – the faculty, instructors, students, researchers and staff, whose positive attitude and willingness to adapt to new circumstances creates the foundation on which the other players rest; (b) the learning managementsSystem, which allows faculty to manage their courses, upload their learning materials, and facilitate discussions with students. Tests and quizzes can also be administered and feedback from faculty provided to students; (c) virtual classrooms – to accommodate the differing preferences and requirements of faculty in relation to learning outcomes, it may be prudent to simultaneously host several virtual learning environments such as Big Blue Button, MS Teams and Black Board Connect; (d) content development and management tools such as digitized learning objects that provide faculty with the resources needed to develop their lessons to be delivered in either a synchronous or asynchronous teaching method (Kalimi, & Nachmias, 2013). .

Course curriculum refers specifically to a planned sequence of instruction, or to a view of the student's experiences in terms of the course facilitator's or University's instructional goals. It is based on a syllabus which merely specifies what topics must be understood and to what level in order to achieve a particular grade or standard. It is vital that a post-Covid-19 course is at least equivalent in depth and scope compared to an on-campus course curriculum. The curriculum development process is often viewed as a seven-step procedure. The last three steps - Step 5: Selection of learning experiences; Step 6: Organization of learning experiences; Step 7: Determination of what to evaluate and of the ways and means of doing it – need to be carefully reconfigured to optimize online learning (Commonwealth of Learning, 2020).

Conclusion

The Covid-19 pandemic offers a unique opportunity to reimagine education systems and actualize the ideas by taking meaningful action to bring about that desired future. Universities in the Covid-19 era need to utilize technologies to work and teach remotely. The university of the future needs to be smart in terms of its general infrastructure (smart campus) as well as the stakeholders devoted to optimal tertiary educational outcomes (smart learning). A smart campus links devices, applications and people to deliver two key value propositions: enabling new experiences and improving operational efficiency.

A smart learning framework improves on traditional on-campus approaches to education by requiring learners to be motivated, technologically adept, and self-paced in their learning activities. Smart universities are implicitly committed to overhauling their course curricula so as to better reflect real world challenges and to assure that the delivery and assessment of courses are appropriately enhanced with technology to facilitate optimal learning and retention. The learning environment is expanded to consider new realities such as the dominance of mobility, which has opened vast opportunities for mobile learning. With Covid-19 realities universities now more than ever have the opportunity to redesign service delivery and mobilize collective action to transform the university experience into cyborg centres with affordable and contemporary courses featuring rich content that is accessible to most eligible learners through the leveraging of technology.

References

Al Awar. (2017). 'Pioneering smart learning'. Ellucian. URL: https://www.ellucian.com/emea-ap/insights/pioneering-smart-learning Accessed 30 April 2019.

Anderson, T., Rourke, L., Garrison, R., & Archer, W. (2001). 'Assessing teaching presence in a computer conferencing context', *Journal of Asynchronous Learning Networks, 5*(2). URL: https://auspace.athabascau.ca/bitstream/handle/2149/725/assessing_teaching_presence.pdf;jsessionid=20295CBD91B05F1B21964132E80E803C?sequence=1 Accessed 10 June 2019.

Chatti, M. A., Agustiawan, M. R., Jarke, M., & Specht, M. (2010). 'Toward a Personal Learning Environment Framework'. *International Journal of Virtual and Personal Learning Environments*, 1(4), 66-85. doi:10.4018/jvple.2010100105

Cohen, A., Kalimi, S., & Nachmias, R. (2013). The use of digital repositories for enhancing teacher pedagogical performance. Interdisciplinary Journal of E-Learning and Learning Objects, 9, 201-218.

Commonwealth of Learning. (2020). Keeping the doors of learning open Covid-19. URL: https://www.col.org/resources/keeping-doors-learning-open-covid-19 Accessed 8 June 2020

Cruickshank, S. (2020). 'How to adapt courses for online learning: A practical guide for faculty'. URL: https://hub.jhu.edu/2020/03/12/how-to-teach-online-courses-coronavirus-response/ Accessed 14 June 2020.

Duran-Sanchez, A., Alvarez-Garcia, J., Del Rio-Rama, M., and Sarango-Lalangui. O. (2017). Analysis of the scientific literature published on smart learning. *Espacios*, *39*(10). URL: http://www.revistaespacios.com/a18v39n10/18391007.html Accessed 10 June 2019.

Future Cities Catapult. (2018). 'Smart Campus - University of Glasgow'. URL: https://futurecities.catapult.org.uk/project/smart-campus-university-of-glasgow/ Accessed 10 June 2019.

HBMSU. (2020). Strategic partnership between HBMSU and UNESCO IITE to launch 'Be an Online Tutor in 24 Hours' course in five global languages. URL: https://www.hbmsu.ac.ae/news/strategic-partnership-between-hbmsu-and-unesco-iite-launch-%E2%80%98be-online-tutor-24-hours%E2%80%99-course Accessed 15 June 2020.

IBM. (2017). 'Reimagining the University at Deakin: An IBM Watson automation journey'. The outsourcing unit working research paper series, paper 17/04. URL: http://www.umsl.edu/~lacitym/LSEOUWP1704.pdf Accessed10 June 2019.

Johnson, M. (2020). Coronavirus forces universities to rapid scale online education capabilities. IT News. URL: https://www.itnews.com.au/news/coronavirus-forces-universities-to-rapid-scale-online-education-capabilities-538849 Accessed 14 June 2020.

Kampouris, N. (2018). 'The Platonic academy of Athens: the world's first university'. Greek Reporter, November 12. URL: https://greece.greekreporter.com/2018/11/12/the-platonic-academy-of-athens-the-worlds-first-university/ Accessed 9 June 2019.

Universities UK. (2020). How Universities are helping to fight Covid19. URL: https://www.universitiesuk.ac.uk/covid19/supporting-national-effort/Documents/we-are-together-case-studies-covid-19.pdf Accessed 10 June 2020.

Zhu, Z., Sun, Y., Riezebos, P. (2016). Introducing the smart education framework: Core elements for successful learning in a digital world. *International Journal of Smart Technology and Learning*, 1, 53 – 66, doi: https://doi.org/10.1504/ijsmarttl.2016.078159

Niyi Awofeso is currently a Professor at the School of Health and Environmental Studies Hamdan Bin Mohammed Smart University (HBMSU), Dubai. He holds postgraduate qualifications in infectious diseases medicine, public health, business administration and health administration.

Adi Arida is Professor and Dean of School of Health and Environmental Studies, HBMSU, UAE. He is actively involved in the management of smart learning initiatives such as curriculum design and content development of online courses.

9

Envisioning Post Covid-19 Higher Education

Reet Cronk
IS Graduate Studies
Graduate School of Business, Harding University, Searcy, AR, USA

Introduction

Envisioning post-Covid-19 anything is challenging but especially so for higher education. The extent of unknowns, the degree of disruptive changes and the diverse mix of institutions that belong under the higher education umbrella increase the difficulty of prediction. Additionally, a range of economic, political, and cultural influences will shape this future. For example, the results of the US election will affect the economy and the level of government support for educational institutions. In microcosms and specifics, one could change their vision of the future on a weekly basis. Hence, timing is also a factor in the vision as we continue to learn through the Covid-19 life cycle. The subsequent examination of general trends and challenges rather than specifics may prove to be helpful.

Firstly, a little context is necessary. The higher education sector was experiencing difficulty before the Covid-19 pandemic. Student numbers have been declining as a factor of fewer college age students (Nadwory, 2016). Declining student numbers have put financial stress on institutions, felt most keenly by smaller colleges with smaller endowments. At the same time, the attractiveness of the traditional university degree is diminishing in favor of micro-credentialing, nanodegrees and the like (Greenberg, 2018) that deliver focused skills without the larger context provided by traditional degrees. One might also argue, without the attention to critical thinking that traditional universities have spent centuries developing and incorporating into their traditional degrees. In addition, businesses have been becoming increasingly dissatisfied with the quality of graduates (JP Morgan, 2020). This factor also contributes to declining enrollments. Against this troubled backdrop, the Covid-19 pandemic forced approximately 1.6 billion (UNESCO) students and teachers to move online quickly. At the time of writing, universities were facing the decision whether to return to campus for the next (Fall 2020) semester. In the words of Dorfman (2020),

> *"On one side of the ledger are the health risks of density if students return to the dorms and classrooms and facilities, especially to older faculty and staff members and surrounding communities. On the other side are disruption and derailment, concern about the isolation of online learning and economic loss for institutions, colleges, towns and regions."*

There will no doubt be a deluge of research analyzing the impacts of these decisions in the years to come. However, the clearest take away at the moment is the financial impact, which is already quite obvious. A further 20% enrollment decline is expected post-Covid-19 (Jaschick, 2020). The perfect storm of the already existing pre-Covid-19 financial pressures together with the losses incurred during the pandemic have culminated in substantial University deficits (Korn et al., 2020). For example, Stanford University saw a $267 million dollar negative financial impact (Tessier-Lavigne, 2020). Tuition and refunds are not the only source of loss. Other potential losses come from the absence of college sports. The National Collegiate Athletic Association (NCAA) generated over one billion dollars in revenue in 2019 (Statistica.com). The pressure brought about by these losses and those to come will see a number of higher education institutions close their doors permanently (Korn et al. 2020) and others reorganize towards online learning. The lessons learned will reach long into the future and accelerate an already existing trend towards online learning, either informally (via educational apps, Duolingo, Khan Academy and providers such as Coursera, and so forth), or formally through traditional universities.

Business

Business has experienced a number of disruptive events such as ecommerce and digitization, so perhaps education can gain some insights from disruption-hardened business and their response to Covid-19 lockdowns? Rubin (May 11) highlights views such as those expressed by an Austin-based CEO, who found that they could now get by with less than half the amount of office space as roughly half of the employees were happy to continue working from home. Similarly, Alphabet pulled out of deals to acquire more than two million square feet of office space, suggesting that many of their employees will work from home. Businesses have been forced out of their comfort zone and pushed to make the required small investments in virtual infrastructure. With the infrastructure now in place, the economic pressures brought about by the Covid-19 pandemic, and the apparent willingness of workers to work from home, it seems reasonable to predict that this trend will continue.

Similarly, the 'working from home' option may also be attractive to students. Given the 'higher education' investment in virtual infrastructure and redesign of classes for the online (or hybrid) environment, together with economic pressures, the future should definitely include an increase in the number of students willing to study online. This of course is a desired outcome for universities as online education is generally less expensive to provide and profit margins are higher. This outcome is especially pertinent in light of early indicators suggesting that the total number of students, at least at the undergraduate level, will see further reductions, as many decide to delay their college education. Community colleges see their low cost on-ground options as an alternate route for students not wanting to move away from home due to finances and uncertainty (Baston, 2020).

Technology

Not only will technology provide the infrastructure required to facilitate online learning, it will also be applied to increase efficiency and effectiveness of higher education institutions. Again, following the lead of general business, machine learning is playing a significant role in a number of industries and business domains. Areas include scalability, improved operations and efficiency, improved customer intimacy via facial, image and speech recognition, virtual assistants, anomaly detection and many more (Squadex, 2020). The efficiencies and insights gained from machine learning, together with intense competition for students and financial pressures, will drive the adoption of these technologies in higher education.

Colleges and universities are already swimming in data, and there is much more on the way in the form of the internet of things. Predictive analytics and machine learning may be applied to student retention and success, recruitment, admissions, reporting, course scheduling, finance and learning, to increase efficiency and effectiveness (Yates & Chamberlain, 2017). These capabilities are currently being built into student information systems (Campus Management Corporation's Nexus product, for example).

Another area where technology will contribute is the continued improvement in telecommunications and video conferencing tools. For example, Google Meet is introducing background noise cancelling features facilitated by artificial intelligence (Porter, 2020).

Challenges

While the main purpose of this article is not to defend face-to-face learning over online, there are some challenges associated with the transition, especially in light of the expected magnitude of transition and time pressure created by increasing losses. Online classes by definition (O'Neil et. al. 2008) take a substantial amount of effort, on the part of both faculty and instructional designers. The shift of paradigm from the face-to-face faculty centered 'what do I want to say to the students', to student focused 'what do I need to do to ensure students are engaged and learn' is considerable and may be too challenging for some faculty. There is concern that the post-Covid-19 financial and hence time pressure may force shortcuts resulting in poorly designed and taught online classes. It may take some time for the market to sort out the poor performers, but it is most likely that universities that already had a mature online program or are prepared to spend a great deal of money developing one, will succeed. In addition to the concern about poorly designed courses, inexperienced students who do not fully understand what they are signing up for may be forced to select online learning for the same financial reasons. Alternatively, the negative impression gained by some students from poorly prepared teachers and inadequate infrastructure during the rapid transition, may steer students away from future online learning.

The challenge not only falls to the educational institution but to the students. Many students attend university or a particular university for the 'College experience', meeting lots of new people, going to parties, sharing a dorm room, participating in sports, being away from parents, being part of the college community and so forth (Dorfman, 2020; Wakefield, 2020), as exemplified by the following student quote,

> *"One of the best things about college is being close to others your age. There were no special memories where I was distant from others". Adam Bassi, rising sophomore, University of Massachusetts Lowell* (Dorfman, 2020).

Studying in isolation without this community experience will be a significant challenge, especially for incoming first year students who have had an expectation of something very different, for many years prior to college. Machine learning algorithms mentioned above may give institutions some insight into actions to assist students, but they cannot fully replace the human connection/community aspect of college life, nor the relationship with faculty. Tom Cavanagh (2010) in his work on developing a 'culture of care', states

> *"if you do not put relationships first, you can still fail to ensure that students meet their potential"* (Cavanagh, 2010).

Whilst college age students have grown up with technology augmented relationships, few would claim that they create the same sense of connection and community that a physical friend group does. Covid-19 lockdowns have not only taught us the utility of technology-mediated communication but also the value of physical connections. The lack of connection may be in part, the reason for significantly lower retention rates (up to 80 percent attrition rate) of students in online classes as compared with their traditional counterparts (Bawa, 2016). Literature reviews indicate that the online attrition pattern is not limited to any specific period or level of graduation. Cronk (2009) discusses faculty-student relationships as predictors of student success outcomes, such as academic self-confidence, intellectual and personal development and intellectual achievement and overall success. In addition, there is a social dimension to knowledge sharing and knowledge acquisition (Cronk & Davis, 2017). By definition, it is difficult to transfer implicit knowledge, particularly in some knowledge areas. As expressed by Sjönell & Qvarnström (2013),

> *"the challenges social interaction bridges are especially related to tacit knowledge, which is foremost shared through face-to-face interaction in social communities."*

Whilst video conferencing tools assist with this type of knowledge transfer, they do not fully compensate for the lack of social community seen in colleges where 'outside the classroom' interaction is more frequent. Hence, special attention is needed to mitigate the effects of non-face-to-face interaction. This is a difficult and complex task, and hence an aspect of learning that will be easy to neglect under the pressure to teach and study online. Fortunately, there is an entire body of work devoted to best practice in terms of quality in online teaching. The question that remains is, 'how many of the new to online institutions will adopt such practices and standards?'

Another issue that moving to online education highlights is the 'digital divide'. The digital divide is still a significant factor in access to online education within the United States. According to Krupnick (2018), approximately three million adults lack the sufficient internet speeds to take online courses. In addition, some lack the funds to pay for adequate internet connection even where available. In a depressed economy, there is typically a reduction in government support for public universities, who may have no choice, but to close some regional campuses and move online.

Finally, security and privacy present significant challenges as more education goes online. Cybersecurity concerns are particularly sensitive in the context of education, where officials must also contend with federal student privacy laws, particularly the Family Educational Rights and Privacy Act, or FERPA in the US. Similarly, GDPR laws apply to European Union students. The terms security and privacy are inextricably linked. In order for information to be private, it needs to be secure so unauthorized users cannot see the data. Privacy may be as concerning as security in cases such as Zoom feeds being hijacked and pornographic content streamed in its place (Griffin, 2020). Arguably even more damaging, is the fact that more than half a million Zoom passwords have been stolen. While this is obviously a privacy issue, the damage potential extends further, given the extent to which passwords are reused for several applications, bank account details for example. In defense of Zoom, they responded quickly and smoothly.

Another potential invasion of privacy is in the use of monitoring systems for remote testing. In this scenario, software such as 'Proctorio', is loaded onto the student's home computer. This type of software takes control of the environment and the student's computer (browser, microphone, and camera). Students are resisting this perceived invasion of privacy as well as the requirement to load the software onto their private machines (Osborne, 2020).

In 2030

Thus far we have discussed immediate trends and challenges, but what might the higher education space look like as far away as 2030? Technological developments will have more far reaching effects than the financial impacts of the Covid-19 pandemic, as technologies such as 5G, machine learning and other forms of artificial intelligence, telecommunications technology supporting knowledge sharing and collaboration, seamless video conferencing, social technologies, virtual and augmented reality, student environment control and testing platforms, simulation software, and artificial intelligence learning analytics and guidance, all have an application in education. As the development and adoption of internet technologies disconnected businesses from their place of operation, so will this suite of technologies disconnect students from a traditional space of study. However, it will connect them to a new place of study, a place that can be explored and massaged to be the new normal place to study. Not being tethered to one place, students will have more options to take classes from multiple universities and tailor their own degree. Universities may take this opportunity to specialize and form consortiums to connect students with the very best offerings in a given subject area. In the words of award-winning CIO of Harding University Keith Cronk,

> *"I can envisage a class designed and taught by a renowned expert, having thousands of students, supported by sound class design and technology."*

Currently we can shop, bank, read, play, be entertained, communicate and the like from anywhere, curating our world. The convergence of technology proliferation in every aspect of life and the lessons we learn about what we are capable of in terms of online education (both from the student and university perspective) will usher in the new norm for education. Traditional universities will still exist but predominantly in the form of elite reputation giants such as Harvard, Australian National University, Oxford and the like, in the same way as name brand products exist for those willing and able to pay extra. Other large state universities with high profile athletic teams will also still exist in the US (though with a smaller number of on-ground students). As mentioned previously, the NCAA is a multimillion-dollar industry and it is difficult to imagine the demise of this culturally significant business. Some discipline areas such as performing arts may also stay closer to the traditional model.

In conclusion, whilst much needed change and innovation has occurred in the online education space since March 2020, government, university and student debt will most likely be the predominant driving factor shaping the higher education landscape in the immediate future (2-5 years). However, technological advances will have the greatest impact in the extended future (5-10 years) as they have the capacity to generate new models of education.

Several challenges lie ahead including creating and maintaining relationships, (student to student and student to faculty), maintaining the quality of learning, the increase of the digital divide and privacy and security concerns. The future may be uncertain, but in the words of Ashton Eaton "If you have done something once, you can do it again or you can do it better. The beauty is the pursuit of the limit, not the limit itself. At least that's what I hope people realize".

Reet Cronk is a professor and Director of Information Systems Graduate Studies in the College of Business Administration at Harding University, Searcy, AR, USA. She holds a PhD in Information Systems and a Master of Science in Molecular Genetics. Research interests include the use of technology in education, gamification, e-learning, knowledge management, and the business value of information systems.

10

University Relevance in a Region's Post Covid-19 Knowledge Economy

Gareth Huw Davies[1], Naomi Joyce[2], David Bolton[1]
[1]School of Management, Swansea University, Wales, UK
[2]School of Medicine, Swansea University, Wales, UK

Role of universities in the knowledge economy

The origins of modern universities as places of enquiry and repositories of knowledge, as well as their role in training, are traced back to medieval Europe (Perkin, 2007). This history shows the initial wave of universities witnessed the world's most deadly pandemic in the Black Death during 1347-1351 (Courtenay, 1980). The emergence of the mass participation form of education and competitive research communities mean universities are now subject to forces that are political and economic, both globally and locally. For Wales, UK it was in 1828, when St David's College received its Royal Charter, that the country first became home to a university, with others established during the next two centuries.

More recently, the evolving university role was discussed as shifting from '*ivory tower to entrepreneurial paradigm*', and described as involving a transition to a 'triple helix' paradigm of engagement between academia, industry and government (Etzkowitz and Leydesdorff, 2000). Specific attention has been given in the context of Wales, a nation within the United Kingdom (Abbey et al., 2008, Huggins et al., 2008), with focus on the role of Smart Specialisations (Morgan, 2013). The Welsh Government Knowledge Economy Nexus review (WAG, 2004) succinctly described economic contributions of universities as;

- *Direct wealth contribution* as businesses themselves with highly skilled workforces
- *Graduate output*, supporting knowledge-based activity through alumni
- *Knowledge transfer and commercialisation,* bringing existing and new knowledge from the university into industry for economic and wider social benefit.

The relationship between institutions and their regions has involved continued consideration of managing both local relevance and a global perspective. This has increasingly emphasised contribution to universities' localities (Charles, 2003) with research undertaken to understand the relationship between different types of university and their local contexts (Hewitt-Dundas, 2012). Pertinent in Wales, this contribution comes from a diversity amongst its universities including older research-focused and younger teaching-led institutions.

For UK universities, the Research Excellence Framework (REF) and the emerging Knowledge Exchange Framework (KEF), examine activities of 'impact', 'commercialisation' and 'problem-solving' (for/with partners). In this context, the Covid-19 crisis has brought specific interest to the application of university knowledge and research in areas ranging from epidemiology through to clinical research for vaccines and therapies, and medical devices such as ventilators. Longer-term framing of such activities in the workplace relating to KEF has already focused on the related concept of Technology Transfer (HEFCE, 2016). The next section briefly presents the regional context for the ILS *Infrastructure* and Accelerate/AgorIP *Activity* examined in this chapter.

The environment: South West Wales

Wales is a semi-autonomous nation within the United Kingdom which presents many of the socio-economic challenges associated with numerous post-industrial regions. These challenges are notable in its south west, where long-term decline of heavy industries has not been matched by economic renewal. The region presents much of the diversity seen across Wales, stretching from the rural west of St Davids to the heavy industry of Port Talbot. Since its role in defining global industrialisation through the coal and steel industries, the region has struggled in transitioning to a knowledge-led economy, for many reasons including persistently low levels of R&D investment and entrepreneurship. However, the region's industrial legacy affects population health as well as its economy. Poor air quality in some areas has resulted in a high prevalence of respiratory disease alongside an ageing population, presenting a challenging context for the Covid-19 crisis (Brunt et al., 2017).

The devolved Welsh Assembly Government (WAG) formed in 1999 took responsibility for economic development policy, shifting focus towards the growth of high value-add sectors (WAG, 2003). Around the same time in 2001, the UK Government identified a 'nascent' life sciences cluster of biotechnology companies in Cardiff and Swansea (DTI, 2001), described by Cooke (2001) as 'mini-agglomerations'. The broader economic weakness across the region has been demonstrated by much of Wales qualifying for the highest levels of EU Regional Aid, bringing focus to the role of universities in helping develop knowledge-based economic activity (WAG, 2004). Initial efforts were met by concern over the existing performance of Welsh HEIs to deliver against ambitions (Gibson, 2007), a view supported by Wales ranking lowly amongst UK regions for the proportion of research-active academic staff (NAW, 2006).

To support University-derived enterprise, Brooksbank and Thomas (2001) recommended the development of incubation facilities and on-campus industrial collaboration environments. This approach was however limited in its potential, considering that existing 'critical mass' of local high technology employment can be regarded as an important precondition for knowledge transfer and substantial local economic effects (Varga, 2000).

The Institution: Swansea University

Established in 1920 within the federal University of Wales as University College of Swansea, Swansea University became fully independent in 2007. Rated as a UK Top 30 institution for research excellence, the university has over 20,000 students across its two campuses. Its relationship with industry was embedded from the institution's first Principal inaugural address, with Davies (2018) noting the "*views of the industrial founders of the University who championed the role of the university in promoting regional competitive advantage through commercialising scientific research*". The institution subsequently developed strengths in materials science and engineering, reflecting its industrial heritage.

Recent significant expansion of the University has also focused on industry engagement. A significant part of this growth has been enabled by (the then renamed) Welsh Government policy support (WAG, 2003, WG, 2014) and EU investment (WEFO, 2014). The 'Science and Innovation' Swansea Bay Campus was established in 2014 as a £450m initiative to embrace the triple helix model for innovation (Davies, 2018). The development followed the creation of the Institute of Life Science (ILS) at the Singleton Campus providing collaborative research infrastructure for the Life Sciences & Health sectors. Collectively, there now exists within the region significant academic and associated industrial research capability, as captured in the South Wales Crucible Science and Innovation Audit for UK Government, and also as noted in observation of Wales' Smart Specialisations (Morgan, 2013, EU, 2017).

The next phase of Swansea University's development is centred on its activity beyond the two campuses, including the Swansea Bay City Region *Internet Coast* City Deal which aims to support a restructuring of the regional economy towards high-growth high-GVA sectors. Built upon Smart Specialisations, the Internet Coast Programme has been developed around four '*Internet Themes*'. In this regard, Swansea University has aimed to become an innovation hub of the nature described by Youtie and Shapira (2008). The next sections explore associated initiatives from perspectives of developing *Infrastructure* and *Activity*.

The interactions: Emergence of open innovation

Institute of Life Science (ILS)

The ILS is a partnership between Swansea University's Medical School, local Health Boards, Welsh Government and the private sector, created to support Life Sciences and Health research and innovation. ILS presents a major effort to develop the regional cluster noted since 2001. Described by Abbey et al. (2008) as part of a sub-regional innovation system, its contribution to the region has been examined through a number of studies (RLP, 2013, Davies et al., 2018). Since 2004, the ILS initiative has developed a set of facilities, primarily at the Swansea University Singleton Campus adjacent to one of the region's main hospitals, and at the nearby major hospital site at Morriston. ILS provides biomedical laboratories for industrial collaboration, a dedicated clinical research facility, a medical imaging research suite, and a business incubator. ILS has also become part of the pan-Wales *Accelerate* initiative, presented later in this case.

Review of the ILS initiative found many of the 646 jobs created with ILS support during the initial (2004-2015) project phase were distributed throughout the cluster (Davies et al. 2018). Collaborations noted in the initiative reinforce the complexity, and non-linearity of knowledge and technology transfer activities described by Hewitt-Dundas (2012) and Bradley et al. (2013). The ability of infrastructure to support job creation in such a high value-add sector is also an important strategic factor for the region, as it aims to develop ~2,000 jobs across the region over the next 15 years as part of the region's City Deal. Incubator initiatives in the region have previously had mixed success and reception (Cooke, 2004, Abbey et al., 2008). However, ILS resonated with the call by Morgan (2013) for more effective consideration of smart specialisation, of which Life Sciences & Health is an accepted Welsh example (EU, 2017). This leads to the question of how *Activity* can then be delivered to exploit this infrastructure, which is explored in the next section through consideration of the open innovation (Chesbrough, 2003) *Accelerate* and *AgorIP* initiatives.

Open innovation: Accelerate and AgorIP

ILS has become a focus for the *AgorIP* and *Accelerate* open innovation initiatives, developed to promote and support the life sciences and health sectors. Both initiatives present the same '*Open Access Open Innovation*' approach to engage across their regional ecosystems and further afield. AgorIP focuses on commercialising academic/clinical research output by bringing the technology transfer process to a point of 'investment readiness'. In parallel, *Accelerate* focuses on progressing opportunities through the provision of specialist support in *addressing unmet clinical need*, *technology development*, *ecosystem engagement* and *user-centric development* perspectives. Each initiative draws opportunities from universities, health boards and industry.

AgorIP, based at Swansea University is a pan-Wales initiative to establish a shared/open Technology Transfer Office, developed in partnership between academia, health service, Welsh Government and industry to commercialise Intellectual Property (IP) derived from university and clinical (primarily Health Board) research. It aims to help respond to the Welsh Government's call for '*a more integrated and holistic support system for commercialisation*' (WAG, 2004). AgorIP operates on a case-by-case basis, providing support tailored to each opportunity. In parallel, the Accelerate initiative provides specialist support through a network of centres with existing academic, industrial and health system networks. This has involved partnerships with specialist facilities/expertise in the regional innovation centres including the Healthcare Technology Centre (HTC) at ILS.

The ILS HTC provides specialist facilities and expertise in fields ranging from medical devices to laboratory diagnostic techniques, supporting delivery of a portfolio of innovation collaborations with companies and health system partners across the region. During the early 2020 Covid-19 crisis HTC was formally positioned as the fulcrum of the University's response to the challenges faced by the health system. Working across the ecosystem this has supported development of ventilator technology with local engineering firms, enabled Health Boards to validate diagnostic techniques, created regulator-approved protective visors, and supported engineering colleagues in hand sanitiser production. This engagement has been critical, as often time-consuming though necessary steps such as approvals from research ethics boards and regulators are particularly difficult to navigate. The ability to repurpose personnel and equipment, and to optimise resource use would potentially have been too difficult and/or too late without the existing ILS/HTC activity and infrastructure. Through Accelerate, HTC also develops broader partnerships including the second mini-agglomeration (Cooke, 2001) around the Cardiff region. This responds to the 'Critical Mass' issue noted in the Wales Smart Specialisation Self-Assessment (EU, 2017), along with observations of key commentators (Gibson, 2007).

Conclusion and Policy Implications

The longstanding relationship between Swansea University and industry stems from its roots formed a century ago and has expanded from the heavy industries to other knowledge-based ones including Life Sciences and Health which have become more prominent during the Covid-19 crisis. The interactions of Swansea University with its region and across Wales through *Activities* such as AgorIP/Accelerate and the *Infrastructure* of ILS illustrate aspects of open innovation and smart specialisation theory in practice. The role of the ILS HTC in particular during the Covid-19 crisis has shown an orchestration role to 'innovation hub' (Youtie and Shapira, 2008), drawing upon both its own resources and those of industry and health system partners across its region.

The Accelerate/AgorIP Covid-19 crisis response through HTC has shown how a portfolio of individual innovation projects can be successfully delivered at pace in response to urgent needs. In parallel, it also presents the non-linear and collaborative nature of the University-Industry interaction and commercialisation. These initiatives present a response to particular challenges of south west Wales during both longer-term endeavours and the recent crisis, offering potential insight for other regions. Maintaining the agility, responsiveness, outcome-focus and collaborative working seen during the health crisis is something that will be critical for the forthcoming economic crisis, facing both the region and wider world.

This chapter has demonstrated how, despite enormous unprecedented contextual changes and challenges, a university's role can remain one of enlarging the world of knowledge to the benefit of the community it serves. The Covid-19 crisis has highlighted how this role is not as an ivory tower, but one to be delivered through outward-facing effective collaboration with industry, health systems and wider society.

References

Abbey, J., Davies, G. & Mainwaring, L. 2008. Vorsprung durch Technium: Towards a system of Innovation in South-west Wales. *Regional Studies,* 42, 281-293.

Bradley, S. R., Hayter, C. S. & Lingk, A. N. 2013. Models and methods of university technology transfer. *Foundations and Trends® in Entrepreneurship,* 9, 571-650.

Brooksbank, D. & Thomas, B. 2001. An assessment of higher education spin-off enterprises in Wales. *Industry and Higher Education,* 15, 415-420.

Brunt, H., Barnes, J., Jones, S., Longhurst, J., Scally, G. & Hayes, E. 2017. Air pollution, deprivation and health: Understanding relationships to add value to local air quality management policy and practice in Wales, UK. *Journal of Public Health,* 39, 485-497.

Charles, D. 2003. Universities and territorial development: reshaping the regional role of UK universities. *Local Economy,* 18, 7-20.

Chesbrough, H. 2003. Open innovation. Boston: Harvard Business School Press.

Cooke, P. 2001. Biotechnology Clusters in the U.K.: Lessons from Localisation in the Commercialisation of Science. *Small Business Economics,* 17, 43-59.

Cooke, P. 2004. *The regional innovation system in Wales,* London, Routledge.
Courtenay, W. J. 1980. The effect of the Black Death on English higher education. *Speculum,* 55, 696-714.
Davies, G., Clement, M., Huxtable-Thomas, R M., Johhnson, G. 2018. Life Sciences & Health in south west Wales: A Sub-regional Innovation System *In:* James, J., Preece, J. & Valdes-Cotera, R. (eds.) *Entrepreneurial Learning City Regions.* Springer.
Davies, I. 2018. The Impact of a Research-led Entrepreneurial University on a Regional Economy: Swansea University's Science and Innovation Campus. *Entrepreneurial Learning City Regions.* Springer.
DTI 2001. Business Clusters in the UK - a first assessment. *In:* Department of Trade and Industry, Crown Copyright. (ed.).
Etzkowitz, H. & Leydesdorff, L. 2000. The dynamics of innovation: from National Systems and "Mode 2" to a Triple Helix of university–industry–government relations. *Research Policy,* 29, 109-123.
EU. 2017. *Wales Smart Specialisations* [Online]. Available: http://s3platform.jrc.ec.europa.eu/regions/UKL/tags/UKL [Accessed 10th April 2017].
Gibson S 2007. Commercialisation in Wales - A Report by the Independent Task and Finish Group., Welsh Government [Online]. Available: www.assembly.wales/commercialisation_in_wales_-_gibson_review.pdf [Accessed 2nd July April 2020].
HEFCE 2016. University Knowledge Exchange (KE) Framework: good practice in technology transfer. Online: Higher Education Funding Council for England.
Hewitt-Dundas, N. 2012. Research intensity and knowledge transfer activity in UK universities. *Research Policy,* 41, 262-275.
Huggins, R., Jones, M. & Upton, S. 2008. Universities as drivers of knowledge-based regional development: a triple helix analysis of Wales. *International Journal of Innovation and Regional Development,* 1, 24-47.
Morgan, K. 2013. The regional state in the era of Smart Specialisation. *Ekonomiaz,* 83, 103-126.
NAW 2006. Review of Science Policy in Wales. *In:* Enterprise, Innovation and Networks Committee (ed.). Welsh Government Cathays Library: National Assembly for Wales.
Power, D. & Malmberg, A. 2008. The contribution of universities to innovation and economic development: in what sense a regional problem? *Cambridge journal of regions, economy and society,* 1, 233-245.
Varga, A. 2000. Local academic knowledge transfers and the concentration of economic activity. *Journal of Regional Science,* 40, 289-309.
WAG 2003. Wales for Innovation. Welsh Assembly Government.
WAG 2004. Knowledge Economy Nexus: Role of Higher Education in Wales. Welsh Assembly Government, (ed.). Cathays Library: National Assembly for Wales.
WEFO 2014. The Economic Prioritisation Framework for Welsh European Funds: Version 2. Welsh European Funding Office, Welsh Government Cathays Library: National Assembly for Wales.
Youtie, J. & Shapira, P. 2008. Building an innovation hub: A case study of the transformation of university roles in regional technological and economic development. *Research policy,* 37, 1188-1204.

Gareth Davies is an Associate Professor in Swansea University's School of Management, with research interests in innovation and regional economic development. His practitioner interests include the AgorIP commercialisation platform and associated initiatives.

Naomi Joyce is a Senior Lecturer in Innovation & Engagement at Swansea University Medical School overseeing a number of regional innovation projects and partnerships including the Healthcare Technology Centre based at the Institute of Life Science.

David Bolton is a Fellow and Director of both CMI and EEUK. Having spent many years in the business support field his focus is on academic development and enterprise skills and entrepreneurship into relevant curricula.

11

Covid-19 and Qualitative Social Media Data Collection

Lakshmi Balachandran Nair
Department of Business & Management, LUISS Guido Carli, Rome, Italy (Incoming)
Methodology & Statistics Department, Utrecht University, Utrecht, The Netherlands

Introduction

The complex and pluralistic nature of the business and management discipline needs to be studied from a subjective, rather than an objective point of view (Reinecke, Arnold & Palazzo, 2016). This dynamic and subjective nature of managerial phenomena requires inductive or abductive theorizing, as afforded by qualitative research methods. However, collecting qualitative data is a cumbersome task, especially for students and early-career researchers. Furthermore, there are several concerns regarding the suitability of conducting qualitative data collection in certain contexts. Collecting qualitative data during an international crisis such as the Covid-19 pandemic is one such context. This chapter therefore discusses the suitability of qualitative data collection during Covid-19. Since the pandemic majorly restricts face-to-face interactions, data collection during this period is predominantly conducted through online sources such as social media platforms (hence, the term 'qualitative social media data'). The aim of this chapter is therefore to familiarize business students and novice researchers (hereafter referred to as 'student-researchers') with qualitative social media data sources, and discuss the risks and benefits of collecting such data during Covid-19.

Coronavirus disease 2019 (Covid-19) was declared as a public emergency of international concern on 30th January 2020. Within a few weeks, the disease was recategorized as a pandemic (Ienca & Vayena, 2020). As per the Google News report on July 6th (6 am, Central European Time), the number of deaths was 533, 780. The managerial implications of Covid-19 spreads from the health sector to real estate, tourism, and even politics (to name a few). Many management researchers are exploring these managerial implications and the effect of Covid-19 on the business world using online modes of data collection. In this chapter, first we elaborate the types of data which come under the umbrella term of social media data. Then we discuss the risks and benefits of collecting qualitative social media data during Covid-19 times, with a predominant focus on the risks.

Qualitative social media data

The advent of Web 2.0 saw the transformation of internet from a static information warehouse to a collaborative, interactive medium of communication where the users are as important as the content. From being controlled by a small, exclusive group of content providers (Cormode and Krishnamurthy, 2008), the web evolved to include participatory, collective platforms named 'social media'. Super-fast communication, interconnections, interactiveness, and participatory culture (Jenkins, 2007) are some features that enable social media to be a very accessible platform to express oneself, communicate, and observe online interactions (e.g. Facebook). Social media is a data mine for topics ranging from sustainability to Covid-19. This data, coupled with the internet's ability to provide suitable research contexts to observe contemporary human interactions, appeals to qualitative researchers. Some categories of online social media data sources are collaborative projects (e.g. Wikipedia), blogs/microblogs (e.g.: Twitter), social networking sites (e.g.: Facebook), content communities (e.g. Youtube) and virtual worlds (e.g. Second Life) (Kaplan & Haenlein, 2010). Some data sources spread across different categories. For example, Yahoo! Answers is a social networking site where users ask and answer questions. Yet, it is also a collaborative project where the users regulate the system by voting for the best answers and marking interesting questions (Agichtein et al, 2008). Regardless of the category, these platforms are useful for extracting both extant (e.g. existing blog posts about Covid-19) and elicited (e.g. participant observation of a Facebook group on Covid-19) qualitative data.

Collecting qualitative social media data during Covid-19

We discuss the risks and benefits of collecting qualitative social media data based on two aspects – the availability and relevance (Tracy, 2010) of data during Covid-19. "Availability" refers to the convenience experienced by the researchers in obtaining data (Cai & Zhu, 2015). Whether a particular piece of data is available depends on its accessibility (i.e. the level of difficulty experienced in obtaining data) and timeliness (which is related to the time delay between the generation of the data and its acquisition and usage).

The dimension "relevance" pertains to the ability of social media data to meet the expectations or demands of the student-researcher (Cai & Zhu, 2015). Relevant data is fit i.e. it matches the concerned study's research objectives; and significant i.e. it is capable of contributing to a deeper theoretical or practical understanding about the research situation or in exemplifying a hidden or ignored occurrence (Tracy, 2010).

Table 1 gives examples of studies involving qualitative social media data, along with a discussion of availability and relevance.

Table 1: Availability and relevance in studies using qualitative social media data

AVAILABILITY	Accessibility	Gurrieri & Drenten (2019) explored the health care narratives of female breast cancer patients and survivors by collecting extant data from their Instagram accounts. The data was accessed through hashtags related to breast cancer (e.g. #breastcancersurvivor, #mastectomy). These hashtags enhanced the accessibility of data by facilitating the detection of 18 self-identified breast cancer patients and survivors with public Instagram profiles.
	Timeliness	Smith (2010) analyzed tweets about relief efforts in Haiti after the major Port-Au-Prince earthquake, to understand social public relations. The earthquake hit Haiti in January 2010. The data was collected between January 22nd and February 11th (2010). The article based on this data was published on 23rd August 2010, within 8 months after the earthquake.
RELEVANCE	Fitness	Ghobadi and Clegg (2015) explored the dynamics of online social activism in Iran by collecting data on a post-election crisis. Three popular YouTube channels were observed for two years. The demographic information, contents, and audience comments of videos were collected.
	Significance	Henninger and colleagues (2016) used Twitter and Facebook data to explore the practical applicability of integrated marketing communications in British fashion industry micro-organizations. The study offered practical advice on the importance of making and maintaining legible social media posts.

Availability of qualitative social media data during Covid-19

To discuss availability, we need to examine the accessibility and timeliness of data. Is it timely to collect real-time social media data during Covid-19? Collecting social media data in real-time provides the possibility of studying social and managerial processes during Covid-19 as they are happening (Edwards et al, 2013). It also provides the opportunity to achieve simultaneity in data collection, analysis, and dissemination of results (Back & Puwar, 2012). Especially in sub-disciplines such as crisis management, this simultaneity is desirable for understanding how firms manage the Covid-19 crisis in real-time. Furthermore, data on social processes collected retrospectively after the crisis might be affected by data loss, biased documentation, and faulty memories (Levick & Olavarria-Gambi, 2020).

On the other hand, focusing too much on real-time data might put one in the "trap of now" (Back & Puwar, 2012). Qualitative research is known for its ability to capture the subjectivities and experiences encountered by people. Too much investment in real-time data produced over a short time might result in less attention being paid to the large-scale picture or longitudinal processes. If postponing will not have any large implications on the research resources, the researchers could do desk-related research duties such as literature review during the pandemic period (Jowett, 2020) and delay the data collection stage to a later period.

Another availability concern is regarding the accessibility of data. There are several qualitative social media data collection techniques for which accessibility is not an issue. A vast majority of social media data is visible, traceable, and in the public domain (British Psychological Society, 2017), making accessibility easier. For instance, many companies are disclosing their Covid-19 solidarity initiatives to their stakeholders and the public through their websites and advertisements. However, an overwhelming accessibility to data can also be challenging. Quantity is the most important indicator neither of social reality (Kitchin, 2014) nor of quality or usefulness of data. Furthermore, expecting inexperienced student-researchers to interpret large quantities of dynamic data might be unrealistic (Latzko-Tot, Bonneau, & Millette, 2017).

Conversely, a student-researcher looking for access to certain private social network accounts might face a different kind of difficulty. For instance, the way several Governments are handling the Covid-19 crisis (Holligan, 2020) are widely criticized by the members of various expat groups on Facebook. Many of these expat groups are private, with 1-2 gatekeepers making decisions about memberships. A student-researcher interested in investigating such criticisms will have to contact the groups' gatekeepers first. Since such groups are specifically intended for members to meet and discuss various topics with each other somewhat privately (Ackland, 2013), the gatekeepers might deny access to a student-researcher whose sole purpose is to collect data.

Availability of data could also involve ethical issues. One major ethical consideration in a social media setting is informed consent (i.e. informing the participants about the nature of the study and the data management plans before obtaining their consent). Extant data collection during Covid-19 often requires access to tweets, blog entries, or Facebook posts made by several participants. In such situations, it might not be feasible to obtain consent from every individual contributor (McKenna et al, 2017). Even if we consider elicited data, for example from an online support group for people who lost jobs during Covid-19, obtaining informed consent might be difficult or stressful to the involved parties. The researcher must consider the risks and benefits of asking for consent in this situation.

Relevance of qualitative social media data during Covid-19

Here, we discuss the fit and significance of qualitative social media data collection. Is data collected during the pandemic fit to answer the research question(s) in hand? If the research question is regarding the impact of Covid-19 on social and business life, collecting online data during the pandemic excludes the members of the society who are not users of social media or digital platforms (Ameripour, Nicholson & Newman, 2010). In normal circumstances, this drawback of social media data can be compensated by collecting other forms of non-digital data. However, during Covid-19 times, the social restrictions regarding movement and face-to-face communication adversely curbs triangulation using non-digital data sources (Hunt & McHale, 2005). This affects the fitness of the concerned study, unless the research objective is specifically looking at the strata of the society which has access to online sources. In that case, the transferability of the results might be compromised (Lincoln & Guba, 1985), since the findings are specific to one small group of the society in a single context only.

Collecting relevant data requires long-time engagement with the field as well as a slow data collection process. Furthermore, an important feature of qualitative data collection is examining said data in its own context and original setting (Latzko-Tot et al., 2017). Given that Covid-19 is changing the social and managerial situations around the globe daily, a novice student-researcher who wishes to collect relevant data would need to engage with and immerse in this extremely volatile context. Simultaneously, he/she is expected to undertake slow, yet real-time and in-depth data extraction. The practical feasibility of a student-researcher collecting social media data during Covid-19 is thus complicated.

Additionally, the concerns regarding relevance also affect the significance of the data in contributing to theoretical or practical solutions for Covid-19-related managerial problems. Analysing volatile Covid-19 related data, which changes drastically over a short span of time, might not be effective in developing long-term or intermediate solutions to pandemic-related business issues. Collecting data retrospectively after the pandemic times might even be advisable in this case (Schröder, 2011). On the other hand, collecting qualitative data involves immersion in the research context and a transformation of the researcher's perspectives over time (Back & Puwar, 2012). A retrospective data collection might affect this process by curbing this immersion and gradual transformation.

Relevance also involves certain ethical dimensions. Some controversial topics (e.g.: employee responses to a company's unsympathetic Covid-19 approach) are significant and interesting. However, the knowledge that someone is observing what you say and do might make the employees overly concerned about their online activities. This, coupled with the inherent impersonality of most digital data collection techniques, might lead to situation in which the participants refuse to give honest responses (Hunt and McHale, 2007). The trustworthiness of any data collected during the pandemic is also thus a matter of concern. Furthermore, even if the data is fit and significant, researchers should decide whether it is appropriate to collect data from specific populations during the pandemic. For instance, it might be insensitive to collect elicited data from healthcare professionals or affected persons (Jowett, 2020) since these people are already under a lot of physical and mental stress and fatigue.

Implications beyond Covid-19

The implications of our discussion in this chapter go beyond Covid-19 times. Business academia has a strong interest in developing high quality research. Student-researchers interested in conducting high quality research should utilize the immense potential of qualitative social media data. Ensuring that potential data is accessible and relevant for the concerned investigation is the first step in this direction. Analysing the risks and benefits associated with the use of probable data sources will save the student-researcher valuable resources during the research process and help in achieving trustworthy findings. From their side, the B-schools and higher education institutions should make sure that they do not put too much pressure on the students. They should be realistic in their expectations regarding the research outputs of student-researchers during times of crisis. Intense pressure to conduct research during stressful times such as Covid-19 might restrict student-researchers from thinking rationally and ethically about their data choices.

The use of suitable, good quality data is also vital for journal editors, funding agencies, and research regulatory bodies who make research policies and assess the value of research. These policymakers should insist that qualitative social media data collection must be preceded by risk-benefit analyses of the availability and relevance of involved data. Lastly, research conducted using appropriate data has a higher chance of leading to trustworthy results, which in turn will have a higher impact on external audiences. This impact subsequently bridges the researcher-practitioner gap by providing student-researchers with opportunities to support the decision-making processes of business practitioners and company policymakers. Moreover, it also enhances the potential of student-researchers to gain from said practitioners' knowledge. Academics of the future should therefore explore the enormous potential of qualitative social media data rigorously, but wisely.

References

Ackland, R. (2013). Web social science: Concepts, data and tools for social scientists in the digital age. Sage.

Agichtein, E., Castillo, C., Donato, D., Gionis, A., & Mishne, G. (2008, February). Finding high-quality content in social media. In Proceedings of the 2008 international conference on web search and data mining (pp. 183-194).

Ameripour, A., Nicholson, B., & Newman, M. (2010). Conviviality of Internet social networks: An exploratory study of Internet campaigns in Iran. Journal of Information Technology, 25 (2), 244-257.

Back, L., & Puwar, N. (2012). A manifesto for live methods: Provocations and capacities. The Sociological Review, 60 (Suppl. 1), 6–17.

British Psychological Society. (2013). Ethics guidelines for internet-mediated research. Leicester, UK: British Psychological Society.

Cai, L., & Zhu, Y. (2015). The challenges of data quality and data quality assessment in the big data era. Data science journal, 14.

Cormode, G., & Krishnamurthy, B. (2008). Key differences between Web 1.0 and Web 2.0. First Monday, 13(6).

Coronavirus (Covid-19). (2020, July 6). Retrieved on July 6th, 2020, from https://news.google.com/covid19/map?hl=nl&gl=NL&ceid=NL:nl

Edwards, A., Housley, W., Williams, M., Sloan, L., & Williams, M. (2013). Digital social research, social media and the sociological imagination: Surrogacy, augmentation and re-orientation. International Journal of Social Research Methodology, 16(3), 245-260.

Ghobadi, S., & Clegg, S. (2015). "These days will never be forgotten…": A critical mass approach to online activism. Information and Organization, 25 (1), 52-71.

Gurrieri, L., & Drenten, J. (2019). Visual storytelling and vulnerable health care consumers: normalizing practices and social support through Instagram. Journal of Services Marketing, 33 (6), 702-720.

Henninger, C. E., Alevizou, P. J., & Oates, C. J. (2017). IMC, social media, and UK fashion micro-organizations. European Journal of Marketing, 51 (3), 668-691.

Holligan, A. (2020, April 5). Coronavirus: Why Dutch lockdown may be a high-risk strategy. Retrieved May 1, 2020, from https://www.bbc.com/news/world-europe-52135814

Hunt, N., & McHale, S. U. E. (2004). Reported experiences of persons with alopecia areata. Journal of loss and trauma, 10(1), 33-50.

Ienca, M., & Vayena, E. (2020). On the responsible use of digital data to tackle the Covid-19 pandemic. Nature Medicine, 1-2.

Jenkins, H. (2007). Confronting the challenges of participatory culture: Media education for the 21st century (Part One). Nordic Journal of Digital Literacy, 2(01), 23-33.

Jowett, A. (2020, April 20). Carrying out qualitative research under lockdown – Practical and ethical considerations. Retrieved May 1, 2020, from https://blogs.lse.ac.uk/impactofsocialsciences/2020/04/20/carrying-out-qualitative-research-under-lockdown-practical-and-ethical-considerations/

Kaplan, A. M., & Haenlein, M. (2010). Users of the world, unite! The challenges and opportunities of Social Media. Business horizons, 53(1), 59-68.

Kitchin, R. (2014). The data revolution: Big data, open data, data infrastructures and their consequences. Sage.

Latzko-Toth, G., Bonneau, C., & Millette, M. (2017). Small data, thick data: Thickening strategies for trace-based social media research. The SAGE handbook of social media research methods, 199-214.

Levick, L., & Olavarria-Gambi, M. (2020). Hindsight bias in expert surveys: How democratic crises influence retrospective evaluations. Politics, 0263395720914571.

Lincoln, Y.S., & Guba, E. G. (1985). Naturalistic inquiry. Newbury Park, CA: Sage.

McKenna, B., Myers, M. D., & Newman, M. (2017). Social media in qualitative research: Challenges and recommendations. *Information and Organization*, *27*(2), 87-99.

Reinecke, J., Arnold, D. G., & Palazzo, G. (2016). Qualitative methods in business ethics, corporate responsibility, and sustainability research. *Business Ethics Quarterly*, *26*(4), xiii-xxii.

Schröder, M. (2011). Concepts and Topics. In *Retrospective data collection in the Survey of Health, Ageing and Retirement in Europe. SHARELIFE methodology* (pp. 11–19). Mannheim: Mannheim Research Institute for the Economics of Ageing (MEA).

Smith, B. G. (2010). Socially distributing public relations: Twitter, Haiti, and interactivity in social media. *Public relations review*, *36*(4), 329-335.

Tracy, S. J. (2010). Qualitative quality: Eight “big-tent” criteria for excellent qualitative research. *Qualitative inquiry*, *16*(10), 837-851.

Lakshmi Balachandran Nair is Assistant Professor (Senior) at the Methodology and Statistics Department, Utrecht University, Netherlands. Lakshmi's primary areas of expertise are qualitative research methodology and ethics.

12

Post Corona Adapted Blended Learning in Higher Education

Peter Mozelius
Department of Computer and System Science
Mid Sweden University, Östersund, Sweden

Introduction

The impact of Corona/Covid-19 on higher education is, at the time of writing, quite uncertain and to make any detailed predictions should be avoided. However, the pandemic could be seen as a catalyst for a rapid increase of online activities, and for a further digitalisation of higher education. Several changes that have been discussed for years have now been implemented in just a few weeks. Examples include online seminars, distance supervision, collaborative course development in video conferencing systems and online staff meetings. Not everything is better compared to the face-to-face alternatives, and in a global perspective the response to this new situation is diverse. As identified by Crawford et al. (2020), this is a continuum from higher education providers having no response at all, to pure social isolation strategies and rapid curriculum redevelopment to a fully online setup.

Furthermore, the experiences of this fast digitisation and digitalisation show huge variations due to different universities earlier curricula and blended learning design (Crawford et al, 2020). There also seems to exist different attitudes amongst academics and students towards the technological and pedagogical changes. The aim of this chapter is to discuss if these different attitudes could be related to the differences in existing blended learning models, and to differences in personality traits. Discussions on the variability in individuals' personalities are based on 'the five-factor model of personality' with the five main traits of extraversion, agreeableness, conscientiousness, neuroticism and openness to experience (Jackson & Soto, 2015).

Blended learning

During the last decades there have been substantial investments in information and communication technology (ICT) for technology enhanced higher education, with a mix of more or less successful results (Flavin, 2017). Today, almost all universities use some variation of blended learning with a combination of face-to-face sessions and ICT enhanced online activities. Various models for blended learning have been designed and developed where the blending can be carried out both asynchronously and synchronously. In this chapter the latter and more challenging blend is referred to as Blended Synchronous Learning (BSL), and two variations of BSL developed at the Mid Sweden University are described in the following two sections.

Blended synchronous learning – Model 1

This model was initiated by pedagogues and is still frequently used as the standard blend in the Department of Education at our university. A blend that consists of 'on-campus weeks' where all course participants should attend synchronous face-to-face sessions combined with 'off-campus weeks' with mainly asynchronous activities in a virtual learning environment. The on-campus weeks are often orchestrated with computers and standard software, but without much of other ICT enhancement and rich media tools.

The synchronous on-campus activities are mainly carried out as group work with collaborative problem solving and face-to-face discussions. However, in this model it has been rare to blend the on-campus groups with Internet connected participants, and as mentioned by a teacher in an interview "I've never had any blended groups since I'm afraid that technology wouldn't work" (Mozelius, 2018).

Blended synchronous learning – Model 2

This model, that is sometimes also referred to as 'hybrid learning' (Stewart et al., 2011), is built upon the concept of having on-campus participants and distance students working together on the same synchronous activities. Teachers and learners should be able to collaborate and interact via Internet connected rich media tools. A challenge with this blend is how to break the group barriers, and how to stimulate collaboration between participants from the different groups. This is the standard blend for most courses on Informatics in the Department of Computer and System Science at the Mid Sweden University (Mozelius, 2018).

Student interaction is important and seems to have a positive effect on student satisfaction in this blending model, and a frequent interaction between participants leads to more positive attitudes (Cole, Shelley & Swartz, 2014). Most students are positive towards this blend (Cole, Shelley & Swartz, 2014), but the two groups do have different perceptions about efficiency (Said et al., 2015). Students that prefer distance education tend to perceive it as more efficient (Wong & Fong, 2014). Finally, as highlighted in the study by Blomquist (2017), student attitudes and choice of study mode in this type of blended synchronous learning might be related to their personality traits.

The five-factor model of personality

This five-factor model of personality is a set of five trait domains, that also can be referred to as the Big Five, FFM or OCEAN (Costa & McCrae, 1992; Jackson & Soto, 2015). The latter acronym is created from the ingoing-five factors or aspects of a personality: Openness to experience, Conscientiousness, Extraversion, Agreeableness and Neuroticism. All Big Five have their corresponding counterparts, and as an example Neuroticism can be named by its polar opposite Emotional Stability (Jackson & Soto, 2015). Personality traits should not be categorised as belonging to one of the two polar opposites, but rather as somewhere in the continuum in between.

Individuals with a high degree of openness have a broader range of interests, are sensitive rather than indifferent to art and beauty, and they prefer novelty over routine. Conscientious people are task-focused and organised, and extravert people could be described more as sociable and outspoken, than being quiet and reserved. Agreeable individuals are polite and willing to collaborate, rather than being rude or antagonistic. Finally, neurotic individuals tend to experience negative emotions, such as, irritation, anxiety and also depression with emotional resilience as the polar opposite (Jackson & Soto, 2015). As found in the study by Blomqvist (2017), there seems to be relationships between university students' personality traits and their attitudes towards blended synchronous learning. The assumption in the following discussion is that the same relationship exists for teachers and administrators in higher education.

Discussion

Significant correlations were found between extraversion and conscientiousness, and if students prefer to study independently (Blomqvist, 2017). Opinions amongst university teachers and researchers have also been different in online staff meetings during the Corona period. If the FFM traits are applied to university staff, it would probably be a more positive attitude towards online teaching and learning and online research collaboration for individuals leaning against the poles of introversion and conscientiousness. In Swedish psychology it has been discussed if individual variations in FFM traits could have an impact on how different people react differently to Covid-19 fear and the social isolation during the pandemic (Svenska Dagbladet 2020). My suggestion for a good mix of personality trait for strong quarantine endurance, with many online meetings and seminars, is medium openness, medium to high conscientiousness, a low or medium degree of extraversion, medium to high agreeableness and a low degree of neuroticism.

Furthermore, the attitude towards a Corona adaptation of BSL would probably also depend on the BSL model. The enhancement and upscaling of Model 2, has so far, been undramatic and surprisingly smooth. In the shift towards online activities there have been fruitful discussions about, and also investments in new rich media tools and online conference systems. Except for extending the existing toolbox, there has been no really 'new technology' to master for teachers with earlier experience of the BSL Model 2. It seems like a more drastic shift for teachers used to working with the BSL Model 1, whereby they have not only to learn new tools, but also new technological solutions and digital processes. An issue that has been discussed is how to transform the often very concrete on-campus laboratory work in physics and chemistry. The idea of virtual labs has been explored in research during the two last decades, but the implementation is still mostly work in progress (Perales, Pedraza & Moreno-Ger, 2019).

Like the earlier digitalisation of higher education, the post Corona adaptation must not only be about digitisation, and also truly about digitalisation. As defined by Enhuber (2015), digitisation is the pure analogue to digital conversion of physical items into virtual content, and digitalisation involves the development of processes using the digitised content. This is a two-step process that, with an allusion to Enhuber's field of Art, some digitised paintings do not guarantee a successful vernissage night. Or back to the higher education environment: How should the traditional end of term ceremonies now be carried out in June, and how can the autumn semester kick-off activities be arranged in September?

It can be argued that a Bachelor or a Master programme could survive without such auxiliary arrangements as kick-offs and end of term activities. However, considering the FFM traits of extraversion agreeableness and neuroticism, social activities must not be underestimated. Quality content, active learning, interaction and good learning outcomes should always be prime goals in higher education, but the FFM might serve as a helpful checklist to achieve these goals.

To summarise, the pandemic has kick-started a lot of interesting initiatives that will lead to further development of existing models for online learning and blended learning. However, as with all other development, this must be carefully done and with the aim of inclusion and heterogeneous student groups. This will be of great importance during the coming years, where the increasing and historically high unemployment rates must be met by new initiatives for professional development at our universities. How should the existing blended learning models be adapted for adult learners in groups where the average student is around 45 instead of 25 years old?

Conclusion

Researchers in healthcare have during the pandemic emphasised the need for an immediate digital revolution (Keesara, Jonas & Schulman, 2020). Higher education could probably better be described as a heterogeneous evolution of existing blended learning models and online collaboration, where the heterogeneity should be seen as positive, and as an opportunity to enhance the existing blended learning models with a more inclusive design. Although a difference in the attitudes towards online and on-campus activities will probably always remain, with a thoughtful redesign, reservations can be reduced. Finally, what healthcare researchers and higher education in general both have to deal with are what changes should be made permanent after the immediate crisis has resolved (Crawford et al, 2020; Keesara).

References

Blomqvist, E. (2017). Attitudes and personality traits among students in hybrid learning environments: a survey among students in higher education, (Attityder och personlighetsdrag bland studenter i hybrida lärmiljöer: En enkätundersökning bland studenter i högre utbildning), Bachelor's Thesis, Department of Computer and System Science, Mid Sweden University, Östersund

Cole, M. T., Shelley, D. J., & Swartz, L. B. (2014). Online instruction, e-learning, and student satisfaction: A three year study. *The International Review of Research in Open and Distributed Learning*, *15*(6).

Costa, P. T., & McCrae, R. R. (1992). Four ways five factors are basic. Personality and Individual Differences, 13(6), 653-665.

Crawford, J., Butler-Henderson, K., Rudolph, J., & Glowatz, M. (2020). Covid-19: 20 Countries' Higher Education Intra-Period Digital Pedagogy Responses. *Journal of Applied Teaching and Learning (JALT)*, *3*(1).

Enhuber, M. (2015). Art, space and technology: How the digitisation and digitalisation of art space affect the consumption of art—A critical approach. *Digital Creativity*, *26*(2), 121-137.

Flavin, M. (2017). *Disruptive technology enhanced learning: The use and misuse of digital technologies in higher education.* Springer.

Jackson, J. J., & Soto, C. J. (2015). Five-factor model of personality. *Oxford bibliographies in psychology*, 1.

Keesara, S., Jonas, A., & Schulman, K. (2020). Covid-19 and health care's digital revolution. *New England Journal of Medicine*.

Mozelius, P. (2018). Furnishing Active Learning Classrooms for Blended Synchronous Learning In: Roberta V. Nata (ed.), Progress in Education. Volume 54 New York: Nova Science Publishers, Inc.

Perales, M., Pedraza, L., & Moreno-Ger, P. (2019). Work-In-Progress: Improving Online Higher Education with Virtual and Remote Labs. In *2019 IEEE Global Engineering Education Conference (EDUCON)* (pp. 1136-1139). IEEE.

Said, H., Kirgis, L., Verkamp, B., & Johnson, L. (2015). On-line vs. face-to-face delivery of information technology courses: Students' assessment. *Journal of Information Technology Education: Research, 14*, 297-312.

Stewart, A. R., Harlow, D. B., & DeBacco, K. (2011). Students' experience of synchronous learning in distributed environments. *Distance Education, 32(3)*, 357-381.

Svenska Dagbladet (14/05/2020). Psykologen, "Am I unusal, when not taking the virus so seriously?" ("Är jag ovanlig som inte tar viruset på stort allvar?") (Accessed 20/05/2020) from: https://www.svd.se/ar-jag-ovanlig-som-inte-tar-viruset-pa-for-stort-allvar

Wong, L., & Fong, M. (2014). Student attitudes to traditional and online methods of delivery. *Journal of Information Technology Education: Research, 13*(1), 1-3.

Peter Mozelius is a senior lecturer and researcher in the Department of Computer and System Science at the Mid Sweden University in Östersund, Sweden. His research interests are in the fields of Technology Enhanced learning, Game-based learning, Programming education and Artificial Intelligence.

13

Higher Education, Student Protests, a Virus and Ethics

Penelope Engel-Hills
Professional Education Research Institute
Cape Peninsula University of Technology
South Africa

The 2020 higher education environment

Higher Education (HE) across South Africa was disrupted in 2015 by the #FeesMustFall, student social movement and the accompanying protests (Buttelli, and Le Bruyns, 2017). In the list of demands was a well-crafted call for decolonisation of the curriculum that was addressed by Mbembe (2016) at the level of decolonising the university. Although many institutions reached a tenuous stability in the 2018 academic year, there continue to be unresolved conversations. At some institutions the student protests resurfaced in 2020, at a time the severe acute respiratory syndrome virus (SARS-CoV-2) was taking a toll in many countries. Resolution of the student unrest had not been reached when the coronavirus disease 2019 (Covid-19) pandemic arrived in South Africa in March 2020. The onset of the hard national lockdown, imposed by the government, in a bid to flatten the curve and allow the health service to prepare for a high case load (Du Toit, 2020) meant that contact teaching institutions ceased to offer campus-based classes.

In South Africa, where the academic year follows the calendar year, the Higher Education Minister Blade Nzimande and the Deputy Director-General for Higher Education Diane Parker, proposed a risk-based plan to save the 2020 academic year within the national agenda to save lives. The suggested adjustments were for an academic year going beyond the usual closing in late November. Operationalisation of saving the academic year included HE institutions transitioning, with varying degrees of speed and acumen, into what some (e.g. Bozkurt and Sharma, 2020) have termed Emergency Remote Teaching (ERT) until the phased return of students to campus and the resumption of face-to-face teaching that required attention to health and safety in order that students and staff would be in as safe an environment as possible. There was simultaneous continuation of remote modes of teaching and learning, and the provision of digital devices and data to solve the challenges of the many students who were unable to access learning material delivered through the use of technology-based learning.

Covid-19 in South Africa has exposed the gaping inequalities in society as well as across the higher education sector. There are those institutions with resources and infrastructure that enabled the rapid shift and those that struggled to re-establish teaching and learning online. Similarly, the spectrum of students is from the well-resourced who were able to transition to online learning, juxtaposed to the many who were unable to engage in the alternative mode of delivery. At the time of writing, South Africa faces an increasing burden of infections, hospitalisations and deaths related to the pandemic and it is apparent that recovery will be on an extended path. This places a threat on the goal to complete the academic year amidst this unprecedented disruption to the achievement of successful educational outcomes. Return to campus was focused on final year students, leaving many students in the lower levels unable to be on campus and/or in residence. This forced a multi-modal approach, including the low technology distribution of printed material, and continued learning activities offered through the Learner Management System (LMS) or other e-platforms over an extended period. The human-centric focus was all but lost, and in this environment the inequalities in Cape Town, known to be the most unequal city in a country, one of the most unequal in the world (The World Bank, 2018) have been highlighted. The gap between those who have and those who have not is wider than ever amidst the harsh realities of further unemployment and growing poverty due to the pandemic.

The approach

We do not yet have the benefit of hindsight and cannot know for sure how things will transpire as countries across the globe face the pandemic on different time scales and degrees of risk and harm. However, we will be remiss if we do not find ways to reflect on the lessons learnt from the student protests and the pandemic to find a new direction for the university of the future in Africa. If we believe that on this continent the university will survive into the next century, then this is the most likely point in time when we must focus not only on saving this one academic year (Dell, 2020) but also on saving the institution to serve the needs of society.

The author was inspired by future scripting to engage in a futuristic scanning process of scenario thinking (De Laat, 2000; Den Boer, Rip and Speller, 2009) to identify themes related to the values and ethics of leadership and structure in HE. In this analysis the construction of an organisational structure to place ethical decision-making at the core of the university was emphasised. The creation of a theoretical system to enable "mutual appreciation" (Engel-Hills, Winberg, and Rip, 2019) is proposed to allow the gaze to shift from strongly policy driven endeavours to the facilitation of an environment with strong human relations in the university of the future that would be more responsive to the social needs of the post-pandemic society.

Emergent theme

Post Covid-19 it will be imperative to consider the ethics of the university through the lens of the impact of the pandemic on the people occupying the teaching and learning spaces. It emerged that the focus should shift from the selfish "own-interest" model of vertical silos to a flatter interdisciplinary approach to support the broader institutional purpose. This implies saving the integrity of the university through changing the system in ways that are yet to be determined but that must be flexible and agile in the unfolding post-Covid-19 environment.

In South Africa the stressors of the pandemic came on top of serious financial and social challenges (Van der Berg, 2020) impacting the HE sector. The convergence of student protests and Covid-19 created a perfect storm. Pressure was placed on the university leaders in this complex and complicated environment, and those content to just survive the battering can be forgiven. However, to slip back into old ways without putting a spotlight on what can be learned would be a missed opportunity to take a proactive stance (Du Toit, 2020) to nurture the reconceptualisation of the role of the university. We should take the chance to transform this entity for the full achievement of the ethical purpose of serving society or hasten the demise of the university as valuable to Africa. Leaders now must create a platform to push back against the exclusion of those in poverty and speak against the structural injustices in the system to drive an agenda of radical reform (Buttelli & Le Bruyns, 2017).

It is premature to present a vision of the university of the future, but it is timely to promote reflection and debate as key post-Covid-19 activities to seek answers to what the university of tomorrow must be. In the grip of the pandemic we cannot imagine what should or could change but if the stretched elastic of the university system simply returns to its old pre-Covid-19 position we will have failed in our duty as HE stakeholders to learn from this global crisis and improve the world. Only by viewing the future through a transformative and ethical lens with integrity and morality at the centre, will we answer questions such as what a university should look like if it is to be of service to the populations of such an unequal society – something we need to be concerned about in South Africa.

It is argued that for any possibility of creating an ethical higher education system, there is the urgent need to scrutinise the university. It is too simplistic and undesirable to suggest that the technology innovations incorporated into saving the 2020 academic year will bounce universities into quasi-distance institutions with ever reducing face to face teaching. The recommendation that emerged is rather to focus on the structural and human ethics of HE in the dual stress of ongoing student protests and Covid-19. The drive to save the academic year was tempered by the call to leave no students behind in this unequal society that will continue well past the pandemic. These contradictions raise the dubious ethical foundation of the HE response to shift to a technology-based approach. However, there can be redemption if this is a catalyst for imagining how a higher education system can be created that will more determinedly speak to the social needs of an unequal society. Without this, many will stay pegged in escalating poverty (Van der Berg, 2020) and therefore now is the time to show our humanity as a university sector and to speak to the ethical and moral dimensions of social justice in HE. This chapter is one stimulus for that conversation, but more will be needed to engender hope and avoid HE leaders reverting to what was considered normal or settling into a new normal that closely resembles the old ways. What is needed post-pandemic is to face the challenges and create a new identity for the university within a framework of ethical values.

Enabling change

In this book of looking to the future of universities from the present crisis, other authors will engage fully with possible scenarios and visions. Therefore, the purpose of this chapter is to provide the message that there must be learning from the lessons of the pandemic to enable positive change in the sector. Meaningful engagement and scholarly deliberation on the ethics of knowledge acquisition will be the cornerstone of a service-oriented university intended for the benefit of all and not just the few. To answer questions such as what will a university of the future look like, how will it behave if it is to serve the people of such an unequal society as South Africa and how can it contribute to closing the gap rather than contributing to the widening socio-economic divide, there will need to be open spaces for emotional conversations in a climate that adheres to the ethics of listening (Beard, 2009). It is proposed that only through such channels will the answers emerge in a changed world. We can start now and use scenario planning to project possible outcomes and influences of this pandemic on the education of tomorrow if we can truly listen to each other. The need will be to place ethics on the university agenda by a leadership that promotes wide sectorial engagement and student involvement in a paradigm of social justice. The unfolding of the university of the future, post the pandemic, is a process that should not be limited by how we think it might or should look as for now that is uncertain. What is more sure from the scenario planning conducted is that if we return to the position of pre-Covid-19 then we have lost the opportunity to be different in a meaningful way.

The pandemic will continue to have an impact on society and the HE sector in the years ahead. Much is written about the technology driven solutions and how the delivery of qualifications will be changed forever. Forums are needed for technology training but also forums for academics, students and administrators to share their problems, realities, needs and solutions so that we can construct the future and enable a socially just higher education system. By strengthening ethics in higher education we will place a vision on new societal values, contribute to closing the massive economic gap (Van der Berg, 2020) and build on a firm foundation for the continuation of HE in a technology driven landscape with a humanness and robust value system.

Concluding Reflections

The aim was to consider the university of the future but what emerged were the immense ethical challenges and questions arising from the current global crisis in an unequal and economically constrained environment where student unrest is not abating. Transitioning to online learning exposed the gaps related to access to devices and data and again highlighted the need to transform the curriculum and decolonise the university. In HE, the students and academics should take a leading role to create a new vision for changing society and achieving ethical higher education; the characteristics of which are still to be debated. In the present we are in survival mode to save the academic year but later we must dedicate sufficient time to pondering the lessons that could come out of this pandemic in what might look like a 'reflexive hub' (Engel-Hills, Winberg, and Rip, 2019). This perfect storm should not allow us to return like an elastic band back to an equilibrium or lead us into a new normal that closely resembles the old. This is the opportunity to make the world of HE a better place so as to reduce the economic divide. The HE landscape changed radically with Covid-19 and suddenly students needed to engage from their own homes which in many cases were not conducive to learning. Even staff in many instances lacked the resources and capacity for ERT. The focus at the time was positioned on technology but we need to shift and focus on the person and the social impact so as to glean all the learning needed to face the future. We have a golden opportunity and should make good use of it.

References

Beard, D. (2009). A Broader Understanding of the Ethics of Listening: Philosophy, Cultural Studies, Media Studies and the Ethical Listening Subject. International Journal of Listening, 23: 1, 7-20, DOI 10.1080/10904010802591771

Bozkurt, A., & Sharma, R. C., (2020). Emergency remote teaching in a time of global crisis due to Corona-Virus pandemic. Asian Journal of Distance Education, 15(1), i-vi.

Buttelli, F.G.K. & Le Bruyns, C., 2017, '#FeesMustFall as social movement and emancipatory politics? Moving towards an apocalyptic theological praxis outside the limits of party politics', HTS Teologiese Studies/Theological Studies 73(3), a4789. DOI: 10.4102/hts.v73i3.4789

De Laat, B. (2000). Scripts for the future: Using innovation studies to design foresight tools. In N.

Dell, S. (2020). HE department unveils plan to 'save the academic year'. University World News: Africa Edition, 15 May 2020. Accessed 28 June 2020. Available: https://www.universityworldnews.com/post.php?story=20200515152947531

Den Boer, D., Rip, A., & Speller, S. (2009). Scripting possible futures of nanotechnologies: A methodology that enhances reflexivity. Technology in Society, 31, 295–304.

Du Toit, P. (2020). Beyond Covid-19 lies turbulence, change and opportunity. News24. Available: www.news24.com

Engel-Hills, P., Winberg, C.& Rip, A. (2019). Ethics "upfront": Generating an organizational framework for a new university of technology. Science and Engineering Ethics: Ethics at Modern Universities of Technology, 25(6), 1705-1720, DOI: 10.1007/s11948-019-00140-0

Mbembe, A.J. (2016). Decolonizing the university: New directions. Arts & Humanities in Higher Education, 15(1), 29-45, DOI: 10.1177/1474022215618513

The World Bank. (2018). Overcoming Poverty and Inequality in South Africa. An Assessment of Drivers, Constraints and Opportunities. Washington: International Bank for Reconstruction and Development.

Van der Berg, S. (2020). Poverty rises, inequality shifts as Covid-19 impact continues unabated. News24. Available: www.news24.com

---

Penelope Engel-Hills is an Associate Professor and Acting Dean in the Faculty of Health and Wellness Sciences at the Cape Peninsula University of Technology (CPUT) in Cape Town, South Africa. She balances intersecting roles in higher education with a keen interest in professional education, research ethics and community engagement.

14

The Post Covid-19 University: *Quo Vadis?*

Mandla Stanley Makhanya
Principal and Vice Chancellor, University of South Africa, Pretoria/Tshwane South Africa

Background

The Education 2030 Incheon Declaration and Framework for Action Towards Inclusive and Equitable Quality Education and Life-long learning for all (2016) asserts "We reaffirm that education is a public good, a fundamental human right and a basis for guaranteeing the realization of other rights. It is essential for peace, tolerance, human fulfilment and sustainable development. We recognize education as key to achieving full employment and poverty eradication" (p. 7). The UNESCO Position Paper on Education Post-2015 (2015) addresses emerging considerations in the remit of responsibilities ascribed to universities and higher education. These include a social and sustainably transformative dimension of teaching and learning that focuses on the wellbeing of people and their right to an improved quality of life through quality education, as well as the notion of 'responsible (global) citizenship' (p4). We thus note a strong focus on the sustainability, social justice, inclusivity and equality aspects of higher education, as well as a growing emphasis on the responsibility of ordinary citizens to participate actively in their own development, that of their communities, and the spaces that they inhabit. This signals a transition from education that is tasked to develop a critical citizenry to education that will ensure that individuals will simultaneously be developed as responsible global citizens by incorporating the ethical stewardship of our planet and a commitment to the sustainability of its ecosystems. Perhaps Sustainable Development Goal (SDG) 4 best encapsulates the preceding policy trajectory and intent when it states that in the 21st Century, the intention is to "ensure inclusive and equitable quality education and provide life-long opportunities for all by 2030" (UNESCO 2015). While efforts towards achieving Education for All (EFA) have yielded some progress (UNESCO Jomtien Statement, 2011), more recent data indicate that progress has come to a standstill and that it is virtually certain that the EFA and Millennium Development Goal (MDG) education agendas will not be realised by the envisaged dates (Montoya & Mundy, 2018). There is thus a need to revisit education agendas within the prevailing contexts, so as to deliver agreements and actions that will resurrect the momentum for both EFA and MDG 4 (UNICEF/UNESCO, 2007). However, the emergence of the Covid-19 pandemic in December 2019 has thrown the proverbial "spanner-in-the-works", halting and even reversing much of the already limited progress that has been made and plunging global higher education into and even greater crisis.

Current societal dynamics and challenges require higher education solutions that are flexible, integrated and holistic and which should not only include transdisciplinarity and engagement with professional bodies, business and industry in the development of courseware and teaching practice, but also an openness to different modes of assessment and credentialising to meet different societal requirements. Furthermore, higher education institutions should be open to very fundamental restructuring (including administrative) to ensure the responsiveness and agility that is required to ensure ongoing relevance. This is particularly true in the current global context of massive socio-economic inequality, where in OECD countries for example, ".... the richest 10% of the population earn 9.6 times the income of the poorest 10%. In the 1980s, this ratio stood at 7:1 rising to 8:1 in the 1990s and 9:1 in the 2000s...While there is always a gap in education outcomes across individuals with different socio-economic backgrounds, the gap widens in high-inequality countries as people in disadvantaged households struggle to access quality education" (OECD, 2015).

It is from this platform of inequality (or abundance) that rapid, ongoing and accretive advances in technology are propelling societies forward in virtually every sphere of endeavour and inducing higher education institutions to provide a level and quality of education, student experience and support that equips students for relevance in the workplace and which simultaneously inculcates responsible and critical global citizenship for the sustainability of the planet (Barnett, 2000; Castells, 2009; Oblinger, 2003). 21st Century graduates need to be contextually relevant, socially mobile, ethical, critical, responsible, adaptable and appropriately equipped to navigate an opaque future.

Poverty is often scaffolded on pre-existing socio-economic inequality, and this is directly linked to a lack of digital equity, which entails ensuring that everyone has equal opportunities to use the tools and resources needed to fully participate as a citizen in today's digitally-powered world (ISTE, 2006). To date, the affordances of the digital revolution, when it comes to access to a quality and affordable education have not been realized to the extent that it could be claimed to have made a measurable impact on the lives of those who need it most (Bennet & Kent, 2017; Kalman, 2016).

The Covid-19 pandemic has brought to the fore these gross inequalities, which exist in both developed and developing societies when it comes to access to both appropriate devices for learning and the internet itself. As soon as the pandemic struck, and lockdown measures were imposed, most parents, teachers, children and students were forced to stay at home, sharing devices and internet access, where these were available, for both home schooling and higher education studies. There was a scramble by the majority of institutions to move fully online into what many have dubbed "emergency remote teaching". Thus far it has been a sobering experience. There has been an uncomfortable realisation for most, that Open, Distance, and e-Learning is a distinct education model requiring its own types and levels of expertise, from pedagogical design and delivery for quality education, to ensuring that the appropriate IT infrastructure is in place to facilitate online teaching and institutional operations.

Higher education in transition

Higher education is at once responsive to, and a driver of change to the extent that higher education institutions could be microcosms of, or even proxies for their State and their national developmental aspirations. Seen through the lens of this symbiotic transformational relationship with the State, broader society and global membership, it could be suggested that many of the current challenges faced by universities had their genesis in the advent of the internet (in 1991) and subsequent digitisation, which contributed to, and facilitated burgeoning globalization, massification and the internationalisation of higher education.

It is important to note that there is a move from the more traditional understanding that higher education institutions exist to educate students for lives in public service, to advance knowledge through research, and to develop a critical citizenry and leadership, to one where universities are increasingly pressured to prepare graduates with the requisite knowledge and skills and the ethical and social responsibility to meet the very dynamic and transient workforce needs arising from what is increasingly being dubbed 'the 4th Industrial Revolution'.

There is also a rise of the new industrial model of privatization, commercialization, and corporatization which has altered higher education's traditional mission, and increased the mission differentiation in higher education systems in preparing all graduates for democratic participation, active citizenship, and personal development (Kezar, 2004; Lambert, 2014). In other words, we note quite fundamental mission drift. Institutions of higher learning are not only under pressure to promote access, affordability, and graduation in today's uncertain future, but also enhance individuals' core competencies and dispositions (i.e., "noneconomic" benefits) such as the ability to think logically, the capacity to challenge the status quo, and the desire to develop sophisticated values for entry into the highly competitive global labour market (Brennan, Durazii, & Sene, 2013; Selingo, 2016; Tilak, 2008; Washburn, 2005). Technological innovation and digitisation continue to play a fundamental role in this transformation trajectory.

Accelerated technological innovation and influence

For higher education institutions in developing societies, the aspects of both 'peril' and 'promise' hold true. On one hand, most are struggling to navigate an unparalleled nexus of complex and (potentially) destructive socio-economic and political forces (including the as yet unclear outcomes and impact on higher education of the Covid-19 pandemic), while on the other, the potential and promise that 4IR offer a platform from which to transition into a more equitable, relevant future. Furthermore, even as institutions of higher learning in developing societies grapple with their contextual realities *vis a vis* 4IR (and technological innovation *per se)* they are obliged to deal with the fundamental institutional change that will be required to derive benefit from its affordances, and the disruptive impact that this will have regarding institutional leadership and management, and the need for staff (academic, professional and administrative) and students of all ages to unlearn and relearn for a future that holds little certainty. It is this transition that has been made painfully real, and increasingly imperative, as the global pandemic wreaks its havoc globally.

There is a view that those higher education institutions that are not willing or able to make the necessary changes are likely to suffer a decline in relevance and impact. Most certainly, the virtually compulsory forays into "emergency remote learning" have brought home the need to be technologically proficient and able when it comes to higher education delivery, and it is likely that once the pandemic has passed, many institutions of higher learning will adopt those aspects of education delivery or practice which they implemented, that are likely to have some form of financial benefit or cost saving going forward, in a world teetering on the brink of depression.

The advent of Covid-19 has had (and will have, going forward), a serious impact on jobs, required skills and even business and institutional operations going forward. It is evident that a harsh reprioritisation and reorientation is taking place. Everyone has noted those businesses and jobs which became immediately redundant while on the other hand, note was taken of services that remained relevant and essential to the functioning of society. Job security appeared to be vested in (for example) teaching, policing, medical manufacturing services and provision, some forms of transport, food production and provision, funeral services, technology and the sciences, especially the biomedical and analytical sciences. On the other hand, leisure pursuits such as travel, eating out, sport, musical concerts etc, and niche businesses related to these and other non-essential production, came to a halt, literally overnight. As businesses have closed and the recession has taken hold, hundreds and thousands of people have been retrenched, livelihood lost, and millions have been plunged into new, or greater, poverty.

A tangential outcome of the pandemic has been a process of revisiting operational needs at most businesses and institutions that have managed to stay in operation, especially where staff have needed to work from home (as is the case for many higher education institutions). There has been a realisation that institutions can actually function adequately with fewer members of staff and that a number of institutions and businesses have a lot of unproductive or even unnecessary staff. The likely outcome of this is that staff complements will be streamlined for maximum efficiency and productivity as necessary adjustments are made for their survival and future sustainability. The unfortunate consequence of this is twofold: not only will more people become redundant and unemployed, but those fortunate enough to remain employed are likely to find that their workloads have increased, and their current work stresses and concerns exacerbated. What all of this means is that current societal dynamics and challenges require higher education solutions which are flexible, integrated and holistic and which should not only include transdisciplinarity and engagement with professional bodies, business and industry in the development of courseware and teaching practice, but also an openness to different modes of student support, assessment and credentialing to meet different societal requirements and student expectations. There is a growing emphasis on the recognition of prior learning as a means of drawing more experienced yet non credentialised students onto the system, and acknowledgement that concerted attention should be given to the upskilling of mature learners as a means of ensuring their ongoing employability in the transforming world of work.

Key to achieving this, is an invested academe, which is currently not the case in many institutions. Reports from across the globe attest to disgruntled, depressed and even suicidal academics (Farber, 2018; Oswald, 2019; Orozco *et al,* 2018; Pitt, 2018; Richardson, 2019). This scenario is likely to be exacerbated by the consequences on the profession of the Covid-19 pandemic.

Conclusion

Globally, higher education is becoming increasingly fragmented and polarised and the notion of education is being reshaped in line with technological advancements and the entry into higher education of an avalanche of for-profit providers eager to leverage the affordance of technology for financial gain, and more latterly, the Covid-19 pandemic. Traditional higher education providers, both in the distance education and face-to-face contexts have entered the fray, with varying degrees of success and influence.

One also notes a move into online education, which is defined and understood differently depending on the location and context (this was exposed by Covid-19 and the leap into emergency remote teaching), as well as public or private and for-profit entities, but again, it is fragmented, with little research on its general implementation and success.

Finally, universities that wish to survive and thrive have no other option than to reinvent themselves through a future-centric mindset that includes a multi-stakeholder, broadly participative leadership and management, collaborative business models, a fundamental commitment to sustainability through ethical stewardship of the institutional and the planet's resources, a genuine appreciation of the people who comprise the university community, and high quality, relevant courseware, assessment practices and student support, that will prepare graduates for an uncertain future and provide a foundation for future flourishing.

References

Barnett, R. (2000). Thinking the University, again. *Education Philosophy and Theory, 32 (3).* 319-326, https://doi.org/10.1111/j.1469-5812.2000.tb00457.x

Bennet, R. & Kent, M. (2017). *Massive Open Online Courses and higher education: what went right, what went wrong and where to next.* New York. Routledge, Taylor &Francis.

Brennan, J., Durazzi, N., & Sene, T. (2013). *Things we know and don't know about the Wider Benefits of Higher Education: A review of the recent literature*. London, UK: London School of Economics and Political Science (LSE).

Castells, M. (2009). *Communication power*. Oxford: Oxford University Press.

Farber, T. (2018). *UCT sets up inquiry into Bongani Mayosi's suicide*. 03 August 2018 - 13:38. Sunday Times, Times Live. Retrieved from: https://www.timeslive.co.za/news/south-africa/2018-08-03-uct-sets-up-inquiry-into-bongani-mayosis-suicide/

Kalman, Y.M. (2016). Cutting through the hype: evaluating the innovative potential of new educational technologies through business model analysis. *Open Learning: The Journal of Open, Distance and e-Learning,* 1(31), 64 – 75. https://doi.org/10.1080/02680513.2016.1164592

Kezar, A. (2004). Obtaining integrity? Reviewing and examining the charter between higher education and society. *The Review of Higher Education*, 27(4), 429-459. http://dx.doi.org/10.1353/rhe.2004.0013

International Society for Technology in Education (ISTE) (2006). *Digital Equity Toolkit – Working Draft*. Retrieved from: http://www.laurelfelt.org/digital-equity/

Lambert, M. T. (2014). *Privatization and the public good.* Cambridge, MA: Harvard University Education Press

Oblinger, D. (2003). Boomers, Gen-Xers & Millennials: Understanding the New Students. *EDUCAUSE Review*. July/August (pp37-47).

OECD. (2015). *In It Together: Why Less Inequality Benefits All.* OECD Publishing, Paris. http://dx.doi.org/10.1787/9789264235120-en

Orozco, R., Benjet, C., Borges, G., Moneta Arce, M. F., Fregoso Ito, D., Fleiz, C., & Villatoro, J. A. (2018). Association between attempted suicide and academic performance indicators among middle and high school students in Mexico: results from a national survey. *Child and adolescent psychiatry and mental health*, 12 (9). doi:10.1186/s13034-018-0215-6

Oswald, A. (2019). *Middle aged academics are at greater suicide risk than students.* Times Higher Education. Retrieved from: https://www.timeshighereducation.com/opinion/middle-aged-academics-are-greater-suicide-risk-students

Pitt, C. (2018). News 24. *UCT must take responsibility for Prof Mayosi's death* – former Fees Must Fall leader

News 24. 2018-07-31 14:03. Retrieved from: https://www.news24.com/SouthAfrica/News/uct-must-take-responsibility-for-prof-mayosis-death-former-fees-must-fall-leader-20180731

Richardson, H. (2019). University counselling services 'inundated by stressed academics'. Retrieved from: https://www.bbc.com/news/education-48353331

Sciences Pro.(2019). U7+ ALLIANCE: A UNIVERSITY ALLIANCE TO WEIGH IN ON THE G7 AGENDA. o710 2019. Retrieved from: https://www.sciencespo.fr/en/news/news/u7-alliance-47-universities-commit-to-tackle-global-issues/4248

Selingo, J. (2013). *College unbound: The future of higher education, and what it means for students*. New York, NY: New Harvest

Tilak, J. (2008). Higher education: A public good or a commodity for trade? *Prospects,* 38, 449-466.

UNESCO. (2006). *Global Education Digest. Comparing Education Statistics around the World.* UNESCO Institute for Statistics. Montreal. (pp 76-79).

UNESCO/UNICEF. (2007). A Human Rights-Based Approach to EDUCATION FOR ALL. A framework for the realization of children's right to education and rights within education. *A Human Rights-Based Approach to Education* © United Nations Children's Fund/ United Nations Educational, Scientific and Cultural Organization. Retrieved from: https://www.unicef.org/publications/files/A_Human_Rights_Based_Approach_to_Education_for_All.pdf

UNESCO. (2015). Sustainable Development Goals. Available at: http://www.un.org/sustainabledevelopment/sustainable-development- goals/. Accessed: 2016/04/20

UNESCO. (2015). Position Paper on Education Post-2015 . ED-14/EFA/POST- 2015/1. Retrieved from: https://unesdoc.unesco.org/ark:/48223/pf0000227336 (p4)

UNESCO (2016). Education 2030. Incheon Declaration and Framework for Action Towards Inclusive and Equitable Quality Education and Life- long learning for all. ED-2016/ws/2. Available at http://en.unesco.org/ world-education-forum-2015/incheon-declaration.

UNESCO. (2018). Data for Sustainable development. *Time to Get Serious About Education for All, with Progress at a Standstill.* Posted on February 28, 2018 by UIS Data Blog. Data for Sustainable Development. UNESCO Institute for Statistics Blog. By Silvia Montoya, Director of the UNESCO Institute for Statistics (UIS) and Karen

Mundy, Chief Technical Officer, Global Partnership for Education (GPE). Retrieved from:
https://sdg.uis.unesco.org/2018/02/28/time-to-get-serious-about-education-for-all-with-progress-at-a-standstill/

Washburn, J. (2005). *University Inc.: The corporate corruption of American higher education.* New York, NY: Basic Books.

Mandla Stanley Makhanya is Vice Chancellor of the University of South Africa and is a prominent proponent of higher education leadership and advocacy, nationally, continentally and globally, more especially as it pertains to Open, Distance and eLearning.

15

Blended Learning as a Response to Covid-19 in Syrian Universities

Dima M. Dayoub
English Language Teaching Department, Higher Institute of Languages, Tishreen University, Lattakia, Syria.

The Syrian higher education context

The emergence of a handful of reported Covid-19 cases prompted the Syrian Ministry of Higher Education and Scientific Research (MHESR) to take immediate measures announcing a nation-wide temporary closure of public and private universities and campuses. This was coupled by continually updated guidelines on how to resume the teaching-learning process during the lockdown period and, later, on how to compensate for the "learning gap" upon re-opening. The disruption started on the 14th of March and ended on the 31st of May, 2020. The ministry of education that governs schools took even more drastic measures. The second term was terminated and exams were cancelled with automatic passes for all students in the hope of providing intensified tuition at the beginning of the next term. This unprecedented measure excluded the 9th-graders and baccalaureate students due to the importance of their end-of-year exams for entry into secondary schools and universities respectively. In the meantime, an Educational TV channel was launched to ensure the delivery of their curricula.

Unified guidelines vs individual initiatives during lockdown

The main official requirement during the lockdown period was the digitalization of lectures through uploading: 1) electronic PDF versions of textbooks that are not available in print, and 2) lectures as narrated PowerPoint presentations. Despite the unified guidelines issued by the MHESR, the actual implementation varied widely across universities, departments and even staff members. This diversity was manifest in the lecture digitalization format: PDF versions of textbooks uploaded into universities' sites, narrated PowerPoint Presentations, live streaming of lectures, selected readings as email attachments, dedicated YouTube channels, and WhatsApp and Facebook groups, among others. The virtualization of content greatly depended on lecturers' prior experiences and preferences, the available resources and the numbers of targeted students. Indeed, this phase witnessed collaborative and creative contributions, but also highlighted deficiencies. The lack of clear pedagogical policy nurtures innovative and flexible instruction on one hand, but compromises quality monitoring on the other (Crawford et al., 2020, p. 12).

The Syrian Virtual University (SVU), an accredited fully-fledged online university, took the initiative to collaborate with traditional universities by making available its live virtual class platforms for free use by the teaching staff:

Due to the exceptional circumstances that our beloved country is going through and in line with the precautionary measures endorsed by the Cabinet, and in order to ensure the continuity of the educational process; the Syrian Virtual University offers its virtual class platform to enable faculty members to record lectures using simple tools and small file sizes, which facilitates the upload and download of lectures. Lecturers can record and upload their sessions to their universities' websites or to any other forums they deem appropriate. Students can download and re-play the lectures using the same tools.

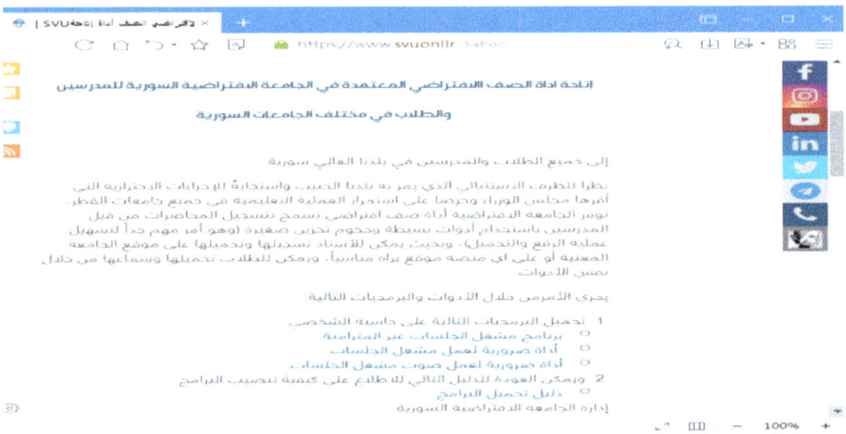

Figure 1: The SVU's announcement of making available its virtual classes, listing the technical requirements for operating them

Given the lack of open-source educational technology, this initiative was invaluable. However, the SVU's inherently educational platforms are not easily utilized as operating them requires downloading a set of programmes and becoming familiar with the basic functions of their virtual tools. Given the unprecedented breadth of disruption it was not possible to ensure that faculty members at traditional universities had meaningful access to technology, to say nothing of students. Although access to technology, in its material sense, was a tangible obstacle; the digital divide extended beyond physical resources and was shaped by motivational, usage and skills access. As Dijk (2006, p. 232) puts it, the digital divide is best understood by "addressing issues such as attitudes toward technology (e.g. technophobia and computer anxiety), the channels used in new media diffusion, educational views of digital skills, and cultural analyses of lifestyles and daily usage patterns". Analysis of the Covid-19 induced transition to online learning in a Chinese university concluded that negative student attitudes were due to the "lack of self-discipline" and inappropriate learning environments, rather than being a result of technical challenges (Bao, 2020, p. 114).

An example of disparity in access is the usage of broadband as opposed to prepaid mobile Internet. User access inevitably impacts usage time and the sophistication of the selected applications and tools for online delivery, which enhances or inhibits lecturers' creativity. However, even when a lecturer has the resources to create technology-rich content, asymmetry of usage access makes it hard for students to fully utilize such lectures, or to do so evenly. Unlike shared physical spaces in brick-and-mortar lecture halls and university auditoriums, virtual spaces can paradoxically compromise access equity. Having said that, access to physical universities can also be hindered by commuting expenses or remoteness from the campus.

Another issue related to the use of the SVU tools is that they inherently foster an interactive model of learning and teaching, where students' presence and participation are integral to the educational process. The comparatively large numbers of disrupted students at the Syrian universities (exceeding 650,000, according to the MHESR) and the absence of academic log-in credentials to authenticate students' virtual identities have made it impossible to fully harness the interactive potential of the SVU platforms. The incapacity of conventional universities to offer immediate technical support to faculty and students reflects the large-scale and profoundness of the disruption impact. The SVU recognized this challenge by suggesting that other universities may use its platforms for broadcasting, archiving, and re-playing lectures rather than for interactive teaching and learning, despite the interactive affordances built into the SVU tools.

As an alternative, lecturers resorted to low-technology solutions including generic communication platforms and free familiar applications such as Facebook groups and WhatsApp for interaction with students. The latter was more feasible in the case of postgraduate programmes with limited numbers of enrolled students. However, applications that are not designed for pedagogical purposes have been conceived as inadequate learning tools and merely media for sustained communication with lecturers, according to a small-scale feedback from Masters students and in the English Language Teaching Programme at Tishreen University in Syria.

Evaluating their learning and teaching experiences during the disruption, participants pointed out that the sense the virtualization of classes was a provisional measure and a short-lived experience intensified their alienation and adversely impacted their motivational access. The perception of the transition as transient compromised their commitment and enthusiasm as they felt in a suspension phase that triggered a "waiting mode". The "waiting mode" is attributed to the fact that online courses in the lockdown period were not designed as autonomous models, but rather as immediate under-developed solutions that are secondary to face-to-face sessions. Another reason for students' disengagement as reported in the literature is that online learning environments do not meet students' original expectations of experiencing the "social and experiential" dimensions of university life (UNESCO, 2020, p.42).

In addition to compromising the social aspect of university life, the pandemic has presented unique logistical challenges to nurturing practical skills that require physical presence and interpersonal contact such as laboratory experiments and professional internships. It has also particularly put private universities under financial pressure since such universities are fee-paying and suspension has material implications. Private university students who come from Arab countries faced travel restrictions that extended beyond the national lockdown, leaving them stranded as airports closed and flights were cancelled. In the case of public universities, the ministry arranged the return of Syrian students on scholarships abroad, provided they undergo a 14-day quarantine period.

Reduced close-proximity and increased quality interactions post lockdown

The Syrian Ministry of Higher Education has approached the post-lockdown period as compensatory for the "educational gap" effected by the cessation of face-to-face classes. Regulatory guidelines for re-opening universities targeted three main areas: the academic calendar, the mechanisms for resuming in-person classes and students' assessment criteria. The second term was reduced to two months stretching over the regular summer break. Lecture duration was cut by a half and some were re-scheduled to Saturdays to avoid crowded timetables during week days. Lecturers were invited to concisely go through the key knowledge points of the electronic lectures during face-to-face meetings. More emphasis was placed, however, on lecturers' availability during their office hours (6-8 hours a week) to answer students' questions and to enrich academic discussions. As such, quality one-to-one interactions were structured with the aim of extending and complementing the shorter in-person classes. Further, to ensure social, or rather physical distancing and to guard against large student gatherings, large classes were divided into smaller ones. This has similarly facilitated greater opportunities of student-lecturer interactions. Students' evaluation criteria were more relaxed in the sense that exam questions were required to be proportional with the academic input and with the shorter duration of the second term. At the postgraduate level, research students in the stage of writing their dissertations were granted a period of extension that is equivalent to the suspension phase.

The digitalization of content was not only through uploading lectures to universities' websites, but also through requiring the teaching staff to provide and make available to students a CD containing the theoretical content of lectures. As such, students' access to the learning material has been enhanced, especially in the case of students encountering poor connectivity. A positive outcome of this period has, therefore, been the compilation of faculty-generated open-source academic resources whereas, previously, students resorted to note-taking, recoding lectures and even to some unprofessional businesses that made profit out of selling lecture notes to students. The virtualization of content has enabled the circulation of knowledge and generation of reliable resources in ways that are not possible otherwise.

Overall, the official strategies adopted by Syrian universities to mitigate the impact of the pandemic present a spontaneous experimental model of blended learning where digital content delivery frees time for active engagement in face-to-face meetings. In this emerging model, online and in-person modes of delivery are implemented sequentially rather than simultaneously. In the long run, it may be worth considering the implementation of a hybrid model where some theoretical modules are optionally available online in times of normalcy and mandated in times of crises, health or otherwise. Such models need, however, to become well-established and adequately developed as part of a national strategic plan. "Emergency distance learning" needs to be re-conceptualized to mean well-founded modules and methods that are consistently integrated into courses from the outset rather than reduced to *on-the-spur-of-the-moment sporadic effort*. The literature on inta- period Covid-19 unveils context-/country-specific diversity of responses. A post-pandemic coherent approach would require uniting international endeavors to outline best practice and pedagogy (Crawford et al., 2020).

Post-pandemic: Blended learning as the planned emergency remote higher learning model?

The transition to online delivery of content has been abrupt and has been driven by the urgency to provide instructional continuity. Current debates about a post-pandemic pedagogy cast doubt on conceptualizing such migration as "emergency e-learning" and argue that it is rather a trend to normalize online learning. The normalization of e-learning refers to "strategies that frame the widespread adoption of online learning under Covid-19 as a pathway to a new normal rather than an emergency response", perpetuating thereby issues of educational inequity and posing questions about academic quality (Murphy, 2020, p. 500), rural-urban disparity of access and student welfare (Zhang, 2020, p. 5), among others. In Syria, a full transition to online delivery is beyond the capacities, and may be beyond the interests and objectives, of traditional universities.

The emerging modality in Syrian universities is "emergency remote learning" (Hodges et al., 2020). It is, however, still characterized by a temporary, mandatory, urgent and fragmented nature, falling short of becoming an optimal sustainable online substitute for face-to-face tuition in times of crises. Blended learning needs to become a priority, a national strategic plan that is dynamically developed. The implementation of the online and offline modalities of blended learning should be carried out more deliberately, whether in tandem or sequentially. It may be best to digitalize modules (or parts of modules) that require reflection and self-paced reading, leaving space for hands-on and experiential learning in face-to-face classes. Technologically-speaking UNESCO recommends using an array of diverse educational technologies rather than relying on a single technological tool so that the affordance of ubiquity specific to online delivery is not compromised as a result of excluding the economically and socially vulnerable (UNESCO, 2020, p.44).

To reinvent a disruption-resilient sustainable higher education system is to structure opportunities of virtual access that parallel real-life opportunities in terms of academic quality, equity and preparedness. Future higher education urgently needs to be adaptable through reconfiguring curricula, attitudes, infrastructures, manpower and teaching approaches to reflect readiness in the face of not only present and potentially recurrent Covid-19 but any disruptive adversity. Blended learning, where a balance is created between online courses and in-person meetings, is no longer a luxurious option or a second-hand alternative to traditional learning. It is the way to unburden traditional university resources and maintain human presence, the essence of motivation, without compromising any. Future blended learning models should, however, be re-defined to move from being an unintentional, short-lived, tentative phase to becoming a more deliberate durable response. Innovative individual efforts and diverse pedagogical approaches need to be interwoven into a collective research-based rigorous method of higher education continuity.

References

Bao, W. (2020) "Covid-19 and Online Teaching in Higher Education: A Case Study of Peking University", Human Behav & Emerg Tech, pp. 113-115.

Crawford, J. Butler-Henderson, K. Rudolph, J. Malkawi, B. Glowatz, M., Burton, R. Magni, P. and Lam, S. (2020) "Covid-19: 20 Countries Higher Education Intra-Period Digital Pedagogy Responses", Journal of Applied Teaching and Learning, Vol. 3, No. 1, pp. 1-20.

Hodges, C. Moore, S. Lockee, B. Trust, T. and Bond, A. (2020) "The Difference between Emergency Remote Teaching and Online Learning", Educause Review, viewed 3 June, 2020, <https://er.educause.edu/articles/2020/3/the-difference-between-emergency-remote-teaching-and-online-learning>.

Murphy, M. P. A. (2020) "Covid-19 and Emergency ELearning: Consequences of the Securitization of Higher Education for Post-Pandemic Pedagogy", Contemporary Security Policy, Vol. 41, No. 3, pp. 492-505.

The Syrian Ministry of Higher Education and Scientific Research (2018), viewed 10 June, 2020, <http://mohe.gov.sy/mohe/>.

The Syrian Virtual University (2017), viewed 18 June, 2020, <https://www.svuonline.org/ar/news/4621>.

UNESCO (2020) "Covid-19 and Higher Education: Today and Tomorrow: Impact Analysis, Policy Responses and Recommendations", April, viewed 15 June, 2020, <http://www.iesalc.unesco.org/en/wp-content/uploads/2020/04/Covid-19-EN-090420-2.pdf>.

Van Dijk, J. (2006) "Digital Divide Research, Achievements and Shortcomings", Poetics, Vol. 34, pp. 221-235.

Zhang, W. Wang, Y. Yang, L. and Wang C. (2020). "Suspending Classes without Stopping Learning: China's Education Emergency Management Policy in the Covid-19 Outbreak", Journal of Risk and Financial Management, Vol. 13, No. 55, pp. 1-6.

Dima Moain Dayoub is associate professor of Educational Technology and ELT and head of the English Language Teaching Department at the Higher Institute of Languages, Tishreen university, Syria, where she teaches *Integrating Technology into Language Learning and Teaching* and *Academic Research* to Masters students. She holds a PhD from the University of Manchester. She was awarded an Erasmus+ Teaching Mobility scholarship at the University of Barcelona and a Media and Digital Literacy Academy scholarship at the Lebanese American University in Beirut.

16

Student Readiness for e-Learning Co-Production during Covid-19

Andrews Agya Yalley
University of the Cape Coast, Ghana

Introduction

The ongoing Covid-19 pandemic has led to the implementation of various non-pharmaceutical public health measures including lockdowns, closure of educational institutions, and other social distancing measures by various governments across the globe and traditional universities are not exempt from the impact of these measures. Subsequently, traditional universities have taken initiatives by resorting temporarily to e-learning platforms as a substitute for their usual face-to-face teaching and learning approach. This implies that students have to co-produce teaching and learning through e-learning platforms, thus, raising doubt on students' readiness for this. For instance, in South Africa, Ghana and other parts of the world concerns have been raised on students' knowledge, competence, skills, motivation, and other resources in engaging on e-learning platforms (eg. Larbi-Apau, Sampong and Kwofie 2020; Mukeredzi, Kokutse and Dell 2020).

Addressing these issues is of great concern for universities considering the importance of students in the co-production of teaching and learning. This, motivated Bazana and Nabo-Bazana (2020) to emphasise the importance of students' preparedness for the introduction of e-learning technologies during a pandemic and they called for universities to understand the factors that can enhance and engage students in co-producing teaching and learning online when implementing e-learning technologies. This understanding has implications for universities now and in the post-Covid-19 era in surviving future pandemics and other turbulences.

e-Learning adoption amongst traditional universities

Face-to-face teaching and learning has been a long-established tradition in universities until the emergence of e-learning or pedagogical technologies that transformed the approach to teaching and learning as well as the creation of online universities as new competitors in the university marketplace. Traditional universities differ from online universities by the degree of adoption of e-learning technologies, with traditional universities adopting a face-to-face approach supported by e-learning technologies. Online universities, on the other hand, have adopted e-learning technologies through an open and distance learning approach in facilitating teaching and learning, thus, eliminating the face-to-face encounter.

The adoption of e-learning technologies and platforms including Moodle, Google Classroom, and Blackboard in traditional universities can be attributed to the increasing familiarity and ownership of technological devices particularly amongst millennial students paralleled with the increasing access and speed of internet technologies. This is also attributed to the role of higher education regulatory bodies and other stakeholders in making e-learning technologies a requirement in the accreditation of universities. e-learning technologies have become a popular and essential technology in traditional universities in making education flexible and accessible as well as in bridging the societal information and knowledge need.

Whilst most traditional universities have adopted and implemented these technologies to complement their face-to-face campus based-teaching and learning through the blended learning approach, the degree of adoption varies from partial to limited adoption, particularly for universities in developing countries. Several scholars have documented the slow adoption rate of e-learning technologies particularly in developing countries (e.g. Mutisya and Makokha, 2016), whilst others have identified drivers and barriers of students` adoption of e-learning technologies. These include internet connection, cost and accessibility, cost of computers/laptops, ICT skills, attitude towards e-learning, convenience, flexibility and interactivity with lecturers (e.g. Bhuasiri et al. 2012; Mutisya and Makokha 2016).

Student readiness for co-production

Universities like any knowledge-intensive services are highly dependent on the active participation of students for the production and consumption of teaching and learning materials. As a result, students, as customers are stakeholders in the production of teaching and learning and their active participation and involvement has been referred to as co-production, which relates to situations where students and universities collaborate to produce value through teaching and learning (McCulloch 2009). The success of co-production within universities influences outcomes including service quality, student satisfaction as well as performance, profitability, and sustainable competitive advantage (Sekhon et al. 2016).

For co-production to be effective in universities, the active participation of students is important, and this is dependent on their readiness to co-produce. Student`s readiness to co-produce becomes more important as most traditional universities have had to migrate temporarily to purely e-learning platforms to facilitate their teaching and learning as a result of the current Covid-19 pandemic. However, the reality is that most students have limited or no experience using e-learning platforms as a sole medium for teaching and learning, emphasizing the importance of student`s readiness to participate in co-production.

Customer readiness has been described as a customer's preparedness to perform service-related tasks successfully (Sekhon et al. 2016). Heidenreich and Handrich (2015, p.46) referred to it as "a condition or state in which a customer is prepared and likely to create value together with the company by actively engaging in the service provision and consumption". Yalley and Sekhon (2014), on the other hand, conceptualized this as customer readiness to co-production, which refers to the customer`s preparedness to engage and perform their co-production role successfully. The importance of customer readiness to co-production is related to the attainment of service outcomes and expectations including customer citizenship behavior, customer satisfaction, service quality, productivity, sustainable competitive advantage, and profitability.

Student readiness to the co-production of e-learning

Students readiness to co-produce teaching and learning using e-learning technologies does not happen in a vacuum, and several factors underpin its development. These factors are discussed below:

Resource commitment

Organizational, human and technological resources are vital for effective co-production and competitive advantage. The commitment of these resources to an organizational production process has an effect on customers' attitudes and behavior during co-production. Therefore, for universities to prepare students to engage in co-production through e-learning platforms, the university authorities need to commit appropriate and adequate technological and human resources. Technological resources may include the design and user-friendliness of the e-learning platform, provision of high-quality technical support over the telephone, email, and social media as well as the provision of technological devices, if necessary, to support students. Human resources, on the other hand, may include the quality and expertise of lecturers and tutors in delivering and engaging students through e-learning platforms. This also requires the commitment of students' mental and technological resources (eg. *knowledge, internet, and technological devices*) during co-production.

Communication

Communication plays a significant role in every organizational production process and this becomes of greater significance when it comes to teaching and learning in universities particularly when using e-learning technologies. To engage and enhance students' active participation during co-production, communication between lecturers and students is important. According to Hinson (2020), for universities to survive this 'new normal', clear, accurate and reliable communication is important to ensure an excellent student experience. For universities, this means that lecturers have to communicate effectively, accurately, clearly and enthusiastically with students when teteaching remotely through the quality of voice tone, body language, engagement, as well as a demonstration of knowledge and the use of real-time and two-way communication. The use of social media and video conference technologies including WhatsApp, Facebook, Zoom and Google Hangout may be used to complement e-learning platforms to provide real-time two-way communication in engaging and enhancing students' active participation.

Student motivation

Motivation affects consumer drive and behavior and students as consumers when motivated intrinsically and/or extrinsically can influence their readiness to engage in co-production. Intrinsically, co-production of knowledge through e-learning platforms should be fun, exciting and engaging through the use of emojis, animations, colors, videos, competitions and SMS capabilities. This requires the development of user-friendly and engaging platforms. Extrinsically, e-learning platforms should provide a cost-effective one-stop possibility for accessing learning materials in the cloud; undertaking student assessment and evaluation; tracking student progress and attendance and providing a virtual classroom environment. This also requires the development of an optimized platform for assessing content using different technological devices including laptops, tablets and smart mobile phones.

Student self-efficacy

Students' knowledge, skills, and competence influence their ability to engage and participate in teaching and learning. This also reflects their ability to perform their expected roles successfully whilst co-producing teaching and learning through e-learning platforms. Self-efficacy reflects a person`s judgment of his/her ability in performing an expected co-production role effectively. Therefore, students need to believe that they have the requisite skills, knowledge, and competences to use e-learning platforms. Through self-efficacy the ambiguity of the student role is minimized and co-production behavior is improved, thus, influencing students` preparedness to execute their co-production role effectively.

For universities, this requires the development of students' knowledge, skills, and competence in information and communication technology including e-learning platforms and video conferencing apps as well as developing an awareness of online social etiquette. This can be developed formally through training, workshops, online videos, and FAQs and informally through student`s self-taught knowledge and skills, other students, student reps, opinion leaders, and other external sources.

Conclusion

Successful co-production of teaching and learning through e-learning platforms requires students' willingness and preparedness to engage with university authorities and lecturers and it is incumbent on universities to develop strategies that enhance students' readiness for co-production. This requires effective communication and the commitment of appropriate resources. It also requires that students are motivated, and they have the appropriate level of self-efficacy to engage in co-production. Universities, therefore, in developing and implementing e-learning technologies and platforms to engage students during the Covid-19 pandemic and other turbulences that might affect universities in the future need to consider the readiness of their students to co-produce teaching and learning remotely.

References

Bazana, S. and Nabo-Bazana, S (2020) Going Online - Psychological Support is also needed. Universities World News *[Online]* available from: https://www.universityworldnews.com/post.php?story=20200505105913707 [15 May, 2020].

Bhuasiri, W., Xaymoungkhoun, O., Zo, H., Rho, J. J. and Ciganek, A. P. (2012) 'Critical Success Factors for E-learning in Developing Countries: A Comparative Analysis between ICT Experts and Faculty'. *Computers and Education* 58(2), 843 - 855.

Heidenreich, S., and Handrich, M. (2015) 'Adoption of Technology-Based Services: The Role of Customers' Willingness to Co-create'. *Journal of Service Management* 26(1), 44 - 71.
Hinson, R. E. (2020). The 3Rs – How to Improve Customer Service in the Universities. Universities World News *[Online]* available from: https://www.universityworldnews.com/post.php?story=20200511123436268 [15 May, 2020].
Kisanga, D. and Ireson, G. (2015) 'Barriers and Strategies On Adoption Of E-Learning In Tanzanian Higher Learning Institutions: Lessons for Adopters. *International Journal of Education and Development using Information and Communication Technology* 11(2), 126 -137.
Kotzé, T. G. and Plessis, P. G. (2003) 'Students as "Co-Producers" of Education: A Proposed Model of Student Socialisation and Participation at Tertiary Institutions'. *Quality Assurance in Education* 11(4), 186-201.
Larbi-Apau, J., Sampong, K. and Kwofie, B. (2020) 'Barriers to Online Learning Adoption in Higher Education. Universities World News *[Online]* available from: https://www.universityworldnews.com/post.php?story=20200506200743715 [15 May, 2020].
McCulloch, A. (2009) 'The Student as Co-producer: Learning from Public Administration about the Student-University Relationship'. *Studies in Higher Education* 34(2), 171-183.
Mukeredzi, T., Kokutse, F. and Dell, S. (2020) 'Student Bodies say E-Learning is Unaffordable and Elitist'. Universities World News [Online] available from: https://www.universityworldnews.com/post.php?story=20200422075107312 [22 May, 2020]
Mutisya, D. N. and Makokha, G. L. (2016) Challenges Affecting Adoption of E-learning in Public Universities in Kenya. *E-learning and Digital Media* 13(3–4), 140–157.
Sekhon, H. S., Yalley, A. A., Kumar, R. S. and Shergill, G. (2016) 'A Cross-Country Study of Service Productivity'. *The service Industry Journal* 36 (5/6), 223-238.
Yalley, A. A. (2012) '*Service Productivity Measurement: An Application to Higher Education Business and Management Schools'*. PhD Thesis, Coventry University. Available from:https://curve.coventry.ac.uk/open/file/a4899d9c-dabc-4480-8fac ff06e606ed8a/1/yalleycomb.pdf [22 May, 2020]
Yalley, A. A. and Sekhon, H. S. (2014) 'Service Production Process: Implications for Service Productivity'. *International Journal of Productivity and Performance Management* 63(8), 1012-1030

Dr. Andrews Agya Yalley is a lecturer at the University of Cape Coast, Ghana. He has extensive teaching and consultancy experience in both the UK and Ghana and his work has been published in refereed books and journals. His research is in the area of services marketing and management with an emphasis on higher education service quality and productivity.

17

Post Covid-19 Future of Universities in Low and Middle Income Countries

Cees Th. Smit Sibinga[1], Maruff A. Oladejo[2], Isaac Kajja[3], Arwa Z. Al-Riyami[4]
[1] IQM Consulting, Zuidhorn & University of Groningen, Netherlands
[2] University of Lagos, Akoka, Nigeria
[3] Makerere University, Kampala, Uganda
[4] Department of Haematology, Sultan Qaboos University Hospital, Muscat, Oman

In 1665, 355 years ago, Cambridge University closed because of the plague. Isaac Newton decided to work from home. He then discovered calculus and the laws of motion.

Introduction

The Covid-19 pandemic has caused a serious disruption of both institutional operations and management, and education programmes in all its facets and aspects, including higher education and universities. Universities and higher education institutions, as well as primary and secondary schools were closed one after the other with teachers and students being urged to stay at home and start working and studying from home as much as possible. Communication through social media networks was started up and rapidly intensified. Education programmes were quickly digitalized and prepared for e-distance learning, including chat boxes and the performance of tests and examinations.

This happened all over the world, but unfortunately not to the same extent and with the same speed and financial support, particularly not in the large low- and middle-income part of the world. Additionally, many students that could afford a better level of higher education abroad where called back home or simply told to leave their selected country. Some countries provided support to help return these students home and quarantined them as needed.

Consequences for universities and higher education

Covid-19 from the beginning did cast a long and dark shadow over the academic landscape in the advanced world, but even darker and longer in the less advanced part of the world, starting with inequalities. Globally, many universities, public and private had no choice but to close as part of the universal lockdown measures to contain the pandemic and they had no option but to have resort to the use of information and communications technology (ICT) to deliver their programmes online at a distance to their enrolled students. However, the process immediately has laid bare the digital divide between those countries that have better ICT infrastructure than others; between universities within the same country, with some being far better equipped and experienced than others; and between students within the same institution – the rich who live in urban areas and the poor in rural areas who can barely afford to access the internet, when and if it is available. By and large, only 24% of the rural communities in the developing world has reasonably reliable access to the internet with a reliably regular irregularity of power supply.

It is indeed true that the Covid-19 pandemic has provided an opportunity to all higher education institutions and universities to dynamically improve and maximise their ICT operations. Unfortunately however, the majority of these in middle and low income countries do not have the capacity to fully deliver whole and complex academic programmes online, illustrating that it is not so much the design and construction of the digital programmes, but the art of delivering undisturbed and timely learning, which requires a well-developed, sustained and affordable infrastructure. While a significant number of higher education institutions in Africa for example, have been implementing blended learning (a mixture of face-to-face and online learning) in order to increase access and improve learning, hardly any had intentions for their face-to-face delivery to be completely replaced. There are a few countries and universities that understand the value of investment in these new approaches and provide students with a programmed (software) laptop to facilitate distance digital learning.

That does raise the question - How then can these countries – all low and middle income – and their universities deal with the inequalities arising from the wide use of online learning, even for a relatively short period, where their starting point already was a considerable inequality? (Smit Sibinga et al, 2019)

It is a fiction to believe that online learning can be effective by merely posting a lecturer's notes online or having a video recording of the lecture on a screen. Unfortunately, this is what is largely happening. Experience has shown that quality e-learning requires that the teaching material is prepared by a professional instructional and knowledgeable designer, that the lecturer and professor are pedagogically trained for delivering the programme at a distance, and the students are equally exposed to the pedagogy of online learning. A poor or unprepared online delivery will have an impact on the quality of the programmes. This is extremely unfortunate at a time when significant achievements have been made in improving the quality of teaching and learning in a growing number of higher education institutions and universities in the developing world.

How can universities and their medical schools find adequate alternative approaches to using laboratories and bedsides for clinical practice? Subsequently, how can they mitigate the consequences of poor-quality programmes as a result of unplanned and inefficient online delivery? The worst affected programmes will be in science, medicine and technology as students will be unable to access laboratories for their practicals. However, science, medicine and technology programmes are the ones that are most important for the development processes as part of the world's continuing enlightenment. (Pinker, 2018)

Another relevant problem is in the research function of universities. To improve the research output from less resourced settings, e.g., Africa, known to be the lowest of any region in the world, a plethora of initiatives and projects has been initiated over the past couple of decades, whether at national or regional level. The emphasis has been on increasing postgraduate training, especially at doctoral level, and facilitating research projects in higher education institutions with an emphasis on areas which are a priority to the development in the respective countries. Indicators show that the initiatives are now starting to bear fruit which should continue. However, the majority of research initiatives are funded by European countries and by agencies and foundations in the United States, and increasingly by China and the Middle East. In sub-Saharan Africa there are very few national agencies funding research and hardly any regional ones. Also, almost all the research is undertaken in collaboration with universities in foreign countries and in collaboration with reputed foreign research and science institutes.

What will happen?

How then will post-graduate education and research projects already initiated and funded externally be maintained? To what alternative sources of funding can research institutions and universities turn to continue to undertake their research and postgraduate education?

As Covid-19 is impacting the entire globe, and Europe, the US and China appear to be the hardest hit, can the developing world rely on education and research funding from existing sources in more advanced countries? Several of these countries will probably end up in recession and their universities will understandably give priority to redressing their own situation rather than supporting international education and research collaboration.

The wider use of online learning because of Covid-19 will undoubtedly exacerbate the situation as students will be studying on their own off-site. Here is an opportunity to actively involve employers and potential leaders to assist in providing the skills and competencies they need.

Unemployment as a prospect?

Almost every country has lately been experiencing the challenge of graduate unemployment, and in some low- and middle-income countries these unemployment figures are alarming. From informal feedback obtained from employers, a major cause of the unemployment is the lack of 'soft skills' in graduates – poor communication skills, lack of personal initiative, inability to work in a team, poor guidance and career opportunities, etc.

Unfortunately, for economic reasons, many potential private employers of graduates in the developing world may be forced to lay off their staff, thus increasing unemployment. This will make it even harder for graduates to find employment. The social and political consequences of large-scale unemployment, especially among the educated youth, can be serious and hamper the survival and further future development of these universities.

Loss of intellectual capacity

Secondary schools which feed students to universities have been closed globally and end-of-secondary school examinations are being postponed or cancelled. Before the Covid-19 pandemic it had already been observed in many low- and middle-income countries that with the recent increase in enrolment in secondary schools, resulting from measures taken to improve access, the quality of students entering higher education institutions and universities had deteriorated. What approaches should universities adopt in selecting their next cohort of students if examination results are not available? Here, a national approach covering the entire education sector needs to be adopted. However, the situation could be aggravated by the closure of the primary schools feeding the secondary schools, and universities will have to devise measures to cater for alternative methods of selection and preparation of the students. This may lead to the admission of less prepared students, perhaps requiring remedial courses in the first year.

UNICEF is strongly and loudly ringing the alarm bell about the dramatic additional effects Covid-19 is having on existing problems faced by large numbers of young school children in areas with protracted humanitarian emergencies, including drought, extended poverty and failing governance and leadership. As of May 2020, around 1.5 billion children are out of school and a majority (31 million) of the primary school children are uprooted from their homes, including 17 million internally displaced (UNICEF Education Cannot Wait newsletter 24-05-2020). There is no fair chance that these children will reach secondary education let alone higher education, which is leading to a deplorable loss of human intellectual capacity and is far from stimulating the necessary development of universities.

Economic impact on universities

Two major issues that hold serious implications in the fight against the pandemic are online teaching, which is now championed as an alternative form of educational delivery, and the economic impact of the pandemic on higher education in low- and middle-income countries. Most of Africa's 54 countries now have confirmed cases and fatalities due to Covid-19. Many have closed their borders and banned international flights. Trade is declining at an alarming rate. The Democratic Republic of Congo, Rwanda, South Africa and Tunisia have introduced complete lockdown.

Recent economic forecasts show that Africa's economy could experience a loss of between US$90 billion and US$200 billion in 2020, with the GDP shrinking by three to eight points. The continent's meagre institutional and national capacities, weak health care systems and gregarious way of life may prove catastrophic should the virus continue to spread at the same rate and intensity as in other critically affected countries and areas. The impact of such a calamitous scenario is easy to imagine and frightening to predict. The effects of the pandemic on Africa's nearly 2,000 higher education institutions and universities cannot be over-emphasised. If the crisis persists, it may seriously impact the commitment of governments toward higher education in the face of competing demands from the healthcare, business and other priority sectors serving vulnerable segments of society.

However, on a positive note, this threat – and the approaches to overcome – may be catalytic for long-lasting changes in academic and higher education in low- and middle-income countries. Among others, diversified means of educational delivery, in particular a non-residential model, may become more mainstream, more acceptable and more respectable.

What will be the future post Covid-19?

Despite the extreme disruption caused by the Covid-19 pandemic, there are also opportunities for change and progress such as changing from strategic to vision planning; developing new business models and financial options to stabilize the 'bottom line'; and strengthening collaboration instead of competition. There are a number of remains to be identified for the future beyond Covid-19.

Rolling out e-learning

The list is too long and changes daily of the number of colleges, higher education institutions and universities worldwide that have suspended, or ended, in-person face-to-face instruction and replaced it with online teaching. The wisdom and necessity of increased online and the resurrection of the myths of Massive Open Online courses (MOOC) learning options can no longer be ignored. Presidents, vice-chancellors, provosts and academic deans are forced to reconsider what part of their education delivery in the post-Covid-19 future will be offered still conventionally in person and what part will be offered online.

Less mobility and more students studying closer to home

Specific cohorts of students will opt to study closer to home. According to a report published by QS, prospective Asian students may increasingly look to intra-regional universities for tertiary study. Spencer Hawkes, director of special projects at BMI, told The PIE News (Professionals In Education): "I think there is a clear trend that more Asian students will look to study in Asia. This is happening already." Currently, Malaysia is the leading study destination in Asia. Simon Emmett, CEO of IDP Connect, told The PIE News that a significant number of students are exploring study options in Malaysia, South Korea and Singapore.

Embracing online enrolment methods

Enrolment and admission practices will definitely change. Across Asia and Africa, entrance examinations have been delayed, which will eventually affect the 2020 autumn intake of first-year students. For instance, China's cancellation of SAT, TOEFL, GRE and GMAT examinations will impact future undergraduate and graduate school enrolment in the United States and Canada for the 2020 Fall semester. Admission deans and enrollers in the future will embrace online outreach to prospective students. Flexible application deadlines and a review of qualifying credentials will require re-evaluation of current enrolment and admission practices to universities. Prior algorithms, attempting to calculate expected yields of accepted students, may no longer be valid. College fairs may no longer be valid. Accepted student receptions and traditional orientation programmes may also no longer be possible.

Teleconferencing and the rise of video tele-congressing

Most higher education institutions and universities have banned all non-essential travel for employees. Video teleconferencing opportunities will partially replace long distance travel as both faculty and administrators re-evaluate international travel and attendance at academic conferences. Local, national and international scientific conferences, seminars and symposia are increasingly being organized in a non-physical way through teleconferencing and video technology

Another important element is –

Diversifying supplies and capacities away from China

Supply chains and the internationally mobile student movement have been disrupted and will require diversification in the future. About five million companies worldwide have Chinese suppliers, according to the data base company Altares Dun & Bradstreet (2020). The Covid-19 virus has taught the world hard lessons about a China-only supply chain. Covid-19 has exposed the fragility of overreliance on Chinese suppliers. Amazon, Apple and Microsoft, as well as many Japanese companies, are actively seeking to diversify their supply chain away from China to other countries. Colleges, higher education institutions and universities worldwide, especially those heavily dependent on Chinese student enrolments, such as Australia, Canada, New Zealand and the United States, can no longer expect Chinese students to enrol in the numbers they have for the past decades. According to the Institute of International Education (www.IIE.org, 2020), some 75% of American colleges and universities have reported the negative impact of Covid-19 on recruitment this year 2020. It is important to keep in mind that 370,000 students, or 33.7% of America's total international students, are from China. Decreased enrolment of Chinese students has already impacted the economies of Australia, New Zealand and Canada.

Covid-19 has taught the higher education and university community hard lessons about a Chinese-dependent student supply chain. However, the other side of this Covid-19 coin is that the Chinese master plan to become the #1 importer of international students is in question. University deans and enrollers will be hard pressed to recommend, without reservation, future exchange programmes on Chinese campuses and may thus lead to a larger influx in their own universities. In a survey of over 2,000 students from Africa, Asia and Australia, conducted by QS (QS survey, 2020), nearly 30% reported their plans had changed due to the pandemic. It is impossible to estimate what percentage of students responding to this survey would have studied in China.

What else?

Today we live in a world where norms, standards and morale are constantly unravelling around the edges. At the intersection of disruption and unpredictability will emerge a new model for the world's economy and for higher education at universities.

Covid-19 has created a new world order requiring a shift in perspective and necessitating thinking in different ways, replacing the conventional strategic planning with a vision statement of intent which is fundamentally different from a mission statement, which is a description of the route to follow to realise the vision. Vision statements require thinking from the end backwards.

Important existential and vision questions to raise are: Why should an applicant enrol in your university? What do you do better than any other university? What will your university 'look like' after Covid-19 recedes into the background? What is the vision for your future students? How is that vision different from what it is today? These follow the leader principles strongly recommended by Simon Sinek in his book 'Start with Why' (Simon Sinek, 2009). For heads of state and corporate global leaders, as well as university administrators, a shifting perspective based on such vision, will hopefully encourage re-alignment of academic curricula, markets and students.

Finally, when we slowly move into a post-Covid-19 epoque, a number of important ethical issues needs to be preserved, sustained and re-appraised, starting with ethics under emergency orders. But also integrity of academic leadership and equality in academic treatment resisting conspiracy movements, character building and self-reliance, balanced globalization and the ethics of debt, religious, ethnic and cultural matters and solidarity. Above all the speed addressing the education articles of the Sustainable Development Goals plan highly deserve a continued and focused attention. (Sustainable Development Goals, 2019)

In fact, post-Covid-19 provides a 'golden' opportunity to change and try to narrow the existing knowledge gap in the seriously affected and deprived low- and middle-income world. (Smit Sibinga, Oladejo, Kajja, Al-Riyami, 2019).

References

Altares Dun & Bradstreet Data bases. Accessed May 2020, at https://www.altares.nl/en/our-data/

Institute of International Education. Accessed May 2020 at https://www.iie.org/

Pinker, S. 2018, Enlightenment now. The case for Reason, Science, Humanism and Progress. Penguin House LLC, London, UK

QS survey 2020, Accessible at https://www.surveygizmo.eu/s3/90214070/b8d96142642f?utm_source=TU

Sinek, S. 2009, Start with Why. How great leaders inspire everyone to take action. Penguin House LLC, London, UK

Smit Sibinga, C.Th.; Oladejo, M.A.; Kajja, I.; Al-Riyami, A.Z. 2019, Impact of Knowledge Gaps on the Future of Universities in Low and Middle Income Countries. In: Remenyi, D.; Grant, K.A.; Singh, S, The University of the Future. ACPIL, Reading, UK.

Sustainable Development Goals, 2019. Accessible (pdf) at https://en.wikipedia.org/wiki/Sustainable_Development_Goals

UNICEF 2020, Education Can Not Wait Newsletter 24-05-2020

Cees Th. Smit Sibinga MD. PhD, FRCPEdin, FRCPath is emeritus Professor of International Development of Transfusion Medicine at the University of Groningen, Director of IQM Consulting, The Netherlands and Expert Advisor of WHO.

Maruff Oladejo has a PhD in Educational Management from the University of Ibadan, Nigeria. He specializes in Educational Policy, Planning, and Economics of Education. He currently lectures in the Department of Educational Management at University of Lagos, Nigeria.

Isaac Kajja, MD has a PhD from University of Groningen, The Netherlands. He has specialized in Orthopaedics and Transfusion Medicine and is Associate Professor of Orthopaedics and Chair of the Department of Orthopaedics, Makerere University, Kampala, Uganda.

Arwa Z. Al-Riyami, BSc, MD, FRCPc is a Senior Consultant Haematopathologist at the Sultan Qaboos University Hospital in Sultanate of Oman. She is the programme director of the haematolopathology residency programme at the Oman Medical Speciality Board.

18

Knowledge Management and the Post Covid-19 New Normal in Universities

Eduardo Tomé[1], Pedro Soares de Mello[1], Andrew Hatch[1], Francisco Maurício[1], Elizaveta Gromova[2]
[1]Universidade Europeia de Lisboa, Portugal
[2]Peter the Great St. Petersburg Polytechnic University, Russian Federation

Introduction

In the last six months, the world was taken aback by a very unexpected phenomenon – the Covid-19 disease. Suddenly, routines were changed, and basic social behaviour had to adapt to what was called "the new normal". This new situation was largely driven by a concern for security. People and organizations began to fear basic social contact because contagion that would ultimately lead to death. The daily broadcasting of growing numbers of cases and deaths worldwide only increased this fear and trust evaporated. Table 1 briefly describes a before and after scenario of the situation due to Covid-19.

Table 1 - The old normal and the new normal

	Pre-Covid-19	**Covid-19 crisis**
Rule	Freedom	Confinement
Security	Medium high	Low
General feeling	Trust	Fear
Requirement	Proximity	Social distance
Freedom of movement	Very large	Very limited
Security concerns	Linked to crime and terrorism	Linked to virus
Meetings	Allowed and even encouraged	Restrained if not prohibited
Masks	For Carnival	For normal life
On-line work	Residual	Norm
Office work	Norm	Residual
Face to face meetings	Frequent	Rare
No. of people in gatherings	Hundreds of thousands, even millions	Ten
Borders	Open, with visa and security control	Closed, only exceptional travel
Professional Sport	Permanent	Rare

Source: Authors own work

It is these circumstances that forced universities to face a massive change in their behaviour. Basically, due to the social distancing restrictions, all the work related to classes, teaching, administration, research and scientific conferences, which used to be done face to face and only when needed online, have now become almost exclusively online. This change is described in Table 2.

Table 2: The case of universities

	Pre-Covid-19	Covid-19 crisis
Classes	Basically presential	On-line
Testing	Basically presential	On-line
Administration	Presential	On-line
Research	Online and face to face	On-line
Conferences	Face to face	On-line
Technology	Powerpoints, databases, PDFs, Word, Excel, SPSS	Blackboard or Zoom

Source: Authors own work

At the current stage, we believe that, now and more than ever, "Prediction is difficult, especially when dealing with the future" (Bohr, 1971). However, we believe it is important to analyse what knowledge management (KM) science may say about the Covid-19 "new normal" and particularly how Covid-19 may affect the "new normal" in universities, an specifically with regard to lecturing activities, research and conferences. To answer these two questions, the chapter is divided into the following sections: Theoretical base, Analysis and Conclusions.

Theoretical base

The Economics of post Covid-19 was explained in a recent book by Baldwin and Weder di Mauro (2020). The basic ideas about KM that matter for the analysis of this paper are the following:

- Knowledge is understood information and information is organized data, wisdom being automatic knowledge (Nonaka and Takeuchi, 1995);
- Three basic elements in any KM system are technology, people and processes. Historically KM was first seen as a technological problem, then a human resource problem and finally a processes problem (Edwards, 2011);
- The main types of knowledge are tacit and explicit which are transferred according to the SECI model with Socialization, Externalization, Combination and Internalization (Nonaka and Takeuchi, 1995); this process requires a space, originating the "Ba" concept which is a space in which knowledge creation happens within one of the four phases (Nonaka and Konno, 1998);

Analysis

The new normal as a societal sea change

The significant challenges faced by individuals, organizations, and society during this Covid-19 crisis accelerate the Fourth industrial revolution (Schwab, 2017) and opened a window of opportunity for transformation.

The Covid-19 pandemic made us truly understand how much the technologies of the 21st century — artificial intelligence, the Internet of things, digital learning platforms, augmented and virtual reality, 3D printing, etc. help us. In addition, non-standard conditions encourage a much greater reliance on breakthrough digital, biological, and physical technologies and an increasing inventiveness in how these promising technologies can be used to create new values.

More than 7 billion people (Connor, 2020) live in countries where strict restrictions on the movement of individuals have been imposed, and a third or more of the world's population is in strict self-isolation.

A typical video call requires constant and intense attention to words. Overall, video chat has allowed human connections to flourish in a way that would not have been possible a few years ago. These tools allow us to maintain long-distance relationships, connect work groups remotely, and even now, despite the mental exhaustion (National Geographic, 2020) they can contribute to some sense of togetherness during a pandemic.

The positive aspects that were highlighted indicate a strengthening of the key principles of the agile team (Rigby et al, 2016). This is a cross-functional team that allows engineers and managers from various disciplines to simultaneously work on product and process design taking into account all elements of the product lifecycle from concept to disposal. As a result, new products are designed with all stakeholders in mind. The agile team has a single criterion for success that is to bring the finished product to the customer, satisfy them, and bring profit to the company.

Organizations from all sectors of the economy are increasing their technical capabilities, mastering digital technologies, and transforming business models at a rapid pace.

How does the new normal relate to KM

We believe the "new normal" may be explained in terms of Knowledge Management for the following reasons:

- *Lack of knowledge*: the "new normal" was originated because first and foremost humanity lacked a vaccine related to Covid-19; secondly people and organizations and nations did not have the social knowledge about what to do in the presence of this new and unexpected, silent and unseen menace;
- *Lack of information*: Covid-19 led to measures of confinement and isolation worldwide, which generated economic slowdown and social problems; the solutions to the crisis, other than a vaccine, required information about social routines which were not usually collected by organizations or communities; this in turn led to the understanding that persons, organizations and governments did not have the required information about the situation; and as a result, fear grew;
- *Lack of trust*: lack of trust started the collapse of the stock markets, then the lockdowns, then the closure of business and the announced recession, then the social unrest; if some political and cultural change may derive from the Covid-19 crisis it will be originated first and foremost by the change in the way we face each other and this fact is rooted in trust issues;
- *Relation between technology, people and processes*: The "new normal" implies "hybrid" solutions to organizational management, with more use of technology; people have to deal with trust issues and distancing; in the end it is all, as usual, a question of finding the right and better processes. In

universities, the new optimal mix between technology, people, and processes is as complex and problematic as it is decisive.

The "new normal" as a norm in universities

The coronavirus pandemic has accelerated many digital processes. One of them is distance learning. More than 1.5 billion students (UNESCO, 2020) are currently enrolled in distance learning. But the online learning trend is not new. Coursera was founded in 2012 by Stanford University computer science professors Andrew Ng and Daphne Koller. Ng and Koller were inspired by their experiences offering their Stanford courses online in fall 2011, and soon after, left Stanford to launch Coursera. Princeton, Stanford, the University of Michigan, and the University of Pennsylvania were the first universities to offer content on the platform. The project cooperates with universities that publish and maintain courses in various fields of knowledge in the system. Students take courses, communicate with other students, take tests and exams directly on the Coursera website, and the official mobile app for iPhone and Android is also distributed. As of February 2017, Coursera had 24 million registered users and more than 2000 courses and 160 specializations from 149 educational institutions. Now there are a lot of other digital platforms for education. Many universities around the world have their own digital platforms with authored courses that involve almost all academic disciplines.

Video conferences have become the main tool for organizing training. Microsoft Teams, Zoom, Skype, FaceTime, Google Hangouts, or any other video-calling interface has become part of professors' and students' life. Professors need an additional set of professional qualities as communication between teachers and students becomes more intense. Professors should be mobile, highly professional, creative, responsive, and courageous. During a video lesson, they must present the students with a clearly planned lesson. Clarity is expressed in the deep content of the lecture and hard timing. In addition, they must respond quickly to students ' questions, comments, and suggestions. In turn, students also need a great emotional commitment as the percentage of self-education increases. The control of the teacher's activity increases as the control over the students' decreases. The format of the relationship between a teacher and a group of students in the context of a student performing independent work and the checking of knowledge via the exam becomes more standardized according to the chosen digital platform.

The most important obstacle for all participants in the new educational process is the lack of face to face communication. It has long been known that the personality and charisma of a teacher is especially important. The teacher can captivate a student with personal characteristics and unsurpassed art of teaching. Distance learning reduces the notion of the kind of person a teacher is and the mutual feeling between the teacher and the student becomes less strong. However, online learning opens a range of new opportunities for universities, professors and students that have yet to be fully explored.

Authors reflection on how the new normal relates to universities

The non-referenced ideas listed in this sub-section relate to experiences of elements of the group of authors during teaching in the "new normal" phase.

We analyse first the situation related to lectures and then we consider research and conferences.

In relation to lectures, the first major point was the fact that we began doing digital teaching for digital natives: Suddenly we were confronted with online classes. Within truly short notice, sometimes in 48 hours, we had to begin using online platforms, without time to train. Undergraduate students, which represent most of the public in higher education are digital natives, a fact which led us to the expectation that the classes would go well and would be well accepted.

Quite suddenly we were confronted with the pros and cons of digital communication. Namely, it soon became apparent that the "new communication" in the "new and digital classes" has quite different characteristics from face-to-face communication: Non-verbal communication and paralanguage, which Batista and al (2013) estimate represents 60% to 70% of the information transmitted in face to face communication, are lost. This loss has drastic consequences. We felt we did not have the necessary information to make decisions, so we lost confidence in our actions. The lack of information made it difficult to create empathy with the students, stealing emotion and trust from communication and relationships. Moreover, empathy is a fundamental condition for creating emotional confidence. These two situations (lack of information and lack of confidence) alone were enough to change the entire teaching process.

Digital communication poses major problems to evaluation: How do we know that the student is taking the test and not someone else? Who is the person with whom we communicate? How do we prevent students from plagiarizing? These questions for the most part, remain unsolved.

The underlying conditions of students mattered. Namely the conditions of access to classes are quite different from student to student: poor access to the internet, absence of a computer or with limited capacities, lack of privacy to attend classes, etc are frequent. We also found that another strong conditioning factor is the ability to concentrate in class. Batista and al (2013) indicate that when we communicate online, and we perform simultaneous activities, we are not truly focused on communication, degrading its quality.

The students' reactions to the new situation were complex. On the one hand, students were very happy, as they spent less time in transport, were at home and, and as they often mentioned, "got out of bed straight to class". On the other hand, digital natives reported that it is much more difficult to work in groups, as sometimes is requested. They also reported difficulties in being focused, and in understanding classes, due to communication failures. Furthermore, many students longed for socializing with colleagues. In other words, students realized that despite being digital natives and defending digitalization as the solution of the future, they also have significant "offline" needs.

In our own situation, we have to report bad consequences and good ones. On the minus side are health problems like lower back pain and paraesthesia that increased due to excessive sitting time. On the plus side, not having to travel to work resulted in an optimization of the use of time, and more time for academic activities. A big issue was related to interruption. It is important to have the conditions at home to be able to teach classes without anyone interfering, and also to be able not to interfere in the activities of other people who are also teleworking. Overall, however, the feelings of distance and discomfort prevailed. Teaching in the "new normal" is simply not real teaching because of lack of social contact. We long for the day in which we will meet our students again face to face.

Regarding research and conferences, the "new normal" meant that conferences were cancelled and replaced by virtual events, and therefore that research became based on virtual contacts. This created a process in two phases. During the first days of lockdown, some surge in creativity happened. Loneliness is creative. This first phase was therefore acceptable. But quickly we began to use any digital form of communication available and to find ways to travel and meet again – quite depressingly that intention coincided with the period in which conferences were cancelled or made virtual. We know that research is based in co-opetition (Watson and Mc Gowan, 2020) and co-creation (Dollinger at al, 2019); we also know that people take part in conferences (Smiljanić, 2016) and even make conferences (Corpas and al, 2008) because face to face socialization is essential for the progress of science.

Conclusions

The new normal will "separate the wheat from the chaff". We will certainly increase the use of digital solutions where and when they do bring benefits. After all, digitalization was a trend before the pandemic, which is going to be reinforced. But on the other hand, the extreme social conditions we live in now clearly show the limits of the digital processes – it is as if digitalization was implemented as an experiment in the most drastic circumstances. Digital will be increasingly used when solutions need to be massified and/or there is a lack differentiation. Face-to-face communication will be increasingly used when solutions are unique and need differentiation.

As Plato and Aristoteles in the famous painting of Raphael, we still need to meet our students and our peers and to rub shoulders and to walk with them. This activity is essential to maintain a sustained level a of academic output – both in the classroom and with research. In the Renaissance our ancestors made travelling become the norm in order to foster progress – we are bound to follow their example, and this will be a major conditioning to the "new normal" in Academia.

As ideas to further research we suggest a questionnaire and interviews to students, lecturers, administrators and families worldwide; only then we will really get a grip on the real influence on Covid-19 in Universities and on what the "new normal" in fact means for them.

References

Baldwin R. Weider di Mauro B. (2020) Economics in the Time of Covid-19, CEPR.

Baptista, A,; Sequeira, A D; Veríssimo, I;, Quico, C.; Cardoso, M.; Damásio MJ (2013) Using digital interactive television to promote healthcare and wellness inclusive services International Conference on Digital Human Modeling and Applications in Health, Safety, Ergonomics and Risk Management Pages 150-156

Bohr, Nils (1971) It's Difficult to Make Predictions, Especially About the Future https://quoteinvestigator.com/2013/10/20/no-predict/ As assessed on May 27th 2020.

Connor P. (2020), "More than nine-in-ten people worldwide live in countries with travel restrictions amid Covid-19", Pew Research Centre, April 1st 2020. https://www.pewresearch.org/fact-tank/2020/04/01/more-than-nine-in-ten-people-worldwide-live-in-countries-with-travel-restrictions-amid-covid-19/

Corpas, Manuel; Gehlenborg, Nils; Janga, Sarath Chandra; Bourne, Philip E. (2008) Ten simple rules for organizing a scientific meeting - PLoS Computational Biology. June, 2008, Vol. 4 Issue 6, p1, 3 p

Crary D, Collins D.; Winfiel N. (2020) New 'normal': Countries worldwide slowly get back to business amid coronavirus As assessed on May 26th 2020 https://globalnews.ca/news/6962652/coronavirus-new-normal-countries-reopen/

Dollinger, Mollie; Liu, Danny; Arthars, Natasha (2019) Working Together in Learning Analytics towards the Co-Creation of Value - Journal of Learning Analytics, v6 n2 p10-26 2019

Edwards, John S. (2011). A process view of knowledge management : it ain't want you do, it's the way that you do it. Electronic journal of knowledge management, 9 (4), pp. 297-306.

National Geographic (2020) Zoom fatigue' is taxing the brain. Here's why that happens [Accessed April 24 th 2020]. https://www.nationalgeographic.com/science/2020/04/coronavirus-zoom-fatigue-is-taxing-the-brain-here-is-why-that-happens/

Nonaka, I.; Konno, N. (1998) The concept of "Ba': Building foundation for Knowledge Creation California Management Review Vol 40, No.3 Spring

Nonaka I. and Takeuchi K. (1995) The Knowledge Creating Company. Oxford University Press.

Rigby, D., Sutherland, J. and Takeuchi, H. (2016) Embracing Agile. Harvard Business Review. Pp. pp.40–48, 50. Variation & Change, Mar2015, Vol. 27 Issue 1, p59-87, 29p

Sapienza, Paola; Zingales, Luigi (2012) A Trust Crisis. International Review of Finance. Jun2012, Vol. 12 Issue 2, p123-131. 9p

Smiljanić, Jelena; Chatterjee, Arnab; Kauppinen, Tomi; Mitrović Dankulov, Marija. (2016) A Theoretical Model for the Associative Nature of Conference Participation, PLoS ONE. 2/9/2016, Vol. 11 Issue 2, p1-12. 12p. DOI: 10.1371/journal.pone.0148528.

UNESCO (2020) Covid-19 Educational Disruption and Response", , [Accessed April 21st 2020]. https://en.unesco.org/covid19/educationresponse

Watson, Kayleigh; McGowan, Pauric. (2020) Rethinking competition-based entrepreneurship education in higher education institutions: Towards an effectuation-informed coopetition model. Education + Training, 2020, Vol. 62 Issue 1, p31-46, 16.

Eduardo Tomé is Assistant Professor at Universidade Europeia in Lisbon. He gained his PhD in Economics at Technical University in Lisbon in 2001. Since then he has published extensively in Journals and Conference Proceedings. His main interests of research are Human Resource Development, Knowledge Management, Intellectual Capital and Social Policy.

Elizaveta A. Gromova completed her postgraduate studies in Economics in 2018 and is currently preparing to defend her PhD thesis. She works as an assistant at the Higher school of engineering and economics of Peter the Great St. Petersburg Polytechnic University. Her research interests include agile management, modern organizational technologies.

Pedro Mello holds a PhD in Management from the Universidade Europeia. After 35 years of professional experience in sales management in multinational companies related to the health sector he currently teaches at the Portuguese Institute of Administration and Marketing (IPAM). His research interests are negotiation, commercial management and knowledge management.

Andrew P. Hatch, DC, MBA, PhD is a private practice physician, clinical operations & research Director in Lisbon Portugal. He collaborates with Universidade Europeia Lisbon & GOVCOPP, Universidade de Aveiro with post-doctorate research projects in KM, employee performance, improving productivity, decreasing presenteeism and cost containment strategies for corporations and governments.

Francisco Maurício is a PhD student and researcher at the European University since 2017. His research interests are essentially on Human Resource issues, namely coaching and leadership, particularly in contexts of change.

19

Disruption and the University of the Future

Martin Rich
Faculty of Management
City, University of London Business School, UK

So what does disruption mean?

The term 'disruptive' has found its way into popular discourse around change and innovation, especially in technology businesses but in other contexts as well. This chapter introduces the reasons for the use of 'disruptive' in relation to organisations as a whole, so the first section does not focus on higher education. It then examines what this could mean for changes in universities in the current climate. In discussing universities the focus is on their teaching role, not to diminish the importance of their broader role around research and scholarship, but because it is in teaching and learning that the impact of current upheavals in the world is most acute.

Disruptive innovation as a concept originates with the work of one scholar and one highly influential book, the *Innovator's Dilemma* by Clayton Christensen (2000). Like many scholars, Christensen focused on a specific research question and gathered detailed data to understand it in depth. He had observed that in various business sectors, firms that had been very successful with one generation of technology struggled to compete when they were working with subsequent technologies. Moreover, the firms which were successful with the subsequent technologies often achieved success using tools and approaches which had been explicitly rejected by the firms who had lost their pre-eminence.

Writing in the 1990s, Christensen (2000: 109) cited the example of Digital Equipment Corporation, a manufacturer of mini-computers – that is computers that were larger and more powerful of the personal computers available in the 1980s and 1990s. Digital made repeated and unsuccessful attempts to break into the personal computer market, but failed and ultimately was absorbed by a rival because they collectively did not understand why customers bought personal computers. On the parameters that Digital's established customers used to choose their products, the personal computer looked unattractive. But it opened up new possibilities for businesses and in this context the personal computer was a disruptive innovation.

A similar pattern was replicated in multiple cases in the early 21st century, especially ones in which established large American corporations were involved. Kodak, which had dominated photography for decades and in fact had been a pioneer of digital photography, failed because as a business it did not grasp the consequences of affordable computing power making digital photography commonplace. The firms best placed to take advantage of this were technology companies and not traditional photography companies, ironically because traditional companies such as Kodak knew too much about the market and were reluctant to adapt when the market changed. Whether the smartphone counts as a disruptive innovation is contested purely because, unlike other innovations, it started at the top of the market and not the bottom. Nevertheless Nokia, which dominated the mobile phone market before the introduction of the smartphone, lost ground rapidly once smartphones were available (McCray et al, 2011). Not only did Apple, who in many respects created the ecosystem within which smartphones are sold, adopt a business model that was radically different from Nokia's to secure its position in the market, but in its early days Apple's product was perceived as a niche offering and not regarded as a serious competitor by existing players.

So for all the overuse of 'disruption' in reference to any sort of change, in business it has quite a precise meaning of an innovation which demands new business models, which often catches established players in a sector unawares, and which can threaten the success of the largest and most profitable firms.

The ideas behind disruptive innovation are in fact neither new nor confined to the impact of information technology. Christensen (2000: 89) identifies small-scale, low cost, mini-mills in the steel industry as a disruptive innovation. Lakshmi Mittal, who in the late twentieth century developed a modest Indian-based business into a dominant player in the steel sector, achieved his breakthrough by developing a mini-mill on an unpromising site in Indonesia (Ghoshal et al, 2000). In the mould of other disruptive innovators, Mittal was not regarded seriously by competitors because he operated principally at the bottom of the market. Having established a foothold, Mittal expanded through acquisitions (Economist, 2006) where an understanding of how to set up mini-mills, along with a thorough approach to integrating newly acquired businesses into the parent company, was at the core of the business model.

In the mid-twentieth century, Joseph Schumpeter set out to understand the cyclical nature of economic progress and developed the concept of *creative destruction*. Crucially he argued that as technological innovation changed the types of products and services available, the economic parameters within which businesses operated also changed. While his perception of the disbenefits of innovation was framed in terms of society as a whole (Schubert, 2013) and not of individual businesses there are parallels with Christensen's perception of current assumptions becoming obsolete. McCraw (2006: 242) highlights Schumpeter's use of a theme of 'the extreme difficulty of changing traditional ways of doing things'.

In the late nineteenth century, as described by Nock (1959) the London and North Western Railway made strategic and technical choices on the assumption that there would be no demand to travel at an average speed of more than 40mph. When it became apparent that passengers between London to Scotland needed to go more rapidly than this, they needed to adjust their business model to include not only the provision of faster and more powerful trains, but the provision of fast and convenient food at stations, notably a hearty Victorian lunch served and eaten within twenty minutes. Today if you go through Paddington Station in London and grab a snack from the Japanese bakery on the concourse you are benefiting from the disruptive innovation of around 1870.

Clayton Christensen died in January 2020 after a long period of ill-health (Hill, 2020). In a strange conjunction of events, two months later the world, and the environment within which businesses, nations, and universities operated was transformed by the Covid-19 pandemic. This was an event which had profound, and potentially disruptive, implications on many organisations. It had nothing to do with technology to the extent that, in contrast to the innovations that defined Christensen's academic career, it was not the direct result of new inventions and improved technology. At the same time it had everything to do with technology because the world's collective response, extending to using Zoom for online conferences, using Amazon for online shopping, and even accelerated development of vaccines (Le Page, 2020), depended on technology which had not been available even a decade earlier.

The left-behind university?

For all the rhetoric of disruptive innovation, established universities have over the years proved to be durable and adaptable. The waves of transformation which have affected the British higher education landscape, with new universities opened in the 1960s and the former polytechnics attaining university status mostly in 1992, have not threatened the pre-eminence of the longer-established universities, although several of those classed as 'plateglass universities' (Beloff, 1968) have become extremely prestigious institutions. For undergraduates the transition to university remains an opportunity for a rite of passage, to leave home and to become part of a learning community. And leaving home can mean a change of country: HESA (2020) reports that nearly 500,000 out of nearly 2.4 million students in their first year of a university course in the UK are from overseas. For many professions a university degree is a prerequisite. There is a flourishing sector devoted to using technology to deliver university learning and indeed within this there have been some abortive enterprises. But generally, from the Open University which has delivered distance learning through a succession of technologies since 1965 to the MOOCs (massive open online courses) which were promoted in the early 2010s, these have complemented and not superseded the established universities. Higher education has remained largely unscathed by the most immediate effect of disruptive innovation, that established players can lose their edge.

If anything universities have proved effective at large-scale gradual change to respond to a changing environment. New disciplines have emerged, and new approaches to teaching and indeed to research have evolved. Over time universities are used to setting up new departments and building new initiatives within the existing organisation.

Nevertheless there are concerns, especially in the light of universities' abilities to address the challenges of the Covid-19 pandemic. At the simplest level, an organisation which depends for its success in an international arena on building a learning community, some of whose members have travelled from different continents to join, could be expected to struggle with an event which led to a lot of international travel ceasing almost overnight. How can institutions where the core medium of instruction is a lecture to tens or hundreds of students sitting in one place, address the challenge of social distancing? What are the implications for a city centre university to which students are attracted by the opportunity to attend concerts and nightclubs and football matches, when none of these things are available?

One further factor is that, as far as teaching is concerned, most universities are structurally ill-suited to rapid change. When courses are redesigned or new material introduced, there is typically a planning and approval process lasting for over a year to ensure that details can be included in the prospectus, and that the necessary resources to deliver the course are in place. Universities have proved themselves adaptable over time but they are not necessarily able to alter their approach quickly.

None of this suggests that current universities are likely to be left behind completely by recent events. While Covid-19 has raised concerns about the financial sustainability of some universities, there are no immediate equivalents of Kodak or Nokia in higher education. So the effects on universities which might appear left-behind are likely to be more gradual and subtle, to result in the erosion in their reputation and that of their students. And that introduces another set of challenges, because without an element of urgency it is difficult to make the case for change.

The agile university

An immediate imperative, for universities as for many other organisations in the light of the pandemic, is to respond rapidly to unexpected events. To do this in a systematic and coordinated manner requires structures and processes to support changes. The concept of organisational agility is borrowed from the language of information systems development. Bider and Jalali (2016) note this connection but also observe that whereas agile software development is based on clearly defined requirements and aims, agility in the context of businesses and other organisations is less well understood – a gap which they seek to fill. They build on the notion of a cycle of building up tacit and explicit knowledge (Nonaka and Takeuchi, 1995) but add an additional category of knowledge which is *embedded* in the computer systems used to support an organisation.

Quaadgras et al (2014) highlight business agility, in their terms the ability of a business to adapt to changing conditions, as a non-financial benefit that can derive from the use of information systems, and they focus on management commitments, in their terms a clear agreement for the business to operate in a particular way.

Universities are organisations dedicated to the construction and sharing of knowledge. So an approach to organising with its roots in ideas about knowledge management might offer potential in understanding how they can best respond to a crisis.

The rhetoric behind agile business processes suggests that to move quickly organisations need to develop techniques, and internal processes, which allow for rapid and decisive analysis and actions. They should also ensure that actions are consistent and well aligned with the organisation's aims. Universities adapting to major changes in the environment within which they function need to develop internal processes which ensure that these responses are effective. In particular, given that students' requirements and expectations from teaching and learning have changed in unexpected ways, the processes need to focus on providing adaptability.

The double-loop university

With hindsight, the early stages of the Covid-19 pandemic represented a period when universities were able to change uncharacteristically rapidly. Along with many other types of organisation, they needed to shift within a few weeks not only to an operating model where staff worked from home wherever possible, but to one which obviated the need for students to attend the university in person. Campus-based and city-based universities for whom the location was an integral part of the student experience suddenly needed to shift existing courses to online delivery. Hodges et al (2020) proposed the term *emergency remote teaching* for this immediate shift, highlighting that the requirements for such teaching, and the parameters by which its success would be judged, were very different from those which would apply to a more considered application of an online teaching model.

This placed universities in the position where they need two – or possibly more – distinct responses to the pandemic. Emergency remote teaching was the first of these, deriving entirely from what could be delivered in a short time and what would protect the needs of a group of students already in university who, in many cases, needed to uproot themselves with little notice. The subsequent response, preparing for what could be termed authentic online learning in an environment where there were still considerable constraints on movement, needed to be planned in more depth and according to completely different considerations. A crude factor is that approaches which would be acceptable within emergency remote teaching, because they provided the only way to provide online materials in a hurry, would simply not be sufficient a few months later in an environment of continued online learning.

This contrast between the immediate measures to address a crisis and the longer term measures necessary in its wake has resonances of the concept of double-loop learning developed by Chris Argyris (2002). To achieve double-loop learning it is necessary not only to address immediate events (the first loop) but to address the governing variables that cause them (the second loop). So the implementation of emergency remote teaching should address the immediate needs of educators and of students. Authentic online learning depends on a broader understanding of the social and pedagogic landscape within which it is situated. Argyris (2000) developed his work into an understanding of traps within organisation, with an underlying theme that intelligent and well-meaning leaders could fall into these traps and make bad decisions. Behind both the recognition of organisational traps and the importance of double-loop learning was the distinction between *theory-in-use* – that is the approach adopted in practice by managers – and *espoused theory* as represented by what managers discuss and explain. Organisational traps occur and double-loop learning fails when there is a mismatch between the theory-in-use and the espoused theory.

Reflecting on the author's own institution, it is instructive to reflect on the mapping between the two principal stages of response to Covid-19 and single and double-loop learning. Emergency remote teaching was focused on the choice of tools, and on the adoption of techniques which allowed the learning outcomes already planned to be delivered. With the pandemic taking a grip on life in the UK in March 2020, and a cohort of students aiming to graduate in July, a priority was to ensure that these could complete their studies as planned. Many overseas students had already decided to return to their home countries, often at the behest of worried parents and fearful that international travel would become severely restricted. The situation is complex, but the drivers for the institution's response derive from immediate events and the actions that these require.

Planning for September 2020 and beyond depends on a multitude of factors, many of them unforeseeable. One set of governing variables derives from the direct impact of the pandemic: what limitations on travel, locally and globally, will remain in force and what restrictions on behaviour will apply to ensure social distancing? Another set depends on perceptions of this impact and students' willingness or reluctance to study in a particular setting. How many existing students will decide to interrupt their studies for a while, a move which could look attractive if it means deferring until they can expect to have the university experience that they had hoped for, or might look unattractive if there is a dearth of alternative ways to keep occupied during a pandemic? How many students who were previously tempted by a city-centre university will decide now that they would prefer a campus university away from major centres of population? What will be the response to distance learning from students who had explicitly chosen not to pursue distance learning? And, with a nod to Argyris, how can we ensure that the espoused theory is aligned with the theory-in-use?

Beyond this there are intangibles around the extent to which there will be long-term impacts of the pandemic, both economic and social. As Lowe (2020) points out, the university experience is about participating in a community as an integral part of students' education. While the first loop represented by emergency remote teaching is focused principally on imparting knowledge, the second loop needs to include the creation and development of an effective learning community, which itself entails considerable challenges for a community built through its members, in more usual times, being geographically close to one another.

All these considerations come into play before even considering the financial implications of the Covid crisis, whether these are from the viewpoint of students concerned about what they get for their fees or institutions concerned about their economic viability.

In the author's institution there are arguably four stages to plan for: the first being emergency remote teaching, the second being teaching in the spring and early summer of 2020 which constitutes a transitional stage, the third being the carefully crafted education to be delivered in the autumn of 2020, and the fourth being the unknowable future landscape.

So Argyris provides one source of guidance to universities in the light of Covid-19: to consider both short and longer-term factors, and to establish clarity of the theory and assumptions to be used so as to avoid organisational traps. But it is also worth revisiting Christensen's analysis of businesses threatened by disruptive innovation. Even if, as suggested above, few if any universities are facing the prospect of oblivion as a result of the impact of Covid-19 on their activities, Christensen's recommendations to organisations affected by disruptive change remain relevant. One recommendation is to consider setting up a unit within an existing organisation with a measure of independence, unencumbered by the rigid assumptions associated with earlier situations. In contrast with Digital Equipment Company, Christensen (2000) writes approvingly of how IBM was able to do this and thus, as a long-established company, to take advantage of opportunities in the personal computing sector. Other factors to note are the shortcomings of conventional market research, which fails to take account of people's likely responses to an unknown future, and crucially that organisations need to put resources into responding to disruption. At a time when universities' finances are straitened, perhaps the biggest challenge is ensuring that at least funds are available to support innovative teaching and learning which is right for this changed environment.

References

Argyris C (2010) Organizational traps: leadership, culture, organizational design. Oxford: Oxford University press

Argyris C (2002) Double-loop learning, teaching, and research. Academy of management learning and education 1 (2) 206-218

Beloff M (1968) The plateglass universities London: Secker and Warburg

Bider I and Jalali A (2016) Agile business development: why, how and when – applying Nonaka's theory of knowledge transformation to business process development. Information systems and ebusiness management 14 (4) 693-731

Brown S (2013) Large-scale innovation and change in UK higher education. Research in learning technology 21 (2)

Christensen C M (2000) The innovator's dilemma: when new technologies cause great firms to fail. Boston: Harvard Business School press.

Economist (2006) Lakshmi's Gamble. 31st January

Ghoshal S, Piramal G, and Budhiraja S (2001) World class in India: a casebook of companies in transformation. New Delhi: Portfolio Penguin

HESA (2020) Where do HE students come from? Retrieved 30th June 2020 from https://www.hesa.ac.uk/data-and-analysis/students/where-from

Hill A (2020) Clayton Christensen, author of 'the innovator's dilemma'. Financial times 24th January

Hodges C, Moore S, Lockee B, Trust T, and Bond A (2020). The difference between emergency remote teaching and online learning. Educause review 27th March

Le Page M (2020) 124 coronavirus vaccines are in development – but will any work. New scientist 3rd June

Lowe T (2020) Are community and Covid-19 mutually exclusive? WonkHE 12th June

McCraw T (2006) Schumpeter's Business Cycles as business history. Business history review 80 (2) 231-261

McCray J, Gonzalez J, and Darling J (2011) Crisis management in smart phones: the case of Nokia vs Apple. European business review 23 (3) 240-255

Nock O (1959) Railway race to the North. Shepperton: Ian Allan

Nonaka I and Takeuchi H (1995) The knowledge-creating company: how Japanese companies create the dynamics of innovation. Oxford: Oxford University press.

Quaadgras A, Weill P, and Ross J (2014) Management commitments that maximize business impact from IT. Journal of information technology 29 (2) 114-127

Schubert C (2013) How to evaluate creative destruction: reconstructing Schumpeter's approach. Cambridge journal of economics 37 (2) 227-250.

Dr Martin Rich is Senior Lecturer and Course Director for the BSc in Business Management at City, University of London's Business School. He is interested in how management education should evolve to meet the requirements of a changing business environment and what business and management graduates need to learn.

20

The Idea of a University for the Future

Cathal MacSwiney Brugha
Emeritus Professor
University College Dublin, Ireland

John Henry Newman's "The Idea of a University" explores the nature of knowledge, the role of religious belief in higher education, and the importance of liberal education. It is still the most influential book on the subject 170 years after he started writing it, the most radical, the most revolutionary, and even more relevant today.

Newman flourished in mid-nineteenth century England, a time of great turbulence, change, controversy, and debate about authority of church and state, the individual and society. The famines, floods, fires, and the Covid-19 pandemic we are experiencing suggest that we are in similar challenging times. Global warming, climate change, and planet stress are showing that the old ways of governance are failing and cannot continue. Newman's thoughts about the role of a University could be relevant to us today.

- He believed in inspiring young people to serve the good of all.
- He came to lead several different communities, but was never constrained by them.
- He was an Oxford University academic, and founder of the Oxford Movement.
- He accepted the invitation to be the founder of University College Dublin, where the hierarchy felt there was a need to improve the technical skills of the Irish Catholic middle classes. There he promoted the development of the individual's intellect as more important than skill development going against his brief to the chagrin of the hierarchy.
- He believed in the supremacy of conscience over obedience to church leaders, which irked some of the hierarchy.

That tension between training people to be technically useful to society, and educating people to think, has always existed. Economics was the first business subject to be accepted in universities, as a branch of Adam Smith's moral philosophy. Over time it became convenient for the business world to outsource its training of employees to the universities, especially as markets became more complex. Out of economics came accountancy training bodies, then the engineering profession, followed by business courses, and finally management information systems. Universities filled the demand for courses, but generally only at a skills level.

At the end of the sixties Lancaster University introduced the Systems Thinking and 'Rich Pictures' that Peter Checkland was practicing successfully in the business world. To attract the brightest and best to study under him, Lancaster had to offer them PhDs. A doctor in philosophy had to include philosophy to be a proper PhD. The philosophy professors, Checkland, and his PhD students, were unable to bridge the disconnection between the philosophy that universities taught, and the practice he implemented.

Sociologists tried to bridge this disconnection in subsequent decades, through recourse to Foucault and Bentham, mainly to bring philosophical reflections on the ethical and power implications of social media, and technology in general.

The universities still have not fully embraced the Newman aspiration that their primary role should be to educate. Emphasis on the skills role has meant that universities are currently increasingly captured by corporates who find them an efficient way to commission research. However, by relying increasingly on research funding, universities are becoming research institutes. They are promoting the sciences, not for the science, but for the money. The focus is increasingly on streams of published research that might bring research funds into college. The role of teaching is losing importance in many faculties.

The point at issue in this discussion is not simply to affirm the importance of teaching in universities, or even of pure research, nor is it to start a campaign to save language departments, or history, or even philosophy. An aspiration of the university was always to educate the future leaders of society. Newman wanted education for everyone. The question here is could and should the future university adopt this role again, play a leading and beneficial role in researching, teaching and preparing society to cope with its current and future challenges?

What are these challenges? Should universities address where society is going? Is it time for a radical change in the direction of governance in society? Are there warning signs, challenges to face, problems to overcome, that could be researched, and solved, and solutions taught to this and future generations? The suggestion here is that Newman's ideas could inspire the future university to connect with current challenges: explain them, research them, and educate future leaders to help resolve them.

In the past governance was dominated by colonisers who built corporations and armies, conquered markets and peoples. The colonising approach was self-driven by pioneers, who headed out into the unknown to subjugate markets, centralise control, empower agents, rule territories, analyse opportunities, get organised, and prioritise the capacity to extract.

The second phase focused on getting others to regulate and operationalise markets, encouraging careful design of products for markets, such as the Bauhaus Movement, enabling capabilities by educating.

A third phase was about impacting on the world, using legislation, bureaucracies and enforcing control, to make administrations respond to needs, implementing business plans and institutionalising contributions to effectiveness.

A fourth phase was always optional, the extension of the benefits for the good of all. This is where one might be willing to negotiate and localise agreements, engage and serve people, and give management benefits to the community, emancipating weaker groups and communities.

Table 1 illustrates the same four phase structure, as applied to colonisation, state administration, business, and the relationships between humans and the planet.

Table 1: Four phase structure

Phases:	First	Second	Third	Fourth
Focus:	Self	Others	World	Good of All
Colonisation:	Subjugate	Regulate	Legislate	Negotiate
Control:	Centralise	Operationalise	Bureaucratise	Localise
People:	Empower	Encourage	Enforce	Engage
Society:	Rule	Care	Respond	Serve
Business:	Analyse	Design	Implement	Use
Basic Activity:	Get	Bring	Make	Give
Institutional:	Organise	Enable	Institutionalise	Manage
Focus:	Capacity	Capability	Contribution	Community
Method:	Extract	Educate	Effect	Emancipate

This traditional approach is driven by having capacities that one can extract. It works until the planet's resources can no longer be extracted easily and cheaply, or become scarce. Many global natural resources have already been harvested, are under threat, or are not being renewed sufficiently quickly. Even in the richest countries the proportion of the population who are in poverty is increasing. And the poorest countries are collapsing.

Only recently the oil industry and their collaborators took over United States politics, invested huge resources in the military, and fought resources wars in the Middle East to access their oil. Then they found that fracking meant they hadn't needed to invade the Middle-East to take their oil in the first place.

Another sign of the end is the increasingly poor quality of leaders in many countries, self-driven and often corrupted by power and money, racism, sexism, and slavery: both political and economic.

These are the reasons why John Henry Newman's radical, revolutionary approach of starting by serving the Good of All, is even more relevant today.

But is it practical, realistic, possible, to change society from being rule-driven to serve-driven? It is. It is happening already in business. Markets are changing from product dominated to service-driven. Market dominance based on brand power is giving way to service quality management. To survive, companies have no choice but to respond to what customers and markets want. Corporates are losing control over the channels of distribution, and no longer can impose their products on markets. ("They can have any colour as long as it is black"- Henry Ford) Nowadays customers everywhere use social media to expand their choices, have products delivered in a few days, and return what they don't want. To be competitive companies must continually add services that make their offering more useful to the customer.

How do we generalise this, and apply it to the governance of society in general? And what would be the role of education?

The starting point is Newman's 'good of all', instead of the self. The interconnectedness of the world means we have to look after all others. The idea is to emancipate everyone, with equal effect everywhere in the world, regardless of any division, and give people themselves access to education, which they could use to extract benefits for their own needs wherever they are.

The table below reverses the columns of the table above. Also, the examples in the rows illustrate the new approach, leading by emancipating communities, instead of by subjugation and centralisation.

Table 2: Reversed four phased structure

Phases:	**First**	**Second**	**Third**	**Fourth**
Focus:	Good of All	World	Others	Self
Method:	Emancipate	Effect	Educate	Extract
Focus:	Community	Contribution	Capability	Capacity
Institutional:	Manage	Institutionalise	Enable	Organise
Basic Activity:	Give	Make	Bring	Get
Business:	Use	Implement	Design	Analyse
Society:	Serve	Respond	Care	Rule
People:	Engage	Enforce	Encourage	Empower
Control:	Localise	Bureaucratise	Operationalise	Centralise
Colonisation:	Negotiate	Legislate	Regulate	Subjugate

The first of four phases, driven by the good of all, starts with community, managing it to give useful services, engaging everyone in deciding what they want, finding local solutions to local problems, and negotiating every improvement. It is governance of the people, by the people, for the people.

The next phase makes local initiatives more effective in the wider world, enhancing their contributions, using state institutions to implement and respond, enforcing good practices through bureaucratic support and legislation.

As community needs for services increase, such as for healthcare or housing, this would mean prioritising basic needs rather than lavish state buildings and two-tier health-care systems.

This would mean changing the current system, where state civil servants work for the state as a corporate entity, support the wishes of the people who work there, and the politicians who control it. Changing this mentality will be difficult because corporates have colonised the political parties, the state bureaucracies, and the professional advisors on which both politicians and bureaucracies depend. But education can help.

The key facilitator is the third phase. The universities can help this to succeed, building capabilities to bring in a new era, designing a society that cares and encourages, and operationalising better regulation of society. It can help emancipate citizens who are too weak, customers of state services who are too inarticulate. It can change the attitudes of public servants, and local administrators who are too badly educated or incompetent to know how, or that they could and should, care. A community-based approach would prioritise healthcare and accommodation for everyone, instead of capital investment in hospital buildings, institutions, or housing stock.

Universities embody the capabilities to help enable this process to spread to others, to promote these ideas, initiate them, demonstrate how they would work, bring some immediate benefits, and encourage other communities. University researchers are globally linked through various international federations of societies, and most act for free as referees for international journals vetting the quality of ideas and theories. They could extend this to vetting lectures and courses that are available online internationally, as in massive open online courses (MOOC). In many cases these are state-of-the-art, of highest quality, and available to anyone anywhere who has access to the internet.

Universities are free to carry out research that does not benefit corporates directly. These range from examples such as developing protocols for early diagnosis and prevention of dementia in the community, to researching which extracts from seaweed fed to cattle could radically reduce methane emissions.

The future university will operate over the internet, and consequently need not be confined by historical boundaries.

- It could be of great benefit to people on the margins of society, and poorer nations.
- Refugees who are fleeing from poor areas could be helped to live at home. The best research available internationally could be employed to help re-develop countries that have been devastated by wars, famines, droughts, floods.
- Being boundary-less and community-driven, university education could be integrated across geographical borders, regulated internationally.

The fourth phase would have benefits for the individual. Because of globally integrated education systems and services, citizens, students, lecturers, professionals could have international mobility. Education, qualifications, experience could be transferable from one country to another.

The most efficient and effective healthcare would be the same basic service continent-wide. Why duplicate similar services across Europe? Integrating university education, and medical training, would make this so much more efficient and effective. Having compatible healthcare systems on a continent-wide basis could reduce expensive duplication between countries.

Many medical services are delivered online. Working continent-wide would mean that consultants under different time zones could evaluate test results and consider diagnoses 24 hours a day.

Starting with localised power could lead to a new form of centralisation, based on multiple levels of politics. Within Europe this could mean four levels: EU, national, regional, and local or community. Regions such as Catalonia and Scotland would not have their governance undermined by Madrid or London. And in every country local issues would be better resolved locally, not remotely by centralised bureaucratic desk-rulers from afar.

Another benefit, that would follow integrating university education, would be to promote and develop large projects, such as extracting energy and resources. Harnessing wind, wave and tidal energy from off the coast of Europe could have energy gridded across Europe, without requiring them be justified as individual government projects, or as commercial ventures. The same applies to an offshore marine transhipment logistics hub off the coast of Europe that could serve the European continent.

Community-driven global governance, through the United Nations, could empower peacekeeping throughout the world, and support minorities anywhere in the world.

The same applies at the other end of the scale, where the community that is suffering is everybody on the planet, and it is despotic governments that are causing environmental crises that are impacting on the world, such as the Brazil rain forests. A global response could be to negotiate a trade of protecting the trees in return for interest payments on government debts.

Another example is extracting renewable resources, to increase the capacity of the planet rather than diminish it, organise to get alternatives instead of threatening and endangering native materials and beings, analyse impacts on society, rule against waste and destruction. University education, both teaching and research, could take a long-term, global view of materials needs and uses, what can be sourced and where, and how to do so in the long-term.

Currently, countries badly in need of development, are vulnerable to 'economic hit-men', who get government leaders to accept enormous loans for infrastructure development, for dubious lucrative projects that are contracted to global corporations, and lead to huge state debts, and countries losing their independence.

The future university could provide altruistic advice to governments and politicians in such countries, evaluate the quality of projects, and expose this kind of behaviour, including the agencies and corporates behind these colonising activities.

Newman believed university education could liberate people to think for themselves and, through this, develop their conscience and inspire them to contribute to the betterment of people's lives. I suggest that he would be encouraging the future university to serve what is right for the good of all, at this critical time.

Dr Cathal MacSwiney Brugha, is Professor Emeritus of Decision Analytics, University College Dublin Business School. He is President, Analytics Society of Ireland, and Fellow, Marketing Institute of Ireland. He is co-author of "Doing Business in China: The Irish Experience" (2010), and "Doing Business with China, the Irish Advantage and Challenge" (2016).

Epilogue to the University of the Future: Responding to Covid-19

We hear much about the importance of resilience which is believed by some to be what will save many institutions in the university sector. The problem with this thought is that it suggests the future of universities will be more or less like what it was in the past and that the surviving institutions will be those which have been able to sustain themselves through these most awkward times and return to something quite similar to what they were before. There is no doubt that this will be the case for some if not many universities. However, there is an argument which says that the University of the Future should be something quite different to simply what one would get by springing back to a pre-Covid-19 world. In our previous version of this book, we questioned whether the established model on which most universities were based was still "fit-for-purpose". Just as the pandemic experience is causing many to question other commonly held views on such issues as globalisation and social policies, universities should also be held up to more scrutiny.

Some leading international figures have begun to call for the re-setting of global politics and economics. It is not yet clear precisely what this would entail but it is surely obvious that the current political and economic system has not served the world particularly well over the past 200 years. There is much evidence to support this conjecture other than continuous wars, much global poverty, and corruption in many countries at various levels. Furthermore, it is fairly obvious that the forthcoming climate crisis, which can only be avoided with considerable change to our way of life, has the potential to make the current Covid-19 crisis look like child's play.

Where the University sector would fit into a global political and economic resetting is not entirely obvious. But it is clear that education and especially higher education is an asset which has an important role to play in the forthcoming years. And how to sustain the higher education sector is an issue of considerable concern to many countries as well as individual members of the population. Perhaps it is time for universities and their faculties to be more than scientific observers and to make more direct interventions in the societies around them.

It is difficult to have any real confidence in statistics related to global higher education but there is little doubt that activities related to this important sector are huge. I have seen estimates which suggest that there are globally 40,000 universities and/or colleges and that enrolment exceeds a billion students.

It is easy to list the issues about which universities have been criticised. It is considerably more difficult to suggest a plan for eliminating these problems. There are many reasons why the sector is in the state it is today but perhaps the two most important are the shift in societal values and the remarkable scarcity of bold leadership.

Since the mid-20th century there has been increasing pressure on society to focus on how to develop efficient processes in all aspects of our lives. At the same time there has been increasing concern that we recognised the power of markets to direct general choices in all sorts of ways which had up until then been considered to be outside of the domain of supply and demand. This ended up by eliminating the belief that there were certain things too precious to society to allow their control by market forces. In the early part of the 20th century it would have been said with conviction that the supply of utilities such as water, electricity and gas should not be handed over to the market. And although there has always been some private education it has been understood in many countries that when it came to higher education it was largely a public service.

At the same time this change in values occurred there appeared to be a shift in the type of individuals who were presenting themselves for leadership roles in many facets of society. Organisational leadership became a professional development issue and this resulted in a culture which became fully cognisant of risk both at the organisation and the personal level. This in turn resulted in a generation of leaders whose ability to take bold steps seem to be reduced. This problem is certainly true in higher education and is greatly increased by the fact that universities are intrinsically conservative. There are few institutions where precedence is quite so important as it is in the university sector and change happens very slowly - if it happens at all!

Thus, universities find themselves in a position from which there is no easy solution. Their services are desperately needed by the community but the challenges of increasing access with major pressures on funding threaten many institutions. There is no doubt that possessing a degree significantly improves any individual's life chances. But doubt has been cast on some degrees which may be considered to be of little real value along with debates about whether achieving a degree is an end in itself or something that should be closely linked to employment opportunities. The cost of acquiring a degree has resulted in its value for money being questioned and some young people who could attend a university are deciding not to so do. Issues related to internal management have become a source of contention with members of faculty vociferously condemning managerialism, yet offering little in terms of alternatives other than naïve arguments to return to the past. In short, the status of the University in society has in some cases become an issue.

Nonetheless, all is not lost as the challenges ahead may be difficult but not unsurmountable.

What is required most of all is a re-examination of the basic values on which higher education are premised. This really needs attention to be given to the drifting of universities from public sector institutions towards profit making corporate entities. Once it has been decided that a new model for a modern university is required, as it was when the universities last re-evaluated their role in the early 1800s in Central Europe the actions required should be relatively obvious.

Finding the leaders to undertake this task will not be trivial and certainly the type of people required for this job will not be those who will be attracted by "internationally competitive salaries". A somewhat more committed set of people will need to be found. And this is not just among the high office bearers but also the trustees or governors or others to whom society has offered the privilege of acting as guardians of these most precious institutions. Just as importantly, faculty must find ways to be an active part of the solution and the voices of students need to be heard.

What is being suggested is clearly not easy but if a new mind set is not engaged then the best that can be achieved after the dreadful Covid-19 crisis is a return to the old ways with which so many people were dissatisfied. It is essential that the university sector does not bounce back to what it was before!

A Facebook page has been established to continue discussion on this subject at https://www.facebook.com/groups/2478159529151472

Index

Lightning Source UK Ltd.
Milton Keynes UK
UKHW020732150920
369912UK00003B/8

9 781912 764655